The Business of Liberty

The Business of Liberty

Freedom and Information in Ethics, Politics, and Law

Boudewijn de Bruin

OXFORD
UNIVERSITY PRESS

Great Clarendon Street, Oxford, OX2 6DP,
United Kingdom

Oxford University Press is a department of the University of Oxford.
It furthers the University's objective of excellence in research, scholarship,
and education by publishing worldwide. Oxford is a registered trade mark of
Oxford University Press in the UK and in certain other countries

Published in the United States of America by Oxford University Press
198 Madison Avenue, New York, NY 10016, United States of America

British Library Cataloguing in Publication Data
Data available

Library of Congress Control Number: 2021943269

ISBN 978–0–19–883967–5
DOI: 10.1093/oso/9780198839675.001.0001

Printed and bound by
CPI Group (UK) Ltd, Croydon, CR0 4YY

in memory of Karlo de Bruin

Preface

When the French people gave the Unites States the Statue of Liberty in 1886, they surely could not foresee that their gift would become the most frequently used symbol for freedom globally. The liberty pole, the liberty tree, the cap of liberty, the 'open road', the *Freiheitsglocke*, or even Marianne, are all surely prominent and powerful symbols of freedom. But none covers so many books (or so many T-shirts and mugs) as the Statue of Liberty.

The statue embodies the two ideals defended in this book. It is officially called *Liberty Enlightening the World*. Lady Liberty holds a torch, and some people think that the torch is what represents *liberty*. This interpretation lacks plausibility, though. The torch has since ancient times been thought of as giving us illumination and wisdom, and the image of handing on the torch from one person to another, as in a relay race, has been used as a powerful metaphor for passing on traditions of enlightenment over generations. So the torch does not represent freedom. It is better seen as representing *knowledge*, the result of gathering and processing information.

The key observation driving this book is that you cannot make use of your liberty if you do not have knowledge and information about it. This is, we shall see, a fairly straightforward matter of logic. But that you need freedom and knowledge this way is not without considerable theoretical and practical consequences, or so I argue in this book. The torchlight illuminates our opportunity sets. It makes us aware of all the things we can do, of their consequences and the likelihoods by which these consequences will arise. Without the torch, we would be groping in the dark. We need the torch to use our liberty. But, of course, we also need liberty. We need torch and liberty to enjoy what I call *known freedom*. You have to be informed about your freedom. This is my first normative ideal.

Dave Eggers wrote on Independence Day 2016 in the *Guardian* that the Statue of Liberty was a 'beacon of exuberant and ceaseless welcome' for immigrants fleeing to the US to escape oppression. It was an open manifestation of a commitment to 'secure the Blessings of Liberty', as the preamble to the US Constitution has it. I argue in this book that our freedom becomes more stably realized when others recognize and acknowledge it. We need what I call *acknowledged freedom*. Its location, visibility, and sheer size make the Statue of Liberty a symbol of my second normative ideal.

This book has been very long in the making. Early 2005 I moved to Groningen to join a project devoted to freedom, led by Martin van Hees. One key aim was to contribute to the debate on the value of freedom, in which, besides Martin, Ian Carter and Matthew Kramer had also made big strides. The main methodological tools that I brought to the debate were epistemic, informational, cognitive—that is, related to the way we process information, form beliefs, and gain knowledge. I produced various chapters laying out how the information people possess about their opportunity sets impacts on the type of value they can extract from them, working on doxastic freedom (to do with belief formation), epistemic freedom (to do with knowledge gathering), known freedom, and acknowledged freedom. But, apart from an article that appeared in *Tijdschrift voor Filosofie*, what I published was applied work, often inspired by the 2008 financial crisis that had somewhat intervened. This book completes the project—for now.

This book is written for an audience including such diverse people as business ethicists, political theorists, legal scholars, social epistemologists, normative economists, as well as practitioners, politicians, and policymakers. These people differ greatly in disciplinary backgrounds. This means that I strive to keep technical jargon and methodological details to a minimum, and prioritize simplicity over rigour. The first part of the book is systematic: it introduces theory, even though at most stages I add examples and case studies. The second part reflects my choice of applied topics. These topics are not random, but they are arbitrary in that they reflect what I found most pressing and interesting when I wrote them. They can largely be read in isolation.

Research for this book was financed in part by the Nederlandse Organisatie voor Wetenschappelijk Onderzoek (NWO, the Dutch Research Council), grant numbers 016-048-601, 275-20-017 and 360-20-311. Materials for this book were presented at the Discourse in Philosophy (DIP) Colloquium (University of Amsterdam, Institute for Logic, Language, and Computation, 2011), the Centre for the Study of European Contract Law seminar (University of Amsterdam, Faculty of Law, 2016), the Seventh Annual OZSW Conference (Amsterdam, 2019), the colloquium on Normen im freien Markt at the XXIV. Kongress der deutschen Gesellschaft für philosophie (Berlin, 2017), the Cambridge Forum for Legal and Political Philosophy (University of Cambridge, Faculty of Law, 2009), the Groningen–Cambridge Trust and Belief workshop (University of Cambridge, Faculty of Philosophy, 2016), the University of Delft (Department of Philosophy, 2006), the Annual Dutch Conference in Practical Philosophy (Doorn, 2009), the workshop on Rational Choice and Normative Philosophy (National University of Ireland, Galway, 2005), the workshop on Alcopop TV Culture: Media, Alcohol and Violence in Young People: Research and Policy Perspectives (University of Gothenburg, 2011), the University of Gothenburg (Department of Philosophy, Linguistics and Theory of Science, 2020), the workshop Business Ethics Engaged (Groningen, 2019), the Knowledge, Citizenship, and Democracy conference (Groningen, 2021), the University of Groningen (Faculty of Philosophy, 2006, 2011), the Institute of SocioEconomics (University of Hamburg, 2006), the conference on The Place of Epistemic Agents (Madrid, 2008), the Graduate Center, CUNY (New York, 2017), the University of Southern Denmark, Odense (Department for the Study of Cultures, 2020), the Duty of Care in Finance seminar (Balliol College, University of Oxford, 2011), the workshop on Les concepts de liberté et de pouvoir (Paris, 2008), the workshop on Power and Freedom (University of Pavia, Department of Political and Social Studies, 2011), the Berle XI: Law and Corporate Culture colloquium (Seattle University School of Law, 2020), the Arctic University of Norway, Tromsø (Department of Philosophy, 2019), the Vici Reunion Workshop (Umeå University, 2020), and at the Netherlands Institute for Advanced Studies (Wassenaar, 2006).

I thank the audiences of these events collectively. I would like to thank individually: Han Thomas Adriaenssen, Wouter van Aggelen, Joel Anderson, David Archard, Gustav Arrhenius, David Atkinson, Maria Baghramian, Johan van Benthem, Constanze Binder, John Boatright, Tony Booth, Luc Bovens, Matthew Braham, Bert van den Brink, Tom Brooks, Ian Carter, Olha Cherednychenko, Rutger Claassen, Chris Cowton, Anthony Mark Cutter, George DeMartino, Kayleigh Doherty, Wilfred Dolfsma, Wim Dubbink, Richard Endörfer, Pascal Engel, Amitai Etzioni, Elianna Fetterolf, Marc Fleurbaey, Miranda Fricker, Michael Garnett, Mikkel Gerken, Hans Harbers, Govert den Hartogh, Martin van Hees, Lisa Herzog, Clare Heyward, Claire Hill, Frank Hindriks, Susan Hurley, Sue Jaffer, Muel Kaptein, Simon Keller, Pauline Kleingeld, Jens van 't Klooster, Barteld Kooi, Matthew Kramer, Theo Kuipers, Thijs Lijster, Joe McGrath, Steven

McNamara, Chantal Mak, Quintus Masius, Marco Meyer, Nicholas Morris, Pete Morriss, Laetitia Mulder, Alan Muller, Christian Munthe, Bert Musschenga, Henk-Jan Nanninga, Nikolaj Nottelmann, Alex Oliver, Onora O'Neill, Marc Pauly, Jeanne Peijnenburg, Philip Pettit, Emmanuel Picavet, Graham Priest, Jesse Prinz, Lubomira Radoilska, Jeroen de Ridder, Jan-Willem van der Rijt, Jan-Willem Romeijn, Barend de Rooij, Olivier Roy, Joakim Sandberg, Andreas Schmidt, Stephen Scott, Tom Simpson, Dan Solove, Ulrich Steinvorth, Thomas Teufel, Chris Thompson, Siegfried Van Duffel, Bruno Verbeek, David Vines, Ciaran Walker, Adrian Walsh, Johan Wempe, Chris Zurn, my research assistant Sjoerd Norden, Jenny King and Adam Swallow, editors for OUP, Sharmila Radha, of Integra Software Services, and Hilary Walford, for superb copy-editing, and two anonymous reviewers for OUP. I thank Matthew Kramer for organizing a short stay at Churchill College, Cambridge, in 2009. I thank Alex Oliver for hosting me during the Lent term of 2014–15 at the University of Cambridge.

Very special thanks are due to Martin van Hees. His research project on freedom was what started my interest in freedom. Without his continuous encouragement, curiosity, and creativity there would be no book.

My father was one of the first students in the Netherlands of what in English is called Philosophy, Politics, and Economics (PPE). Born before the war, he talked about freedom—for instance, when we walked along the Iron Curtain in Germany's Harz, when we travelled together to see communism collapse in Berlin in 1989, or when we saw the Statue of Liberty in New York. He was very interested in the project, and knew there would be a book. He died before seeing it to completion. I dedicate it to his memory.

Groningen
15 February 2021

Acknowledgements

This book contains thoroughly reworked materials from various sources. I acknowledge permission from Wiley-Blackwell for reusing, in Chapters 1 and 4, some materials from 'Liberal and Republican Freedom', *Journal of Political Philosophy*, 17/4 (2009), 418–439; from Peeters, for reusing, in Chapter 2, some materials (translated from Dutch into English) from 'Doxastische en epistemische vrijheid', *Tijdschrift voor Filosofie*, 71 (2009), 529–552; from Oxford University Press, for reusing, in Chapter 5, some materials from 'Ethics Management in Banking and Finance', in Nick Morris and David Vines (eds), *Capital Failure: Rebuilding Trust in Financial Services* (Oxford: Oxford University Press, 2014), 255–276; from Taylor & Francis, for reusing, in Chapter 5, materials from 'Socially Responsible Investment in the Alcohol Industry: An Assessment of Investor Attitudes and Ethical Arguments', *Contemporary Social Science*, 8/1 (2013), 58–70 (reprinted in Thom Brooks (ed.), *Alcohol and Public Policy* (Abingdon: Routledge, 2015), 35–48; from Springer for reusing, in Chapter 6, some materials from 'Pledging Integrity: Oaths as Forms of Ethics Management', *Journal of Business Ethics*, 136 (2016), 23–42; from Seattle University Law Review, for reusing, in Chapter 6, materials from 'Epistemic Corporate Culture: Knowledge, Common Knowledge, and Professional Oaths', *Seattle University Law Review*, 43 (2020), 807–839, from Springer, for reusing, in Chapter 7, some materials from 'Media Violence and Freedom of Speech: How to Use Empirical Data', *Ethical Theory and Moral Practice*, 11/5 (2008), 493–505; from Oxford University Press, for reusing, in Chapter 7, some materials from 'Alcohol in the Media and Young People: What Do We Need for Liberal Policymaking?', *Public Health Ethics*, 7/1 (2014), 35–46; and from Springer, for reusing, in Chapter 8, materials from 'The Liberal Value of Privacy', *Law and Philosophy*, 29/5 (2010), 505–534.

Contents

Table of Cases

τὸ δὲ καλῶς κτίμενον ὦ μέγα ναίων
στόμιον, εὖ δὸς ἀνιδεῖν δόμον ἀνδρός,
καί νιν ἐλευθερίας φῶς
λαμπρὸν ἰδεῖν φιλίοις
ὄμμασιν ἐκ δνοφερᾶς καλύπτρας.

Thou tenant of the cave,—great Spirit,
Give to the hero to inherit
His halls ancestral;—may his eyes,
Fearless and bright,
Peer freely forth from sorrow's veilèd night (tr. Anna Swanwick)

Aeschylus, *Oresteia*

Introduction

Why Freedom Is not Enough

Just before the Global Financial Crisis broke out in 2008, the literature on political freedom was in very good shape. Several monographs had helped to reinvigorate the debate about the correct analysis of the concept of freedom.[1] With often great analytical sophistication, these books had offered novel insights into the measurement and value of freedom. They had enriched ethical discourse with so-called *pure negative* or *liberal* as well as with *republican* or *neo-Roman* conceptions of freedom. And they had shown the relative advantages of these approaches over less analytically rigorous contenders.

The analytical insights of this body of research waited only to be extended to more applied branches of moral and political philosophy. But the crisis intervened. Business ethicists, political theorists, legal scholars, and many politicians and pundits returned to earlier criticisms of capitalism and liberalism to understand the crisis. Less freedom-centred views gained popularity. An important literature developed, attacking 'neo-liberalism', and revoking the deregulation, privatization, marketization, and liberalization that had, these critics alleged, been practised during the Reagan–Thatcher era. They proffered neo-Marxist and other approaches as alternatives, and defending freedom seemed to be left entirely to the financial industry, whose credentials were routinely ridiculed by commentators.

But the literature on freedom still has a lot to offer to ethics, politics, law, and practice. I emphasize two points here, reflecting two related aims I have for this book. The first is the practical relevance of this literature: many people make decisions in societies in which corporate law, regulation, and supervision are grounded in views about freedom going back to thinkers in liberal and republican traditions. While neo-Marxist critiques of capitalism may have some appeal, theoretical reflections inspired by liberal and republican thinkers are likely to address the concerns of these people more readily.

The Business of Liberty. Boudewijn de Bruin, Oxford University Press.
© Boudewijn de Bruin (2022). DOI: 10.1093/oso/9780198839675.003.0001

The second point is the analytical clarity of this strand of literature: even to theorists and practitioners who do not identify themselves with the respective positions, the analytical framework developed by Carter, van Hees, Kramer, and others offers great advantages. Oft-cited examples are our increased understanding of the measurement of freedom as well as the specific normative and moral assumptions to which different conceptions of freedom are committed.

In this book I put forward a theory of the epistemic, informational, or cognitive aspects of freedom that, while grounded in the analytical work on freedom, is developed in the broader context of business ethics, political theory, normative economics, and legal scholarship. Using this background, I defend the two ideals of *known freedom* and *acknowledged freedom* in the first four chapters and then put them to use in the last four. For us to enjoy the value our freedom may afford to us, we need to know about our own freedom, and our freedom has to be acknowledged or recognized by others. Overlooked by most theorists, these informational aspects of freedom have been considered by recent advocates of liberal and republican freedom. But, as I show, much needs to be done here to develop a fully fledged view of the informational aspects of freedom, in terms of both analytical rigour and applications. To fill this lacuna is the aim of the book.

Let me give some background, first, and then turn to the plan of the book. Conceptions of freedom are numerous. You may, for instance, think that a person is free to the extent that their actions are not interfered with by others, or to the extent that they are not dominated by others. You may call a person free only if their actions realize their true, authentic selves, or if they contribute to something that we value in common. You could think that what is most important about freedom is the presence of opportunities for action, or rather the absence of impediments to action. You could hold that any conception of freedom should always presuppose a conception of morality, or of an institutional order, or rather hold on to the view that freedom should not make any assumptions concerning what is valuable. You might find that a person's beliefs or desires matter to questions about their freedom, or that freedom should be independent of such attitudes. And you could hold the view that the word *freedom* has only one antonym, *unfreedom*, or that *being unfree* and *not being free* are two different things.[2]

These questions concern the conceptual analysis of freedom and have attracted a lot of attention in the literature.[3] A less often discussed type of question concerns freedom's value. Here possible answers are just as numerous. You might think that freedom matters mostly because it is a sufficient (or necessary?) condition to satisfy our desires, or to maximize expected utility. You could locate the value of freedom in the contribution freedom makes to living an authentic life, to self-realization, self-determination, or self-esteem, or to causal or moral responsibility. You may stress the fact that moral, political, social, economic, scientific, technological, or artistic progress requires freedom. You could note that freedom offers us the opportunity to learn, to develop new interests, and to imagine possible futures. Freedom may also be valued for its contributions to economic efficiency, political deliberation, decreasing conflict, increasing prosperity, and collective welfare.[4]

These thoughts about freedom are by no means only of theoretical interest. Arguments about the conception and value of freedom play a prominent role in politics. British and American politicians explicitly invoked arguments based on desire satisfaction and personal responsibility to defend cutting government spending on public transport and telecommunications, and often cast this in the vocabulary of a 'negative' conception of freedom, according to which freedom consists primarily in the absence of external impediments.[5] These thoughts, it can be shown, were an important ideological driver behind the liberalization of healthcare, the privatization of retirement planning, and the deregulation of finance, witnessed since the 1990s. This applies not only to policy established under such right-leaning governments as those of Margaret Thatcher and Ronald Reagan, but also to the more left-leaning governments headed by Tony Blair and Bill Clinton. How you think about freedom, and why you value it, may therefore determine what policy you favour, at least to some extent.

My main concern in this book is not to defend a particular conception or value of freedom, or a political ideology. Rather what I want to show is that, depending on which conception and value you adopt, you are committed to making certain further claims that have significant policy repercussions. It is, therefore, instructive to keep the following picture in mind. Think of a political ideology such as liberalism or republicanism. I believe that any decent such ideology starts with a fundamental notion seen as valuable, potentially more than one. In our case this is freedom. Secondly, we need arguments for the value of that fundamental notion. In the present case, these arguments will be grounded in the value of such things as desire satisfaction, personal responsibility, self-realization, and so forth, which are somewhat axiomatically assumed to be valuable themselves. Then, thirdly, we need a distributive principle that tells us how the fundamental notion is to be distributed across people (or what determines the conditions under which distribution takes place fairly or equitably) in order to extract the value or values on which it rests. Fourthly, we need institutions to implement all this.[6] This probably requires something like a state, which ideally, I believe, should be thought of, as much as is possible and sensible, as a nexus of contracts between consenting individuals—but this is more than contentious, and it would certainly be too ambitious to defend that idea in this book as well. Finally, we should add a fifth dimension: managerial strategies that organizations (businesses just as much as governmental organizations) should use.[7]

In this book, I am particularly interested in the second element: what makes freedom valuable, and what is needed to generate this value? I am also interested in the fourth and fifth elements, particularly when it comes to the ideal of acknowledged freedom, and the applied last four chapters. So I am not here presenting a view of whether freedom the way I conceive of it should be maximized, maximined, balanced against other values, or organized along lines of Pareto optimality, and whether freedom should be promoted, honoured, expressed, or produced.[8] I do believe, however, that, if one were to design a state with the ideals of known and acknowledged freedom in mind, there would be larger institutional support for the right to education than many liberals might expect. I briefly explore that theme in the Conclusion. All the same, however, the bulk of what I have to say applies to most of the distributive principles that liberals could sensibly put forward.

I have said that the book comes in two parts. The first four chapters present my views of the epistemic presuppositions of arguments for the value of freedom, the concept of freedom of belief, and the two normative ideals of known freedom and acknowledged freedom. The last four chapters consider a variety of cases to which these ideas can be applied, answering such questions as how information may benefit socially responsible investment, how ethics management may contribute to realizing acknowledged freedom within profit and non-profit organizations, how freedom of belief may (or may not) be at stake in the regulation of media violence, and how the normative ideal of known freedom offers a novel way to think about privacy in a host of recent cases. The first chapters build upon each other and form a clear unity. This applies less to the last four chapters, which can be read more or less in isolation.

Let me give an overview of the chapters. Chapter 1 lays the essential groundwork by introducing various concepts of freedom as well as a number of informational notions that form the basis of the book. I introduce the main analytical tools from the literatures on negative, positive, and republican freedom, and such notions as authenticity. I discuss arguments in favour of the value of freedom based on desire satisfaction, personal responsibility, and self-realization, and also consider causal and moral agency, showing, ultimately, that these arguments differ significantly in terms of the types of freedom they support. Subsequently, I show that these arguments for freedom's value are implicitly committed to a number of epistemic or informational assumptions concerning the beliefs of agents whose freedoms we consider. If, for instance, consumers do not know the relevant characteristics of the products or services they are free to buy, the (negative, positive, republican) freedom that these products or services generate does not make a valuable contribution to desire satisfaction or personal responsibility. To illustrate, I consider how fear of being the victim of crime restricts freedom, and conclude with a brief excursion to a well-known case that came before the US Supreme Court, *Wisconsin* v. *Yoder*, on the freedom of Amish education.

Chapter 2 continues the discussion about the informational preconditions of freedom. Its main aim is to develop a novel concept of freedom of belief that is broad enough to be applicable in a wide variety of organizational contexts. *Freedom of belief* here does not refer to freedom of conscience or religion; rather, the idea is to examine, for instance, how individuals and organizations influence the ways in which we gain and process information about products and services. While theorists in the negative freedom tradition have made a start addressing these issues, a fully-fledged conception of freedom of belief has, to my knowledge, not yet been developed. To illustrate what sort of things might constitute interference with belief formation, I consider a number of examples from neuromarketing. These techniques are surely still in their infancy, but regulators have already shown considerable interest here. I also zoom in on particular ways in which organizations such as news media might interfere with people gaining evidence to support and justify their beliefs—for instance, by means of specific framing techniques.

The first two chapters show how freedom and information are mutually dependent: we need information about our freedom of choice to enjoy its value, and to gain and process information we need freedom of belief. In

Chapter 3, I first argue that a result of this is that what one should ultimately consider to be valuable is not freedom per se, but rather freedoms we are aware of. I call this normative ideal *known freedom*—that is, freedom one knows about. I then use insights from various literatures (philosophy, economics, psychology) to highlight the importance of possessing skills and other forms of know-how. Moral and political philosophers have not very frequently discussed skills and know-how under the heading of freedom, because skills involve abilities that are somewhat internal to the agent. I argue, however, that, once we adopt the normative ideal of known freedom, skills and know-how should be recognized as crucial constituents of our freedom. I conclude by looking into the ways in which stereotype and prejudice may limit freedom by affecting skilful behaviour.

The first three chapters move us from assigning value to freedom of choice (Chapter 1) and freedom of belief (Chapter 2) to an argument that what is really valuable is freedom of which you are aware—that is, known freedom (Chapter 3). Chapter 4 concludes this itinerary by one more step. Its main point is to argue for another normative ideal—namely, freedom that not only you but also others are aware of. I call this *acknowledged freedom*. I use insights gained on common knowledge, a concept used by ethicists and economists to study coordination among economic agents. Economists define *common knowledge* of some proposition among a group of people thus: all members of the group know it, they all know that they all know it, they all know that they all know that they all know it, and so on. A proposition that is common knowledge among a group of people is, one could say, entirely *open* among all members of the group. Building on observations about the value of common knowledge, I introduce the ideal of acknowledged freedom: situations where a person's freedoms are common knowledge among relevant beneficiaries or stakeholders. I argue that acknowledged freedom has a number of benefits such as facilitating coordination and cooperation in markets and society at large. The most important benefit from a business ethics point of view is, however, that acknowledged freedom gives extra protection to the freedom of stakeholders. An excursion to the model of informed consent applied to shareholders concludes the chapter.

The last four chapters apply the insights to concrete questions. I begin, in Chapter 5, by offering a new view of socially responsible investing. There seems to exist a fair amount of agreement among business ethicists, finance professionals, and policymakers that socially responsible investing requires investors to shun *sin stocks*—that is, shares in alcohol, tobacco, or other problematic industries. I criticize two arguments that have been proffered in defence of this position: the argument from common goods, according to which sin stocks must be avoided because of the alleged negative effects of these industries on public health; and the argument from religious values, which excludes industries on the basis of religious values, broadly construed. I show that these arguments are flawed, as they sanction interference with the freedom of choice of investors that is incompatible with the value of personal responsibility. Instead I argue for a business ethics approach to socially responsible investing to the effect that investors mutually acknowledge their responsibility vis-à-vis stakeholders to influence corporate decision-making by using such strategies as shareholder activism to address concrete ethical issues in business. I call this the argument from ethical issues. I conclude by considering the question of whether information provides socially responsible investors with a clean conscience.

In Chapter 6 I consider business ethics management techniques fostering the normative ideal of acknowledged freedom. The Global Financial Crisis of 2008 has led to a surprising interest in oaths in business. Perhaps the best known example is the MBA Oath, an initiative that was started by graduates of Harvard Business School in 2009. A more weighty one (because backed by law) is, however, the Dutch Banker's Oath, which almost every finance professional in the Netherlands must pledge. Advocates of these oaths see them as novel—and hopefully effective—forms of business ethics management and corporate social responsibility. In this chapter I first examine the characteristics and functions of these oaths, harking back to research on the use of oaths in medicine. Casting doubt on some of its purported benefits, I argue that nonetheless pledging a well-designed oath is one way for businesspeople to contribute to the ideal of acknowledged freedom—namely, by contributing to mutual respect between businesses and stakeholders.

Chapter 7 considers media violence and aggressive behaviour, and the role of beliefs therein. Several ethicists and commentators have argued in favour of extensive consumer protection regulation concerning violent films and videogames. Such arguments are typically based on the hypothesis that exposure to media violence causes aggressive behaviour. One causal mechanism might be that humans possess an innate tendency to copy behaviour in ways that *bypass*, one could say, free and conscious belief formation. If this hypothesis were true, exposing people to media violence would decrease the extent to which they can enjoy the value of their freedom. It would straightforwardly limit their known freedom. I argue, however, that the empirical data commentators canvass are (as yet) insufficient to demonstrate that media violence diminishes freedom, and that consequently an important argument against the production of violent media fails. I conclude by looking into a recent strand in legal scholarship on an epistemic argument for constitutional protection for free speech.

The main aims of Chapter 8 are, finally, to examine, first, what value privacy has if we take the lessons about the informational aspects of freedom into account, and, secondly, to analyse some of the ethical and legal consequences thereof. I argue that privacy invasions almost always lead to interference with a person's known freedom, because victims of privacy invasions typically lose knowledge about the freedoms they have. I apply this to legal cases involving identity theft—that is, cases where criminals obtain, process, and use personal information about individual people. I argue that lawgivers, courts, and business organizations have a larger array of remedies against such (and other) privacy invasions than is typically recognized.

Notes

1. See Ian Carter, *A Measure of Freedom* (Oxford: Oxford University Press, 1999), Martin van Hees, *Legal Reductionism and Freedom* (Dordrecht: Kluwer, 2000), Matthew Kramer, *The Quality of Freedom* (Oxford: Oxford University Press, 2003), Philip Pettit, *A Theory of Freedom: From the Psychology to the Politics of Agency* (Oxford: Oxford University Press, 2001), Quentin Skinner, *Liberty before Liberalism* (Cambridge: Cambridge University Press, 1998), and Hillel Steiner, *An Essay on Rights* (Oxford: Blackwell, 1994).
2. See, generally, Ian Carter, 'Positive and Negative Liberty', in Edward Zalta (ed.), *The Stanford Encyclopedia of Philosophy*, 2016, plato.stanford.edu/entries/liberty-positive-negative [perma.cc/X8SL-A4UJ].
3. Ibid.
4. Ibid. See also, e.g., Simon Keller, 'Freedom!', *Social Theory and Practice*, 31 (2005), 337–357.
5. Alexander Brown, *Personal Responsibility: Why It Matters* (London: Continuum, 2009).

6. See, e.g., Shelly Kagan, 'The Argument from Liberty', in Jules Coleman and Allen Buchanan (eds), *In Harm's Way: Essays in Honor of Joel Feinberg* (Cambridge: Cambridge University Press, 1994), 16–41, for an attempt using fairly similar categories to think through the consequences of assigning value to freedom only for a defence of libertarianism. See, e.g., Mark Reiff, *Exploitation and Economic Justice in the Liberal Capitalist State* (Oxford: Oxford University Press, 2013), for an attempt to develop concrete policy (regarding just price, minimum and maximum wage, etc.) intended to be compatible with a large variety of liberal ideologies. Philip Pettit, *Just Freedom: A Moral Compass for a Complex World* (New York: Norton, 2014), puts forward a republican political ideal and applies it to questions concerning justice, democracy, and sovereignty, and considers business ethics relevant themes such as corporate responsibility. Robert Taylor, *Exit Left: Markets and Mobility in Republican Thought* (Oxford: Oxford University Press, 2017), examines the economic means through which the ideals of republicanism can be realized.

7. See, e.g., Henri Savall, Michel Péron, Véronique Zardet, and Marc Bonnet, *Le Capitalisme socialement responsable existe* (Cormelles le Royal: Éditions EMS, 2015). They develop the concept of 'socially responsible capitalism' and propose management practices supporting it.

8. See, e.g., Philip Pettit, 'The Contribution of Analytic Philosophy', in Robert Goodin and Philip Pettit (eds), *A Companion to Contemporary Political Philosophy* (Malden: Blackwell, 1993), 7–38, at 32 (honouring and promoting), and Geoffrey Brennan, 'The Contribution of Economics', in Robert Goodin and Philip Pettit (eds), op. cit., 123–156, at 129–130 (expressing and producing). To some extent whether one should honour, promote, express, or produce a value depends also on the argument one has for it. Robert Nozick, *Anarchy, State, and Utopia* (Oxford: Blackwell, 1974), 28–51, argues that, while *S*'s right to life entails a duty on the part of *T* not to kill *S*, it does not entail a duty on the part of *T* to prevent *U* from killing *S*. As Jeremy Waldron, *The Right to Private Property* (Oxford: Clarendon, 1988), 62–105, argues, once we pay attention to the *argument* that underlies the right to life, we should see that the core interest served here is that *S* not be killed, which entails, he thinks, that *T* does have a duty to prevent *U* from killing *S*.

1
From Choice Overload to Discrimination

Arguments for Freedom

In this chapter I first briefly summarize the main key distinctions in the literature. I introduce negative, positive, and republican conceptions of freedom to the extent necessary in this book, which makes treatment correspondingly short. Then I move to the main substance of this chapter: arguments for freedom's value, and the epistemic presuppositions they make.

Conceptions of Freedom

Negative Freedom

Perhaps the oldest version of negative freedom is due to Thomas Hobbes. In *Leviathan* he writes famously: 'By LIBERTY, is understood, according to the proper signification of the word, the absence of externall Impediments.'[1] Or also: 'A FREE-MAN, is he, that in those things, which by his strength and wit he is able to do, is not hindred to doe what he has a will to.'[2] In contemporary parlance: freedom equals *non-interference*. Hobbes is very clear that he means these impediments and hindrances to be external rather than internal to the agent. This is a characteristic most later conceptions of negative freedom share. Hobbes's examples of unfreedom are imprisonment (restrictions by 'walls, or chayns').[3] He explicitly writes that 'when the impediment of motion, is in the constitution of the thing it selfe, we use not to say, it wants the Liberty; but the Power to move; as when … a man is fastned to his bed by sicknesse.'[4]

But saying that freedom equals the absence of external impediments leaves several things unspecified. First: is an illness really internal? Also,

The Business of Liberty. Boudewijn de Bruin, Oxford University Press.
© Boudewijn de Bruin (2022). DOI: 10.1093/oso/9780198839675.003.0002

if I intentionally caused your illness? Or what about internal conditions such as phobias and compulsive beliefs? Do they count as impediments to freedom?[5]

Secondly, are all actions equally important when we consider potential impediments? John Stuart Mill, for instance, thought not. As he maintained that 'liberty consists in doing what one desires', he was committed to the view that external impediments do not decrease your freedom as long as they do not bar you from performing actions you desire to perform.[6] Isaiah Berlin then pointed out that this would force him to call a dictator, implausibly, a *liberator*—namely, if the dictator 'manages to condition his subjects … into losing their original [desires] and embrace … the form of life he has invented for them'.[7] Most contemporary authors in the negative freedom camp agree with Berlin that such an implication should be avoided and that a person's freedom is independent of their desires.[8]

Thirdly, does it matter how the impediments arise? My travelling home is restricted when the police block the road, but also when a highway robber forces me to stop at gunpoint, when a bridge-tender forgets to close a bridge, or when the road gets flooded during a storm. Do all these impediments decrease my freedom to go home? All this depends on how you answer questions about the sources of unfreedom. So you have to decide whether what restricts freedom must be caused by human action (excluding the flood), whether only actual interference count as interference (as in the police case), or also dispositions to interfere (the robber's threatening you), and also whether interference should always be intentional (as in the police and robber cases), or can also be unintentional (as for the bridge-tender, who forgot about the bridge), and whether someone has to be merely causally responsible, or also morally responsible, for the interference.[9]

Matthew Kramer's 'pure negative' conception of freedom illustrates how some of these questions may be answered.[10] While what I say in the this book applies *mutatis mutandis* to other conceptions of negative freedom too, I often work with Kramer's. So let me give some details. According to Kramer, a person P is *unfree* to perform some action A whenever other people's actual actions or dispositions to act prevent P from performing A; and P counts as *free* to perform some action A whenever P is able to perform A.[11]

Kramer adopts an inclusive conception of freedom in that it allows for actual interference and dispositions to interfere and for intentional and unintentional interference. With separate definitions of *freedom* and *unfreedom*, moreover, Kramer is also able to distinguish between cases where, owing to human impediments, people are to be called *unfree*, and where, merely owing to non-human impediments, people should be described as *not free*. I am unable to leave the ski resort because of an avalanche. While as a result of this I am not free to leave, I am not unfree to leave. I would be unfree to leave if, for instance, someone locked me in my lodge, or would lock it as soon as I tried to leave. In both circumstances, the action of leaving the village is not part of my opportunity set. But the reason why is different.[12]

Positive Freedom

For advocates of positive freedom, a different range of questions is important. These are questions not so much about the source of unfreedom, as in the case of negative freedom, but rather about the objects of freedom—that is, about what actions matter to a person's freedom when we look at their opportunity set. Take, for instance, Thomas Hill Green, the British idealist philosopher and politician. He equated freedom with 'a positive power or capacity of doing or enjoying something worth doing or enjoying … something that we do or enjoy in common with others'.[13] Or consider Charles Taylor's view of freedom as the ability fully to realize our authentic selves.[14] For Green and Taylor, when considering a person's freedom, only those actions matter the performance of which they enjoy in common with others, or which they need to perform to realize their authentic selves, respectively. Impediments to actions that a person does not enjoy in common with others, or does not need to realize themselves, do not strictly speaking restrict their freedom. Consequently, someone defining and valuing freedom along those lines does not have an argument against such impediments.[15]

These two conceptions of positive freedom are value-laden in the sense that ethical or social criteria are needed to determine what it means to say that someone enjoys something in common with others, or what it means to say that they need to realize themselves. Both Green and Taylor seem to assume that these criteria are objective. They are grounded in the value of social progress (for Green) and authenticity (for Taylor). Only those actions that contribute to social progress or authenticity affect the extent of a person's freedom. Other actions can be added to, or removed from, their opportunity set, but that will not change the freedom they enjoy.

A value-laden conception risks making freedom dependent on desires—namely, your desire, if you have it, for things that you can enjoy in common with others, or authentically to realize yourself. This opens the door to Berlin's above-mentioned objection (to Mill) about the dictator–liberator. Green perhaps mitigates this risk, as his ultimate value is social progress, which in itself may be incompatible with dictatorship. But, for Taylor, the challenge is less easily handled. Consider, for instance, his example of a person who is 'very attached to comfort', as a result of which they 'cannot do certain things that [they] should like very much to do, such as going on an expedition over the Andes'.[16] Taylor writes that, when the person experiences their attachment to comfort as an obstacle, they may reasonably 'feel that [they] should be freer without it'.[17] It looks as though Taylor thinks that, on a positive conception of freedom, your own desires could constitute impediments to your own freedom, and this is exactly what motivated Berlin's criticism, for a dictator extinguishing these desires would then have to be described as a *liberator*.[18]

Berlin's writings have contributed to the idea that there is an irreconcilable clash between positive and negative freedom, and that negative freedom is conceptually superior. Upon closer inspection, however, the distinction may not be so stark. Gerald MacCallum showed that at its core any account of freedom involves a triadic or three-place relation: statements of freedom involve an agent X, who is free (or not) from impediments Y, to perform some action Z.[19] MacCallum claimed that the debate about negative and positive freedom is primarily concerned with the relative normative importance of Y (impediments) and Z (actions). Champions of negative freedom focus on the impediments and assign highest normative priority to the absence of interference. Champions of positive freedom, by contrast, focus on the actions and value most those actions that contribute to such ideals as social progress or authenticity. But, ultimately, they are talking about the same concept: freedom.

Republican Freedom

A third stream of work has led to the development of republican conceptions of freedom, also associated with such terms as *antipower*, *non-domination*, or *neo-Roman freedom*. The starting point of Philip Pettit's version is the notion of domination.[20] A person is said to dominate another person whenever they have the 'capacity to interfere, on an arbitrary basis, in certain choices that the other is in a position to make'.[21]

By *interference*, Pettit here means intentional obstruction by means of human action that makes the dominated party worse off. So one cannot on Pettit's count interfere for someone's benefit. But the intentional obstruction does not need actually to take place. What suffices is that you could interfere if you were so inclined to, not whether you even have the slightest inclination to.[22] Furthermore, the interference is to be arbitrary, or *ad arbitrium*, which is to say: whether or not you interfere is entirely at your will, decision, or judgement, and there is no need for you to refer, in your judgement, to the interests or concerns of the dominated person. While a police officer has the capacity intentionally to worsen a criminal's situation, this interference is non-arbitrary, Pettit says, because the officer is forced to 'track the relevant interests' of the criminal—namely, 'those that are shared in common with others, not those that treat [the criminal] as exceptional, since the state is meant to serve others as well as me'.[23] This shows that the republican conception of freedom is value-laden, just as the positive conceptions already discussed.[24] What interests are relevant in this regard depends on whom you think the state should serve and how you think the state should do that, which for Pettit and other champions of republican freedom is answered by a republican theory of government.[25]

Arguments for Freedom

It is one thing to debate conceptions of freedom. It is quite another thing to determine what gives freedom its value.[26] For some specific freedoms, this is straightforward. The value of religious freedom or free speech, for instance, is easily accounted for in terms of the value of religion and speech. But what about freedom per se, or *overall freedom*?[27] One might be led to think that what makes overall freedom valuable depends on how you define freedom; for clearly, if you follow Taylor and think of freedom as the ability fully to realize your authentic self, then the value you assign to freedom is to do with the value of self-realization and authenticity. Yet the connection between freedom and value is not always so immediate.[28]

Argument from Desire Satisfaction

The most prominent argument links freedom to desire satisfaction.[29] The main idea is that, in order to satisfy your desires, you need to be able to select actions that help you realize your goals, and that the larger your opportunity set is, the more likely it is that it contains such actions. This argument from desire satisfaction starts with a premiss about the value of desire satisfaction:

(1) Desire satisfaction is valuable.

It then introduces a premiss linking freedom and desire satisfaction:

(2) Desire satisfaction increases when freedom increases.

And from these two premisses it obtains support for the claim about freedom's value:

(3) Freedom is valuable.

Some observations first.[30] For (1) to say that desire satisfaction is *valuable* is more than saying we maximize expected utility.[31] We maximize expected utility relative to a given opportunity set by choosing the best available action. But that action may not yield maximum utility if another action, not in the opportunity set, would lead to even higher expected utility. The core idea of the argument from desire satisfaction is therefore that, when the opportunity set of an expected utility maximizer is enlarged, their chances of reaching higher expected utility increase (or, at least, these chances do not decrease).[32] It is key that this assumption is taken to be about expanding opportunity sets rather than about their cardinality—that is, about the sheer number of elements they contain, as clearly an opportunity set containing few attractive travel destinations satisfies a globetrotter's desires more than an opportunity set containing many stay-home options.

Salmon or Steak?

This line of reasoning is essential to the argument from desire satisfaction. But is it entirely watertight? A classic objection is inspired by an observation due to Duncan Luce and Howard Raiffa.[33] They invite us to imagine a situation in a restaurant in which a waiter tells a guest that they can have steak or broiled salmon. The guest chooses *salmon*. Soon the waiter returns, however, to tell the guest that besides steak and salmon they also serve fried snails today. The guest does not like fried snails, but still changes their order: they order the *steak*.

If this is coherent, then this casts doubt on the above backing of premiss (2). It casts doubts on the idea that, whenever your opportunity grows by one option, your expected utility increases if the added option is better than the best action from the original opportunity set, or remains the same if the best action from the original set is the best action from the expanded set as well. Below I show how an informational perspective helps to put this objection in place.

Choice Overload: *Embarras de choix* and Anticipatory Regret

A second way to put pressure on the argument from desire satisfaction stems from psychology. Psychologists maintain that people are easily overwhelmed when their opportunity set grows too large. Imagine, at Starbucks, pondering a Gingerbread Latte, a Caramel Macchiato, a Java Chip Frappuccino, or a simple espresso, or think of the challenges selecting mobile phone subscriptions or health insurance, and you get a feel for what this objection is about. In a well-known experiment, Sheena Iyengar and Mark Lepper examined the phenomenon of choice overload in the context of consumer behaviour.[34] In one setting, consumers visiting an upmarket grocery store in Menlo Park (California) were offered sample tastes from six flavours of a brand of jam at a tasting booth. In another condition, they were offered twenty-four flavours of the same brand. Did they subsequently buy jam? In the setting with limited choice, 30 per cent of the people who had tried jam bought a jar of the brand. In the more plentiful setting, the proportion dropped to 3 per cent. This suggests that, if you want to sell jam, you should make sure consumers have only limited choice. You should limit their freedom, for otherwise they may feel upset, and you will not sell as much.

That consumers feel upset may be due to various factors, according to the psychologists. You may feel encumbered by an excess of options— that is, by an *embarras de choix* that you experience as a very obstacle itself, barring you from choosing. You are simply charged with too big a task. But another factor may arise out of your anticipating the possibility of regretting a bad choice. The more options there are, the more likely it may seem to the decision maker that, when they select one option, another option may in the end turn out to be better. This form of anticipatory regret seems to affect especially what might be called *maximizers*, consumers possessing Oscar Wilde's 'simplest tastes' of being 'always satisfied with the best'. So-called *satisficers*, who are satisfied provided a certain threshold level is met, would be less prone to be guided by concerns about regret. But, whether or not choice overload upsets people through *embarras de choix* or through anticipatory regret, the bottom line is that an increase in freedom does not seem to increase desire satisfaction. Exit premiss (2).[35]

Type and Extent of Protection of Freedom

A third line to criticize the argument from desire satisfaction proceeds on conceptual rather than psychological grounds. The main issue here is not whether the argument is sound (a question about the plausibility of its premisses) but rather what conception of freedom it could be an argument for.

This translates into two questions: one is about the extent of freedom; the other is about the type of freedom protected by the argument. Let me first talk about extent of freedom. If it is only desire satisfaction that makes you assign value to freedom, then it is enough for you to possess very limited freedom. You need only the freedom to perform the best action, as no other actions are relevant to your desire satisfaction. In other words, reducing a person's freedom is compatible with the argument from desire satisfaction as long as their expected utility does not decrease while reducing their freedom. This is a variant of Berlin's objection against Mill's conception of freedom. The extent of protection the argument from desire satisfaction offers to your freedoms is very small, which, as we shall see, contrasts this argument with the argument from responsibility. As Hayek wrote:

> The case for individual freedom rests chiefly on the recognition of the inevitable ignorance of all of us concerning a great many of the factors on which the achievement of our ends and welfare depends. … If there

were omniscient men, if we could know not only all that affects the attainment of our present wishes, but also our future wants and desires, there would be little case for liberty.[36]

Let me now turn to type of freedom. The challenge here is that the argument from desire satisfaction does not specifically engage with the political character of freedom that many scholars assume. Some hold on to the view that freedom is curtailed only by impediments caused by the actions of other people. A police officer can make me unfree to leave the village; an avalanche, according to such a view, cannot. The focus on human impediments is often justified by the observation that our interest in freedom is political—for instance, motivated by the ambition to develop a political theory about legitimate state interference. This is particularly clear in such undertakings as Pettit's defence of republicanism. If you adopt such an approach, you should expect that the disvalue faced as a result of a police officer's interference is different in size or character from the disvalue faced because of an avalanche.

The objection now is that making such a distinction is not something the argument from desire satisfaction can do. Whether interference is due to the police officer or to the avalanche, I am unable to leave the village. If leaving the village is what I desire most, then both cases should be judged equally, from the point of view of the argument from desire satisfaction. Following that logic, removing the police force has the same value as removing the avalanche.

To take stock, I listed three objections that may be raised against the argument from desire satisfaction: the salmon–steak case, the choice overload objection (*embarrax de choix*, anticipatory regret), and a conceptual objection about extent and type of freedom protected by the argument. Before proceeding to the argument from responsibility, let me make a general observation that is brought into relief by the third line of criticism (about extent and type of freedom): arguments for freedom and conceptions of freedom are often mutually dependent on one another, and can be in tune with each other, or not. Consider republican freedom. For there to be a reduction of republican freedom, someone has to have the capacity intentionally to worsen another person's situation. If desire satisfaction is what gives republican freedom its value, then it is unclear why the worsening (certainly something that decreases desire satisfaction) has to be intentional: unintentional worsening reduces desire satisfaction just as much.

This shows that the argument from desire satisfaction is not really in tune with the republican conception of freedom. The republican needs another argument.

Argument from Responsibility

The argument from responsibility partly addresses the empirical and conceptual objections against the argument from desire satisfaction. Its logic is similar. It is based on a premiss about the value of responsibility:

(4) Responsibility is valuable.

And on a premiss linking responsibility and freedom:

(5) Responsibility increases when freedom increases.

These two premisses are claimed to support the desired conclusion about freedom's value:

(3) Freedom is valuable.

The plausibility of the two premisses (4) and (5) very much depends on what one takes *responsibility* to mean.

Consequentialist and Kantian Praise and Blame

One approach is to consider the practice of holding people responsible for their deeds.[37] A consequentialist may value responsibility because of the alleged beneficial effects of such a practice. When we blame and praise others in more or less predictable ways, we establish incentives for people to conform to moral norms, at least if people value praise and disvalue blame. A more Kantian merit-based approach, by contrast, values the practice of holding each other responsible on the grounds that it is a reflection of the fact that people genuinely deserve praise (or blame) for their actions, when these actions are in accordance with morality (or not). Probably this presupposes a more objective view about morality.

On both counts, the link between freedom and responsibility as captured by (5) has some plausibility. For the Kantian, freedom is likely to figure as a conceptual presupposition for someone genuinely to deserve praise (or blame).[38] Take a bank employee who is offered money for deposit from a client involved in money laundering. If the reason why the banker does not accept the client's money is that the software at the bank automatically bars employees from opening an account for such clients, then the banker does not deserve praise for their behaviour. But, if the banker takes that decision all by him or herself, fully aware of the potential attractions of doing business with the client—there is great demand for the client's sizeable wealth, as money is scarce—then the banker does merit the praise. So whether or not the banker merits the praise depends on whether or not the banker was free.

For the consequentialist, on the other hand, the link between freedom and responsibility can be understood in terms of incentives. The consequentialist thinks that the practice of holding people responsible obtains its sense because of the fact that it creates incentives for people to behave ethically. But incentives work by virtue of the fact that some courses of action get more, and others less, utility. When alternative courses of action are absent (or when the available actions are equally good or bad), the creation of incentives is senseless. This shows that, for incentives to play the role the consequentialist assigns to them, there has to be freedom.

Agency, Causal Efficacy, and Responsibility

The Kantian and consequentialist stories about the practice of responsibility provide support for both premises of the argument from responsibility. They tell us why responsibility matters (premiss (4)): to incentivize or praise moral behaviour. They also tell us that responsibility thus conceived presupposes freedom (premiss (5)): no incentives or praise without freedom. But we do not need the consequentialist or Kantian approach to appreciate this point. Here is a different way to defend the argument from responsibility.

Consider, first, Thomas Hurka's more formal argument.[39] He contrasts an agent with an opportunity set comprising ten options (A, B, C, and so on) with an agent with only one option (A). Then he imagines that both select A, and that this satisfies their respective desires maximally. From a desire-satisfaction perspective, there is no difference between the two agents. Yet their responsibilities diverge widely. The first person is responsible, Hurka says, not only for selecting *A*, but also for selecting not-*B*, not-*C*, and so forth. They are responsible for the non-realization of all available alternatives to *A*. The second person is, by contrast, responsible only for selecting *A*. Surely also for this second agent this leads to a situation in which *B*, and *C*, and so on, are not realized. But, in Hurka's words, in that case 'the responsibility for their non-realization rests with nature, with whoever constrained [the second person]—in any case not with [the second person]'.[40] This line of reasoning offers a much more direct defence of premiss (5): enlarging the freedom of the second person makes their responsibility grow. This connection between freedom and responsibility is quite strong. Freedom and responsibility are perfectly correlated, for Hurka, in that an increase in freedom is an increase in responsibility, and, conversely, an increase in responsibility is an increase in freedom.

About the argument from desire satisfaction we asked: what extent and what type of freedom does it support? We saw that, since desire satisfaction is compatible with minimal freedom, the extent of freedom it supports or protects is exceedingly small. We also saw that it does not offer support for a specifically political conception of freedom. How does the argument from responsibility fare in these respects? It is straightforward to see that the argument from responsibility protects large extents of freedom, particularly construed along the lines of Hurka's approach: the addition of one action to a person's opportunity set increases the set of actions the non-realization of which they are responsible for. This is very different from the case of the argument from desire satisfaction, where it is possible to increase freedom without increasing desire satisfaction (but not of course conversely).

Hurka seems, however, less interested in construing his argument so as to offer special protection to a specifically political conception of freedom. Here, however, going back to the consequentialist and Kantian lines of defence might help. One way of posing the question is whether we should assign specific *disvalue* to a decrease in a person's extent of responsibility, if this decrease is due to a decrease of that person's freedom resulting from other people's actions, or dispositions to act. It seems to me we can answer this question affirmatively, at least if we approach the issue in specific ways. To see this, consider a case, slightly different from above, in which a banker is tempted to accept a money launderer as a client. In one version of the case, the banker overcomes the temptation and rejects the client. In another, a power shortage makes it impossible for the banker to log on to the system to open a client account. In a third version, a colleague overhears the conversation with the criminal and decides to intervene, perhaps rather drastically by switching off their colleague's computer system.

The task now is to show why the third scenario should be seen as a restriction of the banker's responsibility, but not the second. Let us distinguish the Kantian and the consequentialist again. The consequentialist might point out that the practice of holding people responsible is less effective in realizing its aim (that is, creating incentives for moral behaviour) if some person P anticipates that some 'moral expert' Q may intervene when P is tempted to engage in immoral behaviour. When you know your colleague intervenes when you are about to act wrongly, it makes no sense for you to acquire knowledge of the relevant moral and legal norms. So the consequentialist can plausibly argue that an organization relying on the interventions of a small group of moral experts (the Q just mentioned) is unlikely to acquire and maintain morality in a very stable way. The third scenario is exactly of this kind, and therefore the limitation of the banker's opportunity set frustrates their personal responsibility in a way that the consequentialist would not want to sanction. In the second scenario, by contrast, this does not apply, and hence there is no lamentable reduction of their responsibility, from the consequentialist point of view.

A Kantian line of defence can be developed if we assume, not just that people should get praise when they merit it, but rather more that people desire and vie for merited praise in situations where merited praise can be obtained. I do not want to make too much of this, so I offer this only as a tentative suggestion. We would need to introduce something like an economy of praise and blame, in which people (sometimes) compete with each other for praise and (sometimes) resent others taking away opportunities to gain praise.[41] In the first version of the money launderer case, there is an opportunity for merited praise, both for the banker (who seizes the opportunity) and for their colleague (who could in principle have intervened). The power shortage removes that opportunity for both of them in the second scenario, so there is no change in the economy of praise and blame there. In the third scenario, however, the colleague does seize the opportunity to intervene and thereby frustrates the banker's desire for merited praise. The colleague's intervention (say, by switching off the computer system) leads to a situation in which the banker cannot obtain the praise that they may have desired to merit, which means that the third scenario can be construed as one in which the personal responsibility of the banker was decreased.

Self-Determination and Self-Employed Workers

We have three ways of defending premisses (4) and (5) of the argument from responsibility: one along Kantian lines (merited praise), another along consequentialist lines (incentives), and one due to Thomas Hurka. It is important to appreciate a peculiarity of these three lines. Consider premiss (4) again, according to which responsibility is valuable. A natural question to ask is to whom it is of value that some person P is responsible. The consequentialist should generally be inclined to say that it is valuable to bystanders, because it incentivizes or 'responsibilizes' P to act ethically. The Kantian, on the other hand, might find that it is primarily P who benefits, for it is P who gets or does not get the praise they merit. (The Kantian might find it more difficult to explain why P should be interested in getting merited blame, but that is a question I ignore.) Hurka's approach seems to agree with the Kantian, which becomes clearer once we realize that part of what makes responsibility so defined attractive to person P is that it endows P with 'agency' or 'causal efficacy'.[42] The more P can exclude ('non-realize'), the larger their agency and causal efficacy.

But why should P value agency and causal efficacy?[43] Here it is interesting to turn to the psychological research on self-determination, which is due to Edward Deci and Richard Ryan.[44] To the extent that we are justified in equating responsibility and agency or causal control, this literature offers some additional evidence for premiss (4). Consider, for instance, the degree of agency that workers enjoy in the workplace. A recent review by Lea Cassar and Stephan Meier suggests that fostering the control and responsibility of workers increases their intrinsic motivation in the job, is associated with positive health effects (through, among others, a reduction of work-related stress), higher productivity, enhanced job safety, and a host of other beneficial effects.[45]

One way to make this more concrete is to investigate a question such as whether individuals are willing to pay (or forgo income) in order to increase their agency. It seems they do. Self-employed individuals generally have lower initial earnings than employed workers, and the growth of their earnings is also likely to be less (a median difference of 35 per cent after ten years). But they are willing to lose out on the benefits of employment because they value the control they have over their working day.[46] It offers them greater flexibility in their schedules, which may help them to realize various other projects—and they may also simply value being their own boss.

Argument from Self-Realization

Before turning to epistemic or informational topics that form the centre of this book, I briefly discuss a third argument for freedom, the argument from self-realization. Self-realization comes in various guises. The common core is the ideal of developing one's capacities to the fullest. Wilhelm von Humboldt, perhaps its most eloquent champion, describes the ultimate goal of a human being as developing their powers into a consistent whole, downplaying the contributions of disparate activities to their self-realization, or such actions that draw less from their capacities, or even go against them. Humboldt observes that, in order to reach this ideal, we need freedom as well as what he calls 'variety' or 'manifoldness of situations'.[47] John Stuart Mill largely followed Humboldt. Twentieth-century conceptions of self-realization due to scholars such as Charles Taylor linked it with authenticity, the ideal of acting in accordance with what one is 'really' or 'deeply' convinced one's desires are or should be.[48] Alternatively, this could be linked with a more socially determined or 'welfarist' conception of a social good, as envisaged by Jon Elster.[49]

Whatever way you read the concept of self-realization, it is clear that the argument from self-realization does not offer protection to all freedom. Its extent of protection is those freedoms you may need to realize yourself, and it has very little that makes it typically political. If, as Elster has it, you think that 'juggling with a chain saw' can contribute to self-realization, whereas 'talking with friends' and 'making love' cannot, then preventing the latter does not reduce freedom's value.[50]

Informational Assumptions

Let me continue and turn to the epistemic analysis of the arguments for freedom's value. The surveyed arguments offer support for freedom by showing that freedom contributes to desire satisfaction, responsibility, self-realization—or really any other value that might plausibly be linked to freedom using the logic from above. Not everything that contributes to anything valuable is something that we should promote, though. Some things have morally unacceptable side effects, are too costly, or are not sufficiently aesthetically pleasing. And some things contribute only marginally. So, if we want to contribute to something valuable, then we should be particularly interested in what makes a large and significant contribution, perhaps even a maximal one. The idea that I develop in this section is that, if large or maximal desire satisfaction, responsibility, or self-realization is what we want, then freedom per se (whether construed in negative, positive, or republican terms) is not what we should focus on most. What contributes more to desire satisfaction, responsibility, and self-realization is freedom accompanied by adequate beliefs. Only a decision maker who is informed about their opportunity set can use their freedom for desire satisfaction, responsibility, or self-realization. That, in a nutshell, is the main claim defended in this section.[51]

Argument from Desire Satisfaction

I now consider the arguments from desire satisfaction and responsibility from this informational or epistemic point of view. The argument from desire satisfaction is based on the observation that, if a person's opportunity set grows by one option, say A, that person's expected utility may increase, and does not decrease. It may be that there is an option B that yields greater expected utility than A (or equal expected utility). In that case, the addition of A does not boost desire satisfaction. Or there is no such B, and then the addition of A increases desire satisfaction. Or does it?

If the decision maker is unaware of the fact that A is available, then they may not use A to increase their desire satisfaction. The same applies if they do not know what consequences A has, or when they do not know how likely these consequences are. In order to make use of their freedom, decision makers generally need to be informed about their choice situation.[52] Freedom, that is, contributes to desire satisfaction when particular informational assumptions hold true. This insight is reflected in the following rendering of the argument from desire satisfaction. Here the term *known freedom* is a placeholder for freedom satisfying these informational assumptions, a concept on which I make expand towards the end of this chapter.

The first premiss is unchanged:

(3) Desire satisfaction is valuable.

But the second is different:

(6) Desire satisfaction increases when known freedom increases.

Whence a different conclusion:

(7) Known freedom is valuable.

One way to summarize this is to say that the informational perspective makes clear that, to the extent that you accept the argument from desire satisfaction as an argument for freedom, you should a fortiori accept it as an argument for known freedom.[53]

Connoisseurship

The informational perspective brings considerable theoretical benefits: it allows us to address some of the objections already surveyed—that is, Luce and Raiffa's salmon–steak case, the worry about choice overload (about *embarrass de choix* and anticipated regret), and the worries about the extent of protection offered by the argument.

Let me start with choice overload: individuals confronted with large opportunity sets experience overwhelm or choice overload, which bars them from choosing, and in such circumstances Oscar Wilde type maximizers are more likely to anticipate future regret. Consider the jam experiment due to Iyengar and Lepper again. The authors of the study interpret their results as showing that the more flavours consumers can select, the larger the likelihood is that consumers will face choice overload.[54]

But a different reading is in epistemic terms: the participants in the experiment have rather incomplete information concerning their choice situation. While they certainly know how many actions are available to them (they see the jam jars), they are probably less fully informed about the likely consequences of selecting them, and perhaps also about their actual desires vis-à-vis the various flavours. They do not fully know the precise gustatory and olfactory sensations that the consumption of the various jams will lead to, nor how the various jams combine with the toast they have for breakfast, for instance. They do not know how to distinguish, say, Little

Scarlet Strawberry Conserve from East Anglian Strawberry conserve, and, as a result, they do not know which one they would prefer. My claim is then that, once consumers gain knowledge about their choice situation and reach a bit of 'connoisseurship', they are much less likely to face *embarrass de choix*. They then simply know what to buy.[55]

It is, of course, an empirical question what the level of known freedom is that consumers minimally need for the level of connoisseurship to be high enough to maximize sales. The takeaway from my example here is that at least a one-off sample tasting as provided in the experiment by Iyengar and Lepper is insufficient to provide the requisite information to consumers. Generally, however, I am inclined to think that most people have mastered sufficiently high levels of relevant known freedom in such everyday routine environments as the grocery store. The European visitor experiences some choice overload the first time they walk through the proverbial cereals aisle of an American supermarket. But they quickly adjust.

Consumer Obfuscation and Naïveté-Based Discrimination

It is equally clear, however, that in other domains we radically lack known freedom. As an influential study by Paul Heidhues and Botond Kőszegi demonstrates, phone-subscription plans may be a case in which service providers intentionally exploit the lack of knowledge on the part of consumers about the consequences of taking out particular subscriptions.[56] This form of consumer obfuscation they call *naïveté-based discrimination*. In particular, consumers may underestimate the number of minutes of an average (or maximum) call, therefore may take out too lean a subscription, and as a result will have to pay more in overage charges than they had expected (and also more in total than they would pay with a more suitable plan).

Anticipating Future Risks

Let me turn to the second objection against the argument from desire satisfaction, concerning anticipatory regret. Here there are two possible scenarios. One ground for anticipatory regret may lie in the decision maker's realization that, when they select some jam, or some phone plan, another jam or phone plan may turn out to be more desirable. They do not know everything about the jam or phone plan as yet, and it is because of this uncertainty that they cannot exclude that such a form of regret will arise. With more and better information about the choice situation, though, this uncertainty decreases.

But regret may also arise out of the probabilistic nature of the consequences of the available options. Let us assume I can spend some sum of money on either bonds or shares. The general idea is that bonds are less risky than company shares. If I buy shares, I may earn more, but also lose more, as compared with the situation in which I spend the whole sum on bonds. A decision maker who is prone to anticipate regret will realize that, while they may earn more with the shares than the bonds, they may also end up in a situation where they regret having selected the shares rather than the bonds. In such a case, extra knowledge is of no avail. The decision maker is facing a process that determines the outcomes of their actions indeterministically, or at least unpredictably, and they have to live with it. More information about, say, the volatility of the shares (roughly, the amount of variation) may help them to manage their anticipatory regret (and may help them select some less volatile shares). But it will not eliminate anticipated regret.

Before proceeding, it may be relevant to consider an objection to the effect that the acquisition of information is also costly. Acquiring known freedom may require money and effort, and will always require time and attention, and so known freedom comes with opportunity costs. The perceived need for information search (or the search activities themselves) may therefore be a cause of distress as such, hindering decision-making. This is a valid point. Think about the amount of effort it would take really to turn yourself into a jam connoisseur or an expert on phone subscriptions. Yet, more theoretically, the force of this objection is weakened once we include information acquisition activities in the decision maker's opportunity set as well, and so make it explicit in the model that they trade off the advantages of getting more information against their costs.

Good Salmon or Good Steak?

Back to the objections against the argument from desire satisfaction. What about Luce and Raiffa's salmon–steak case? The guest was told there were steak and salmon on the menu, and ordered salmon. Then the waiter returned to tell them there were also snails, which made them change their order to steak. The waiter will certainly have been surprised, but the strangeness of the guest's order disappears when we consider the broader informational consequences of the waiter's announcement. Luce and Raiffa explain that the guest first thought the restaurant's quality was average, and, since they prefer an *average salmon* over an *average steak*, they ordered salmon. Learning about the snails, however, the guest updated their beliefs about the restaurant on the grounds that (they believed) only good restaurants offer snails. And, since they prefer *good steak* over *good salmon*, they changed their order to salmon. In other words, what happened here was not just an expansion of the guest's opportunity set, but rather also a belief update concerning the characteristics of the available options. The guest's freedom increased (they could now get snails), but the guest also increased their knowledge about freedom (as they learned that they could get a *good* steak).

Argument from Uncertainty, and the Ignorance Trick

Before proceeding, let me put things in relief by considering the role of knowledge and freedom from a slightly different angle. Recall Gerald Mac-Callum's triadic analysis of freedom as a relation between an agent X who is free to do or become Y, unhampered by constraints Z.[57] Isaiah Berlin famously objected to MacCallum's analysis:

> This seems to me an error. A man struggling against his chains or a people against enslavement need not consciously aim at any definite further state [the Y]. A man need not know how he will use his freedom; he just wants to remove the yoke.[58]

For Berlin, then, it seems that an agent X and potential constraints Z are the only necessary components of an analysis of freedom. Ian Carter argues that Berlin's objection rests on a mistaken (or insufficiently precise) analysis of the value of freedom.[59] For Carter, we need to realize that there is a difference between the *specific* value that some freedom may have (say, the value of freedom of speech to a person who wants to express their opinion on a particular matter) and what he calls its *non-specific* (or also *independent*) value:

> A phenomenon, x, has non-specific value … [if and only if] the value of x cannot be described wholly in terms of a good brought about or contributed to by a specific instance of x or set of specific instances of x.[60]

We should, therefore, say, according to Carter, that what a person struggling against their chains values is not certain specific instances of freedom such as the freedom of speech. Rather they attach non-specific value to the freedom to do things 'in general'.[61] The third element is still there. Berlin is mistaken.

There are, however, at least two ways to think of Carter's definition of non-specific value. These ways are not necessarily mutually incompatible, but they put the focus on different aspects of Carter's account. One might, first, read the definition as suggesting something primarily to do with the metaphysics of value. We have some property F that applies to a range of instances a, b, c, and so on, and F's value is *not* reducible to the respective values of its instances a, b, c, and so on, nor to properties these respective instances have. Secondly, one could give the concept of non-specific value an epistemic reading. Carter has hinted at such a reading himself at various places. He writes:

> The reason for seeing freedom as nonspecifically instrumentally valuable lies in an awareness of the unavoidability of human ignorance and fallibility.[62]

Carter quotes Hayek to illustrate the point (a quote we have seen already):

> if there were omniscient men, if we could know not only all that affects the attainment of our present wishes but also our future wants and desires, there would be little case for liberty.[63]

For our purposes, the relevance of this is that, if we accept this epistemic reading of non-specific value, and if we attach value to freedom primarily on the basis of its non-specific value in this sense, then we have a most direct line of argumentation for taking the epistemic assumptions of arguments for freedom's value into account.[64] In fact, what Hayek and Carter write about ignorance can be turned into something like an ignorance trick. The argument from desire satisfaction as such offers no special protection to actions that an agent will never desire to perform. It is, in that sense, a very weak argument for freedom. But, if we apply the ignorance trick, it becomes quite powerful: for it then protects all actions about which we do *not* know that we will never want to perform them.[65] That may be quite a few.[66]

Argument from Responsibility

Knowledge about our choice situation (opportunity set, consequences, probabilities) helps us to satisfy our desires, and that is why the argument from desire satisfaction is really an argument for known freedom. Is the argument from responsibility an argument for known freedom too? To see it does, requires little work, given what I have explicated about the epistemic assumptions of the argument from desire satisfaction. The argument from responsibility is grounded in the value of the practice of holding people responsible, construed along consequentialist or Kantian lines. On a consequentialist defence, praise and blame work as carrots and sticks—that is, as incentives that, the hope is, induce people to comply with the demands of morality. For such incentives to work in the long run, people should generally be aware of sufficiently many alternatives: it makes no sense to incentivize people into some form of behaviour if they do not see that they have anything to choose from. Praising a person for their good deeds in an environment where they are not aware of any attractive, yet immoral, courses of action makes little sense: what you are unaware of cannot tempt you. This gives us a way to appreciate the value of known freedom for personal responsibility, from the consequentialist viewpoint.

The Kantian line is a bit different. Here what matters is not whether the practice leads to some desired end. The idea rather is that holding people responsible by praising and blaming them is the right thing to do to the extent that they deserve the praise or blame. There may, as we saw, even be some sort of competition for merited praise. Consider again the banker confronted with a money launderer offering the money for deposit. If they are unaware of the client's criminal activities (and could not have found out about them), then they do not deserve blame, because for a person to be blameworthy for something they must have been able somehow to foresee it. But, even if they were aware of the client's criminal background, they may not be blameworthy by accepting the deposit—namely, if they were unaware of (and could not have found out about) alternative courses of action. For instance, the banker may have reasonably entertained the thought they had no choice because rejecting the deposit would endanger some of the bank's employees (say, the gun was clearly displayed to communicate these intentions). Similar observations hold for praise. It is decidedly odd to praise the banker for not giving in to the temptation of opening an account for the money launderer if, for instance, the reason why they did not open the account was that they thought the relevant computer system was temporarily out of order. Using Thomas Hurka's terminology, in order to be held responsible for not-A (so for the non-realization of A), one has to be aware of the fact that A is in one's opportunity set. This shows that the Kantian reading of the argument from responsibility is also better seen as an argument for known freedom.[67]

Known Freedom

This chapter has introduced conceptions of freedom, outlined arguments for freedom's value, and shown how these arguments should really be seen as arguments for known freedom. For I have argued that our freedom generates its intended benefits (desire satisfaction, responsibility, and so forth) only if we know about it. In the next chapter I continue looking at freedom through the epistemic lens. There I consider *doxastic freedom* (freedom of belief) and *epistemic freedom* (freedom to know). Before turning to these topics, however, let me say some words about the concept of known freedom, which has so far not been defined with great precision. A small excursion into fear of crime and freedom of education concludes this picture.

Known freedom is best explained using the standard economics model of rational choice.[68] A decision maker's choice situation consists of a set of opportunities—that is, actions available for choosing. Actions have consequences that arise with particular probabilities, which generally depend on the actions of other people as well as on 'nature' (how and when I arrive in the office depends on the weather and other cyclists). The decision maker desires some outcomes more than others, a fact that can be modelled by a preference ordering over the consequences of all available actions. In addition to that, agents have a range of beliefs: about the opportunity set, the consequences, the probabilities, the preferences.[69]

Known freedom obtains when all these beliefs are correct, maximally accurate, and complete.[70] Can known freedom ever obtain? Whether it can is not so much the point. Known freedom is something to be aspired. We are hardly ever fully informed about all details of a choice situation. What matters, however, is that we see how we can increase known freedom. To do that, we do not always need to increase freedom. When agents are unaware of certain aspects of their choice situation, gaining more information increases known freedom. Nor is increasing freedom sufficient to increase known freedom: an agent whose opportunity set is expanded by some option does not gain in known freedom unless they become aware of the expansion. A call for maximizing known freedom is therefore a call for increasing freedom and knowledge about freedom.

A Case: Fear of Crime

As with many important moral and political ideals, the value of known freedom is perhaps best illustrated when we look at situations in which it is somewhat absent. A telling case is drawn from work in media studies scholarship concerning fear of crime among US citizens in the 1990s, carried out by Dennis Lowry, Tarn Ching, Josephine Nio, and Dennis Leitner.[71] Great reductions in crime were witnessed during these years, making American cities safer places than they had been for a long time. Homicide rates almost halved, from 9.4 in 1990 to 5.5 in 1999, per 100,000 inhabitants. Nevertheless, these researchers show that public perceptions of crime (as measured, for instance, by asking people what they considered the most important social challenge) went up. People perceived American cities as increasingly unsafe, as places to avoid, at least without car or company.

One explanation for this discrepancy between reality and perception, Lowry and his team argue, was the agenda setting that went on in broadcasting companies: crime obtained more and more (prime-time) attention. Coverage of homicide rates went up from 80 evening news items in 1992 to a stunning 587 items in 1999, excluding the civil war in former Yugoslavia (300 minutes of coverage in night shows), the Oklahoma City bombing (400 minutes), and the O. J. Simpson trial (1,591 minutes). For people getting most of their information from such television shows, it is unsurprising that they ended up believing that their environment was rapidly becoming more and more dangerous. In 1999, you would on an average see more than one news item per day reporting a homicide case.

Fear of crime is reflected in the beliefs people have about their choice situation. Relative to some benchmark, a fearful person assigns higher probability to events such as theft, robbery, assault, and homicide, and may also tend to believe that certain actions are not part of their opportunity set (such as walking home at night undisturbed). This clearly affects their behaviour. Someone who thinks that there is a significant chance that they will be robbed if they walk to the theatre will rationally take a taxi. Now, if these higher probabilities reflect reality, knowing about them adds to your known freedom. They inform you about your opportunities and their likely consequences in a way that helps you decide. But, if they do not reflect reality, you are not adequately informed, and your known freedom decreases.

Consequently, crime prevention faces significant challenges here. Some crime-prevention techniques are quite successful at reducing crime rate, typically by reducing the number of opportunities for crime. But, as long as people do not realize that these techniques reduce crime, their fear level remains the same. Other techniques reduce fear of crime without necessarily reducing opportunities for crime.[72] In between these two types of policy is an approach inspired by the broken-window theory, proposed by James Wilson and George Kelling in the *Atlantic*, according to which police attention to small disorders would promise large reductions of crime.[73] This approach has caught on in the US, as New York, Chicago, and Los Angeles have adopted measures inspired by the theory—for instance, through more aggressively enforcing minor misdemeanour laws. While this may increase subjective feelings of safety, it is dubious whether it has reduced crime rates.[74] This means that potentially the policy has decreased rather than increased known freedom.

A Worry: Amish Education

A worry might be that focusing on the value of knowledge to desire satisfaction and personal responsibility might lead to an instrumentalization of knowledge—that is, a view of knowledge as only a tool to satisfy our desires and gain responsibility or self-determination. We would not, that is, need to know more than we need to satisfy our desires and assume responsibility, and, if these desires and responsibilities are 'small', then our knowledge can be 'small'.

In an oft-discussed case that came before the US Supreme Court in 1971, the thought was that indeed sometimes we do not need to know much.[75] The court ruled that certain groups of Amish in Wisconsin are allowed to stop education of their children at the age of 14 instead of the usual 16 years, because among other things Amish children need to know only things that are necessary for living in what Russell Hardin has called the 'extraordinarily restrictive Amish society, in which a low level of education is sufficient for a normal level of success in occupational life'.[76] Perhaps this education gives Amish children the knowledge they need to satisfy the desires and to assume the responsibilities that are typical of Amish life.[77] It surely does not offer them a great deal of further knowledge, though. My argument says that what people in any society should know is at least the things they need for what could be called a 'normal level of success in occupational life'.[78] So in a sense what I say may be congruent with this line of reasoning. But there is so much more to know that, while not strictly speaking necessary in that sense, is still very worth having. To make more specific what knowledge that is should not be my aim here, though.[79]

Notes

1. Thomas Hobbes, *Leviathan, or the Matter, Forme & Power of a Common-Wealth Ecclesiasticall and Civill* (London: Andrew Crooke, 1651), 64.
2. Ibid. 108.
3. Ibid. 107.
4. Ibid.
5. Ian Carter, *A Measure of Freedom* (Oxford: Oxford University Press, 1999), 153 ff., and Matthew Kramer, *The Quality of Freedom* (Oxford: Oxford University Press, 2003), 264 ff., discuss this type of impediment in the context of a theory of negative freedom.
6. John Stuart Mill, *On Liberty* (London: John W. Parker, 1859), 172–173, where it is stated: 'If either a public officer or any one else saw a person attempting to cross a bridge which had been ascertained to be unsafe, and there were no time to warn him of his danger, they might seize him and turn him back, without any real infringement of his liberty; for liberty consists in doing what one desires, and he does not desire to fall into the river.' It seems, then, that Mill thinks we can remove a strictly dominated action from a person's opportunity

set without diminishing their freedom—that is, an action for which there is an alternative that is strictly better. Yet he continues: 'Nevertheless, when there is not a certainty, but only a danger of mischief, no one but the person himself can judge of the sufficiency of motive which may prompt him to incur the risk: in this case, therefore … he ought … to be only warned of the danger; not forcibly prevented from exposing himself to it.' Mill seems to suggest an epistemic policy rather than paternalistic interference once matters become probabilistic. But this may make matters worse by making the argument dependent on the decision maker's attitude towards risk. Should the person also only be warned and not interfered with if there is a 99 per cent chance of the bridge collapsing? Mill might think that the 'public officer' knows that most people do not want to take such risks. But, if knowledge of another person's preferences is what drives the inference here, then it looks as though any paternalistic interference becomes justifiable again, which was exactly what Mill wanted to avoid.

7. Isaiah Berlin, 'Two Concepts of Liberty', in Berlin, *Four Essays on Liberty* (London: Oxford University Press, 1969), 139–140. This qualification does not occur in the 1958 version of the essay (Berlin's inaugural address). Berlin acknowledges an anonymous reviewer for having pointed out that he criticized a conception of freedom dependent on desires, while adopting such a conception himself. This reviewer was Richard Wollheim. See Henry Hardy (ed.), *Isaiah Berlin: Liberty* (Oxford: Oxford University Press, 2002), 30, n. 1. William Parent, 'Some Recent Work on the Concept of Liberty', *American Philosophical Quarterly*, 11 (1974), 149–167, at 152, doubts whether Berlin succeeded in avoiding desire-dependence himself. A slightly related point was raised by Felix Oppenheim, *Political Concepts* (Chicago: University of Chicago Press, 1981), 74 ('We must be careful not to confuse the degree of an actor's freedom with the degree of value he attaches to his freedom. The degree of my freedom is a function of the possibilities left open to me, but does not depend on whether these do or do not include actions that I desire to perform').

8. Keith Dowding and Martin van Hees, 'Counterfactual Success and Negative Freedom', *Economics and Philosophy*, 23 (2007), 141–162, note the problems with a 'preference-free' conception of freedom, and suggests a way of overcoming them by including the intentions of the interferer into the description of what renders people unfree. See also Keith Dowding and Martin van Hees, 'The Construction of Rights', *American Political Science Review*, 97 (2003), 281–293. Cf. Ian Carter, 'How Changes in One's Preferences Can Affect One's Freedom (and How they Cannot): A Reply to Dowding and Van Hees', *Economics and Philosophy*, 24 (2008), 81–89. Ian Hunt, 'Overall Freedom and Constraint', *Inquiry*, 44 (2001), 131–148, suggests an account of freedom dependent on

desires. Cf. Simon Keller, 'Freedom!', *Social Theory and Practice*, 31 (2005), 337–357, at 345 n.

9. See, generally, Ian Carter, 'Positive and Negative Liberty', in Edward Zalta (ed.), *The Stanford Encyclopedia of Philosophy*, 2016, plato.stanford.edu/entries/liberty-positive-negative [perma.cc/X8SL-A4UJ] on the types and sources of the constraints of freedom. See Friedrich von Hayek, *The Constitution of Liberty* (Chicago: Chicago University Press, 1960), for a requirement of intentionality or coercive intervention, Matthew Kramer, *The Quality of Freedom* (Oxford: Oxford University Press, 2003), for dispositions and causal responsibility, and David Miller, 'Constraints on Freedom', *Ethics*, 94 (1983), 66–86, and Frank Hindriks, 'Freedom under an Indifferent Dictator: Intentionality and Responsibility', *Economics and Philosophy*, 33 (2016), 25–41, for moral responsibility.

10. Matthew Kramer, *The Quality of Freedom* (Oxford: Oxford University Press, 2003). The term pure negative is due to Richard Flathman, *The Philosophy and Politics of Freedom* (Chicago: Chicago University Press, 1987). For further scholarship in the pure negative camp, see, e.g., Ian Carter, *A Measure of Freedom* (Oxford: Oxford University Press, 1999), Martin van Hees, 'On the Analysis of Negative Freedom', *Theory and Decision*, 45 (1998), 175–197, Hillel Steiner, 'Individual Liberty', *Proceedings of the Aristotelian Society*, 75 (1974–1975), 33–50, and Hillel Steiner, 'How Free: Computing Personal Liberty', *Royal Institute of Philosophy Supplements*, 15 (1983), 73–89. These authors are also interested in developing precise ways to measure the degree of freedom people possess. For other proposals of measuring freedom, see, e.g., Stanley Benn, *A Theory of Freedom* (Cambridge: Cambridge University Press, 1988), Lawrence Crocker, *Positive Liberty: An Essay in Normative Political Philosophy* (The Hague: Martinus Nijhoff Publishers, 1980), Charles Humana, *World Human Rights Guide* (London: Hodder and Stoughton, 1986), and United Nations Development Programme, *Human Development Report* (Oxford: Oxford University Press, 1991). It is interesting to note that for Hayek law does not make people unfree because, even though it is coercive in a sense, it is predictable. This introduces an epistemic element in the definition of constraint.

11. This is a fairly loose rendering. For details, see Matthew Kramer, *The Quality of Freedom* (Oxford: Oxford University Press, 2003), 3.

12. In line with standard economic terminology, I use *opportunity set* here to refer to one of the elements of a choice situation that a decision maker faces. The other elements are outcomes or consequences, and the likelihood with which they arise. Availability of actions may be thought of in probabilistic terms (with 10 per cent probability I have the option of buying a visa for the US), but the probability may equally be modelled as attached to the consequences (with

10 per cent probability my attempt to apply for a visa will result in my getting one). Probabilities are here objective. Agents attempt to estimate these
probabilities, making them subjective. See, e.g., Keith Dowding and Martin
van Hees, 'The Construction of Rights', *American Political Science Review*, 97
(2003), 281–293. Stanley Benn and William Weinstein, 'Being Free to Act, and
Being a Free Man', *Mind*, 80 (1971), 194–211, at 203, add a category of *eligible*
actions to the choice situation ('Even so, it might still be objected that though
Esau was not free to refuse Jacob's offer, this was because there happened to
be no other alternative course that a reasonable, prudent man would consider
eligible—not that Jacob had deprived him of alternatives to accepting. For he
had not'). This makes the account dependent on desires again. See Salvador
Barberà, Walter Bossert, and Prasanta Pattanaik, 'Ranking Sets of Objects', in
Peter Hammond and Christian Seidl (eds), *Handbook of Utility Theory: Volume 2: Extensions* (Amsterdam: Kluwer, 2004), 893–977, for the use of decision
theory to measure freedom.

13.   Thomas Green, *Liberal Legislation and Freedom of Contract* (Oxford: Slatter
and Rose, 1881), 9. See also Avital Simhony, 'On Forcing Individuals to be
Free: T. H. Green's Liberal Theory of Positive Freedom', *Political Studies*, 39
(1991), 303–330. As in the case of many republican thinkers, Green's definition
of freedom is given in what is a plea for designing particular political institutions, such as banning child labour and other deplorable practices on the shop
floor, prohibiting the renting of unhealthy houses, a strict regulation of alcohol
stores, the criminalization of various kinds of contracts between farmers and
landowners, and plans to revise education.

14.   Charles Taylor, 'What's Wrong with Negative Liberty', *Philosophy and the
Human Sciences* (1985), 211–229.

15.   John Christman, 'Liberalism and Individual Positive Freedom', *Ethics*, 101
(1991), 343–359, at 347, proposes an account of positive freedom in terms of
autonomy. For a desire to be formed autonomously, the agent has to have been
in the position to reflect on it, should not resist the desire, and should satisfy
some rationality conditions. As for Taylor, for Christman certain obstacles do
not restrict one's freedom: 'a Tibetan monk who has spent the last several years
in the same room meditating and sitting quietly … and from which he will
never desire to move' does not experience a change in his freedom of action
'[i]f chains are then put on the door to the room, a room he does not want to
leave' (ibid. 354). This analysis is incomplete, if not unsound, from the epistemic perspective defended later in this chapter. It should be added that the
Tibetan monk knows he will never desire to leave the room (so he will have
to know, for instance, that there will not be a fire emergency or similar). Cf.
Peter Jones and Robert Sugden, 'Evaluating Choice', *International Review of
Law and Economics*, 2 (1982), 47–65, at 59, for an observation to the effect that

economic theory overlooks the fact that we are somehow responsible for our preferences, potentially close to Christman's, but without proposing a positive account of freedom. See also Lawrence Crocker, *Positive Liberty: An Essay in Normative Political Philosophy* (The Hague: Martinus Nijhoff Publishers, 1980), and Steven Wall, *Liberalism, Perfectionism, and Restraint* (Cambridge: Cambridge University Press, 1998).

16. Charles Taylor, 'What's Wrong with Negative Liberty', *Philosophy and the Human Sciences* (1985), 211–229, at 221.

17. Ibid. 224.

18. Christopher Megone, 'One Concept of Liberty', *Political Studies*, 35 (1987), 611–622, at 620, calls such type of action 'free intentional irrational action'.

19. Gerald MacCallum, 'Negative and Positive Freedom', *Philosophical Review*, 76 (1967), 312–334. See Frank Hindriks, 'The Freedom of Collective Agents', *Journal of Political Philosophy*, 16 (2008), 165–183, for the view that collectives can be agents in this relation, and Andreas Schmidt, 'Persons or Property: Freedom and the Legal Status of Animals', *Journal of Moral Philosophy*, 15 (2018), 20–45, for the view that animals can be.

20. Philip Pettit, *Republicanism: A Theory of Freedom and Government* (Oxford: Oxford University Press, 1997), 52. For further republican scholarship, see Iseult Honohan, *Civic Republicanism* (Abingdon: Routledge, 2002), Christian List, 'Republican Freedom and the Rule of Law', *Politics, Philosophy and Economics*, 5 (2006), 201–220, Quentin Skinner, *Liberty before Liberalism* (Cambridge: Cambridge University Press, 1998), Jean-Philip Spitz, *La liberté politique: Essai de généalogie conceptuelle* (Paris: Presses Universitaires Françaises, 1995), and Maurizio Viroli, *Repubblicanesimo: Una nuova utopia della libertà* (Bari: Laterza, 1999). See also Eric MacGilvray, *The Invention of Market Freedom* (New York: Cambridge University Press, 2011), for an account of how republican thought was replaced by liberal market freedom ideologies. Critics of republican thought include Boudewijn de Bruin, 'Liberal and Republican Freedom', *Journal of Political Philosophy*, 17 (2009), 418–439, Boudewijn de Bruin, 'A Note on List's Modal Logic of Republican Freedom', *Politics, Philosophy and Economics*, 7 (2008), 341–349, Ian Carter, 'How are Power and Unfreedom Related?', in Cécile Laborde and John Maynor (eds), *Republicanism and Political Theory* (Oxford: Blackwell, 2008), 58–82, Matthew Kramer, 'Liberty and Domination', in Cécile Laborde and John Maynor (eds), *Republicanism and Political Theory* (Oxford: Blackwell, 2008), 31–57, and Jan-Willem van der Rijt, 'Republican Dignity: The Importance of Taking Offence', *Law and Philosophy*, 28 (2009), 465–492. One's political ideology may be republican because of its commitment to a republican conception of freedom, but also because one favours a particular distributive principle or institutional implementation. Quentin Skinner, *Liberty before Liberalism*

(Cambridge: Cambridge University Press, 1998), may be an example of such a form of republicanism. It is not conceptually impossible that on the basis of a cost–benefit analysis one should recommend the republic as a way to maximize negative freedom.

21. Philip Pettit, *Republicanism: A Theory of Freedom and Government* (Oxford: Oxford University Press, 1997), 52. See also Stefan Gosepath, *Gleiche Gerechtigkeit: Grundlagen eines liberalen Egalitarismus* (Frankfurt am Main: Suhrkamp, 2004), 308.

22. See Fabian Wendt, 'Slaves, Prisoners, and Republican Freedom', *Res Publica*, 17 (2011), 175–192, for a critical discussion of this condition.

23. Philip Pettit, *Republicanism: A Theory of Freedom and Government* (Oxford: Oxford University Press, 1997), 55–56.

24. Whether or not a conception of freedom is desire-dependent is only one of the questions one can ask about it. It can further be asked whether it is individualist (dependent on individual values) or collectivist (dependent on collective values), whether the conception is moralized or not, and so forth. For specific values in republican thought, see, e.g., Cécile Laborde, 'Critical Republicanism vs. Conservative Republicanism: Rethinking "Reasonable Compromise"', *Critique internationale*, 44 (2009), 19–33, for a distinction between critical and conservative versions of republicanism, in France, and Tom O'Shea, 'Socialist Republicanism', *Political Theory*, 48 (2020) 548–572, for a republican defence of public ownership and economic democracy.

25. In the paradigm case of republican unfreedom, the slave-owner does not give a further thought to what the slave might wish, desire, or need in present circumstances, in the absence of relevant legal prohibitions. These interests are the place to situate the desire-dependence of republican freedom, for they need desires to distinguish between the predicament of the prisoner and the plight of the slave. Both face interference, but, while the slave's desires to leave are relevant, the criminal's desires are not, for the republican. Note that a more direct route to show desire-dependence is that republican freedom is defined in terms of actions that worsen the interferee's situation, which is to do with their desires.

26. Interesting empirical work on the meaning and value of freedom compares Western and Eastern Germans in the years after the fall of the Berlin Wall. Thomas Petersen and Tilman Meyer, *Der Wert der Freiheit: Deutschland vor einem neuen Wertewandel?* (Freiburg im Breisgau: Herder, 2009). Around a fifth of both populations adheres to something like Mill's desire-dependent conception ('Freedom means that you can do what you like …'). 23 per cent of Western and 38 per cent of Eastern Germans have a conception of freedom as social security ('Freedom means to be free from social needs, poverty, homelessness, and unemployment'). 52 per cent of Western and 39 per cent

of Eastern Germans use a conception of freedom in terms of responsibility ('Freedom means to be responsible for yourself …'). Ibid. 41. This is consistent with the differences between value ascriptions. Western Germans prefer freedom over equality, Eastern Germans the other way round, over a period spanning the last quarter of the 20th century. Ibid. 56 ff.

27. See, e.g., Ian Carter, 'The Independent Value of Freedom', *Ethics*, 105 (1995), 819–845.

28. See also Stephen Darwall, 'The Value of Autonomy and Autonomy of the Will', *Ethics*, 116 (2006), 263–284, Joel Feinberg, 'The Nature and Value of Rights', *Journal of Value Inquiry*, 4 (1970), 243–257, Martin van Hees, 'The Specific Value of Freedom', *Social Choice and Welfare*, 35 (2010), 687–703, Martin van Hees and Marcel Wissenburg, 'Freedom and Opportunity', *Political Studies*, 47 (1999), 67–82, Simon Keller, 'Freedom!', *Social Theory and Practice*, 31 (2005), 337–357, Felix Oppenheim, 'Evaluating Interpersonal Freedoms', *Journal of Philosophy*, 57 (1960), 373–383, and Itai Sher, 'Evaluating Allocations of Freedom', *Economic Journal*, 128 (2018), 65–94. See, generally, Prasanta Pattanaik and Yongsheng Xu, 'Freedom and Its Value', in Iwao Hirose and Jonas Olson (eds), *The Oxford Handbook of Value Theory* (Oxford: Oxford University Press, 2015), 356–380. I ignore various more or less prominent accounts of the value of freedom (and also the question of whether it has intrinsic value), including those of Ronald Dworkin, *Taking Rights Seriously* (London: Duckworth, 1977), 266 ff., Friedrich von Hayek, *The Constitution of Liberty* (London: Routledge and Kegan Paul, 1960), 22 ff., Karl Popper, *The Poverty of Historicism* (New York: Harper and Row, 1964), 152–159, John Rawls, *Justice as Fairness: A Restatement* (Cambridge, MA: Harvard University Press, 2001), 42 ff., Joseph Raz, *The Morality of Freedom* (Oxford: Clarendon Press, 1986), 407 ff., and Amartya Sen, *Inequality Reexamined* (Oxford: Oxford University Press, 1992), 39 ff.

29. The three arguments I discuss are the arguments from desire satisfaction, personal responsibility, and self-realization. For other arguments, see Ian Carter, *A Measure of Freedom* (Oxford: Oxford University Press, 1999) (ignorance), Lawrence Crocker, *Positive Liberty: An Essay in Normative Political Philosophy* (The Hague: Martinus Nijhoff Publishers, 1980) (argument from morality, autonomy), Nicolas Grimaldi, *Ambiguités de la liberté* (Paris: Presses Universitaires de France, 1999) (argument from appropriating life, imagining possible futures, causal responsibility, self-development), Friedrich von Hayek, *The Constitution of Liberty* (London: Routledge & Kegan Paul, 1960) (progress), John Stuart Mill, *On Liberty* (London: John W. Parker, 1859) (learning, 'experiments in living'), and Joseph Raz, *The Morality of Freedom* (Oxford: Clarendon Press, 1986) (autonomy). See, generally, Simon Keller, 'Freedom!', *Social Theory and Practice*, 31 (2005), 337–357, Joel Feinberg, 'The Interest in

Liberty on the Scales', in Feinberg, *Rights, Justice and the Bounds of Liberty* (Princeton: Princeton University Press, 1980), 30–44, and Joel Feinberg, *Social Philosophy* (Englewood Cliffs: Prentice–Hall, 1973).

30. Arguments for the value of freedom can be seen as employing the axiom scheme $((\varphi \rightarrow \psi) \wedge \mathbf{V}\psi) \rightarrow \mathbf{V}\varphi$, which is not of course immediately plausible (take ψ as something that is good and take φ as the conjunction of ψ and something bad). See Lou Goble, 'A Logic of Good, Should, and Would: Part I and II', *Journal of Philosophical Logic*, 19 (1990), 169–199, 253–276, for how this should be spelled out. See also Boudewijn de Bruin, 'The Logic of Valuing', in Thomas Boylan and Ruvin Gekker (eds), *Economics, Rational Choice and Normative Philosophy* (London: Routledge, 2009), 164–172.

31. Nothing suggests that the full force of the Von Neumann–Morgenstern axioms would be needed here. It is only shorthand for desires. Obviously inconsistent desires (and beliefs) are to be excluded, though. One should not at the same time desire to go to Paris and not to go to Paris, or believe that one can go to Paris and that one cannot. But it is fully conceivable that I desire to go to Paris but not to France, as long as I do not believe that Paris lies in France. One may also ask to what extent desire satisfaction is valuable. Richard Arneson, 'Equality', in Robert Goodin and Philip Pettit (eds), *A Companion to Contemporary Political Philosophy* (Malden: Blackwell, 1993), 489–507, at 510, asks 'why matters are improved when someone's perverse or degraded desires are better satisfied'. This might lead to changing the formulation of the first premiss—for instance, using ideas about higher-order volition due to Harry Frankfurt, 'Freedom of the Will and the Concept of a Person', *Journal of Philosophy*, 68 (1971), 5–20, or by specifying along positive freedom lines that the desires be 'authentic' or similar. Clearly the premiss is not meant to entail that desire satisfaction of one person is valuable to another, so desires should not be set aside as 'perverse' or 'degraded' merely on the basis that they might harm or offend others.

32. Talking about expected utility maximization betrays a belief–desire conception of agency. See Donald Davidson, 'Actions, Reasons, and Causes', *Journal of Philosophy*, 60 (1963), 685–700. Cf. Sabine Döring, 'Explaining Action by Emotion', *Philosophical Quarterly*, 53 (2003), 214–230, and John Skorupski, 'Freedom, Morality, and Recognition: Some Theses on Kant and Hegel', in Skorupski, *Ethical Explorations* (Oxford: Oxford University Press, 1999), 160–189.

33. Duncan Luce and Howard Raiffa, *Games and Decisions: Introduction and Critical Survey* (New York: Wiley, 1957), 288. There is a much larger literature on why preference satisfaction may not always be so good. See, e.g., Derek Parfit, *Reasons and Persons* (Oxford: Oxford University Press, 1984), and/or the literature to which it gave rise. I set aside here the difficulties of irrational

preferences, intertemporal inconsistencies, and so on, but do note that it is also good to have good preferences. Another issue is whether there are other things that are good. See Gerald Dworkin, 'Paternalism', *Monist*, 56 (1972), 64–84, for an argument that basing welfare economic policy on anything other than a person's preferences would be paternalistic, as we do not have reliable information about other things they value. I also set aside the question of whether these preferences must be 'informed'—that is, the result of careful thinking through that not everyone will always have the opportunity to carry out. Clearly, we do not even always know what we want ourselves.

34. Sheena Iyengar and Mark Lepper, 'When Choice is Demotivating: Can One Desire Too Much of a Good Thing?', *Journal of Personality and Social Psychology*, 79 (2000), 995–1006.

35. See also Gerald Dworkin, 'Is More Choice Better than Less?' in Peter French, Theodore Uehling Jr, and Howard Wettstein (eds), *Midwest Studies in Philosophy*, 7 (1982), 47–61, and Joel Feinberg, 'The Interest in Liberty on the Scales', in Feinberg, *Rights, Justice and the Bounds of Liberty* (Princeton: Princeton University Press, 1980), 30–44.

36. Friedrich von Hayek, *The Constitution of Liberty* (London: Routledge & Kegan Paul, 1960), 79–80.

37. This discussion is indebted to the literature on free will. See, e.g., John Martin Fischer, 'Free Will and Moral Responsibility', in David Copp (ed.), *The Oxford Handbook of Ethical Theory* (Oxford: Oxford University Press, 2007), 321–351. It is important to point out that I am not interested here to examine the moral epistemology underlying premises (1) (about desire satisfaction) and (4). (1) may be defended inductively, as perhaps Mill thought, while (4) may be seen as synthetic a priori in Kant's sense.

38. I set aside the question of how assignments of responsibility depend on the way the action or consequences are described. You may be responsible for rescuing the child, the heir to the throne, saving the country, and so forth. See Donald Davidson, 'Actions, Reasons, and Causes', *Journal of Philosophy*, 60 (1963), 685–700.

39. Thomas Hurka, 'Why Value Autonomy?', *Social Theory and Practice*, 13 (1987), 361–382.

40. Ibid. 366.

41. See, for related ideas on the economy of esteem, Geoffrey Brennan and Philip Pettit, *The Economy of Esteem* (Oxford: Oxford University Press, 2004).

42. Thomas Hurka, 'Why Value Autonomy?', *Social Theory and Practice*, 13 (1987), 361–382, at 366.

43. Hurka goes beyond ascribing value to causal powers only, as he is primarily interested in intentional agency: 'It is not any causal efficacy that has value, but efficacy that expresses some aim in the mind' (ibid. 367). His argument

for freedom's value may ultimately best be construed as pairing an argument from desire satisfaction with an argument from causal efficacy. Stephen Darwall, 'The Value of Autonomy and Autonomy of the Will', *Ethics*, 116 (2006), 263–284, can be read as providing an argument about the value of being able to do something yourself, as opposed to someone else doing it for you—the toddler's 'Me do it!'—that is, 'the idea that people have a claim to decide for themselves or to exercise a kind of "vote" in matters that concern them' (ibid. 267). Darwall considers the case of parents urging their middle-aged daughter to eat broccoli and imagines a claim to autonomy to involve 'express[ing] or impl[ying] a demand that they back off and let her make her choices for herself' (ibid. 272–273).

44. Edward Deci and Richard Ryan, *Intrinsic Motivation and Self-Determination in Human Behavior* (New York: Plenum, 1985).

45. Lea Cassar and Stephan Meier, 'Nonmonetary Incentives and the Implications of Work as a Source of Meaning', *Journal of Economic Perspectives*, 32 (2018), 215–238.

46. See Barton Hamilton, 'Does Entrepreneurship Pay? An Empirical Analysis of the Returns to Self-Employment', *Journal of Political Economy*, 108 (2000), 604–631. Keith Chen, Judith Chevalier, Peter Rossi, and Emily Oehlsen, 'The Value of Flexible Work: Evidence from Uber Drivers', *Journal of Political Economy*, 127 (2019), 2735–2994, investigate Uber drivers and show they earn more than twice the producer surplus that they would without flexibility. See also Paolo Verme, 'Happiness, Freedom and Control', *Journal of Economic Behavior & Organization*, 71 (2009), 146–161.

47. Wilhelm von Humboldt, *Ideen zu einem Versuch, die Gränzen der Wirksamkeit des Staats zu bestimmen* (Breslau: Eduard Trewendt, 1851), 9–10.

48. Charles Taylor, 'What's Wrong with Negative Liberty', *Philosophy and the Human Sciences* (1985), 211–229. See also Bernard Williams, *Philosophy as a Humanistic Discipline* (Princeton: Princeton University Press, 2006), 141, criticizing the animal liberation movement on account of the fact that a core presupposition of freedom is to speak for yourself ('Oppressed human groups come of age in the search for emancipation when they speak for themselves, and no longer through reforming members of the oppressive group, but the other animals will never come of age: human beings will always act as their trustee'). See Ajume Wingo, 'The Aesthetic of Freedom', in Boudewijn de Bruin and Christopher Zurn (eds), *New Waves in Political Philosophy* (London: Palgrave Macmillan, 2009), 198–219, at 206, on the relevance of this to the relation between self-representation and freedom.

49. Jon Elster, 'Self-Realization in Work and Politics: The Marxist Conception of the Good Life', *Social Philosophy and Policy*, 3 (2009), 97–126.

50. Ibid. 99.

51. It is not that such knowledge is necessary. What is necessary is that you do not believe you are unfree, for if you believe you cannot *A* you will not *A*. Thanks to Graham Priest for discussion.

52. See, e.g., Stanley Benn, *A Theory of Freedom* (Cambridge: Cambridge University Press, 1988), 152–153, for a discussion of the notion of choice situation.

53. To the extent that an agent *S*'s mere freedom increases if their known freedom increases, *S* has reason to value known freedom. Known freedom can, however, also increase through knowledge only. *S* learns at t_1 about an action *A* that had already been available to *S* since an earlier point in time t_0. The obvious case of improved desire satisfaction is when the increased knowledge allows *S* to conclude at t_1 that *A* is better than any other option considered at t_0. Given what *S* knew about available actions and consequences at t_0, *S* would select some *B*, but now that they know about *A*'s being available they opt for *A* instead. In fact, gaining known freedom at t_1 about *A* may help even if *A* is inferior to *B*. At t_0, agent *S* may, for instance, know that *A* is available, but possess false beliefs about *A*'s consequences, or the probabilities with which they arise, and so, at t_0, agent *S* may have the false impression that *A* is better than *B*. Setting these errors right at t_1 increases *S*'s desire satisfaction, as they no longer mistakenly find *A* attractive, and so opt for *B*.

54. Sheena Iyengar and Mark Lepper, 'When Choice is Demotivating: Can One Desire Too Much of a Good Thing?', *Journal of Personality and Social Psychology*, 79 (2000), 995–1006, at 996.

55. This is incidentally also an argument against unreflectively endorsing a policy of nudging citizens into taking 'right' decisions, as proposed by Richard Thaler and Cass Sunstein, *Nudge: Improving Decisions about Health, Wealth, and Happiness* (New Haven: Yale University Press, 2008), even though I do not want to suggest that complete information is always feasible.

56. Paul Heidhues and Botond Kőszegi, 'Naïveté-Based Discrimination', *Quarterly Journal of Economics*, 132 (2017), 1019–1054.

57. Gerald MacCallum, 'Negative and Positive Freedom', *Philosophical Review*, 76 (1967), 312–334.

58. Isaiah Berlin, *Four Essays on Liberty* (London: Oxford University Press, 1969), 'Introduction', p. xliii.

59. Ian Carter, *A Measure of Freedom* (Oxford: Oxford University Press, 1999).

60. Ibid. 34.

61. Ibid. 32.

62. Ian Carter, 'The Independent Value of Freedom', *Ethics*, 105 (1995), 819–845, at 833.

63. Ibid. Friedrich von Hayek, *The Constitution of Liberty* (London: Routledge & Kegan Paul, 1960), 29.

64. The epistemic reading has a lot to recommend also because Berlin's criticism of MacCallum was cast in decidedly epistemic terms. The 'man' struggling against chains 'need not consciously aim at any definite further state. A man need not know how he will use his freedom' (ibid., p. xliii). The 'man' X struggling against certain chains Z is best described as possessing de dicto knowledge about future values which is not de re. (I have de dicto knowledge that you have an email address (I know you have one), but I do not have de re knowledge of your email address (I do not know which one).) In the situation at hand, the knowledge is not de re because 'man' X does not have in mind any particular things he is barred from doing right now which he will value doing in future. There is no thing Y such that X knows of Y that it is blocked by constraints Z at present, and that consequently X would be unfree to but will value in future: $\neg \exists Y \exists Z K_X(Value(Y) \wedge Unfree(X, Y, Z))$. It is de dicto because he knows, nonetheless, that among the things his chains prohibit him at present to perform there is something he will value in future: $K X \exists Y \exists Z (Value(Y) \wedge Unfree(X, Y, Z))$. The 'man' X struggling against chains is as a result concerned with the second element of MacCallum's triadic relation, the action Y, because he knows he will value some action rather than none. Yet X is not concerned with a specific such element, for he does not quite know which action he will value in future. He has de dicto knowledge about the element Y that is not de re. Berlin is right that a 'man' struggling against chains 'need not consciously aim at any definite further state' (ibid.). But he is wrong to take this as refuting the triadic analysis. See also Martin van Hees, *Legal Reductionism and Freedom* (Dordrecht: Kluwer, 2000), 151 ff., Matthew Kramer, *The Quality of Freedom* (Oxford: Oxford University Press, 2003), 242 ff., and Serena Olsaretti, 'The Value of Freedom and Freedom of Choice', *Notizie di Politeia*, 56 (1999), 114–121. James Nickel, 'Book Review: Ian Carter, *A Measure of Freedom*', *Law and Philosophy*, 20 (2001), 531–540, gives an epistemic reading of non-specific value. Cf. Ian Hunt, 'Overall Freedom and Constraint', *Inquiry*, 44 (2001), 131–148, for a critique of non-specific value.

65. It may also be noted that analogously we could introduce a me-do-it trick privileging our own agency at the expense of others, potentially to ward off paternalistic interference and to make the argument from self-realization more precise. Consider two agents S and T, identical in their athletic talents and abilities, and both growing up in California with ample opportunities for skiing and swimming, and some possibilities for rugby. S tried out all kinds of sports (and musical instruments) but decided to spend their time on rugby because it is there that, they thought, their talents are. T was barred (by their parents, say) to go skiing or to become a member of the swimming club, and was forced to turn to rugby. We can only sensibly say of S that playing rugby contributes to their self-realization. While T has the same talent and abilities for playing

rugby, the fact that they exploit these talents is something that happened passively: because of their parents' interference and coercion. If T can be said to have developed their abilities to the fullest (a requirement of self-realization), then in the sense that others have realized them. It is not self-realization, but realization by other peoples. This is where the me-do-it trick comes in, for if it is assumed that, if you do something, it is a good thing that you, rather than someone else, do it, then it is true that, if it is of value to realize yourself, you should do that yourself, rather than your parents. Just as the ignorance trick, the me-do-it trick will come in handy to rescue various other argument for freedom's value that I do not discuss here.

66. See, e.g., Amartya Sen, 'Welfare, Preference and Freedom', *Journal of Econometrics*, 50 (1991), 15–29, who, at 24, gives the example of 'being beheaded at dawn'.

67. I have so far ignored the argument from autonomy, which assigns value to the freedom of an agent S on account of its contributing to S's autonomy and is often cast in terms of a requirement for other agents T to respect S's autonomy. But why would such respect be valuable? The default argument is probably the Kantian one that we have a duty to respect each other's autonomy as a result of the fact that we have to treat others always also as ends in themselves. But, as John Rawls, *A Theory of Justice* (Cambridge, MA: Harvard University Press, 1971), 440 ff., notes, Kantian arguments for what he calls the 'duty of mutual respect' and 'mutual aid' can be supplemented by arguments grounding these duties in certain advantages that ensue from their universal acceptance, even going so far as to maintain that these arguments are more important than the Kantian ones. Ibid. 338. What should interest us here is that the informational assumptions, the topic of the present section, that come with the argument from autonomy differ depending on the primary premiss about how the value of autonomy is fleshed out. While the Kantian defence does not require any epistemic assumptions to be made, the Rawlsian defence gives rise to a kind of precondition not present in arguments from desire satisfaction and responsibility. Take the duty of mutual aid first. Rawls argues that, if it is 'public knowledge' that this duty is followed in society, this endows its members with 'a sense of confidence and trust in other men's good intentions' as well as 'knowledge that they are there if we need them' (ibid. 339). It is not so much the actual aid that one may get from other individuals, because most people will need little aid. Rather, it is the knowledge that, if one were to need aid, one would receive it. In similarly epistemic ways, Rawls grounds respect in the value of individuals possessing a sense of self-respect. For S to possess self-respect entails that they possess, first, a sense of the fact that the ends that they set for themselves are indeed worthwhile pursuing (they need to be confident about their conception of the good). Secondly, it requires that S be confident

that they possess the capacities to pursue these goals, and that they are as capable of determining themselves as of being determined by others. In order for S to possess such form of self-respect, it is necessary that S receives respect from others. This last conclusion is the content of a famous quote from *A Theory of Justice*: a person's self-respect 'cannot withstand the indifference much less contempt of others' (ibid. 338). If S is not treated respectfully by T (and others), then S will not develop a sense of self-respect, or will lose what of S's self-respect remains. It is true that at various junctures Rawls suggests that his concept of respect embraces more than respect for autonomy only, wishing to include such things as one's accomplishments being valued (or even admired) by other individuals. Ibid. 441. An argument grounding respect for autonomy in the value of self-respect is, however, consistent with what Rawls writes. More importantly, both this narrower argument and the more general one ultimately depend on the truth of an empirical statement concerning the effects of (common) knowledge of respect on individual people's (levels of) self-respect, to which Rawls gives only scant attention. See, e.g., Steven Wall, 'Rawls and the Status of Political Liberty', *Pacific Philosophical Quarterly*, 87 (2006), 245–270, at 257 ff., and James Zink, 'Reconsidering the Role of Self-Respect in Rawls's *A Theory of Justice*', *Journal of Politics*, 73 (2011), 331–344, at 333 ff. It should be noted that epistemic assumptions depend on how the premiss is defended. On the Kantian line of defence, no epistemic assumptions have to be put in place, for the primary premiss of the argument from autonomy, then, describes only a situation that arises if others act towards an agent S in ways consistent with the categorical imperative. The categorical imperative does not require that S knows they are being so treated. Under a Rawlsian reading of the argument from autonomy, however, T (and others) have to show respect for S's autonomy on the grounds that this is a precondition for S's developing and/or maintaining self-respect. Clearly an epistemic assumption has to be introduced to the effect that T's respecting S's autonomy is something that S knows about, for, if not, this particular instance of respect will not help S's self-respect. This entails known freedom for S. But, where knowledge of availability and consequences was sufficient in the arguments from desire satisfaction and responsibility, more is needed in the Rawlsian version of the argument from autonomy. S must also possess knowledge about possibilities for T to interfere, because only then will S be able to interpret the availability of a certain action or consequence as indicating that T respects autonomy. This is knowledge about the sources of freedom. In addition, S must have knowledge concerning unavailable actions, because these potentially indicate someone's disrespecting S. Actions may be unavailable because of interference from acts of nature (avalanche) or non-disrespectful actions of others (I am parking my bicycle in front of my house, blocking the pavement). So, for S to find out if the unavailability of some action entails disrespect, S has to possess knowledge about the source of the unavailability—that is, knowledge about the sources of unfreedom. So, in the terminology introduced, *S* has to have knowledge about unfreedom and knowledge about the sources of unfreedom.

68. See, e.g., Boudewijn de Bruin, *Explaining Games: The Epistemic Programme in Game Theory* (Dordrecht: Springer, 2010), or Itzhak Gilboa, *Rational Choice* (Cambridge, MA: MIT Press, 2012).

69. How should we understand knowledge of freedom in the light of such issues as how we individuate actions? You may know that you are free to push a button, but not that this will bring the lift to the eighth floor. (Perhaps the sign is missing, or the sign is in an alphabet or language you don't know.) Such a situation can be represented by means of different beliefs concerning the consequences of the available actions and/or the probabilities attached to them. If the only thing I know is that I can push a button, it is rational to assign equal probabilities to the lift reaching any floor. Many thanks to Jeroen de Ridder for raising this issue.

70. Robert Goodin, 'Liberalism and the Best-Judge Principle', *Political Studies*, 38 (1990), 181–195, defends a related claim that we are in a privileged position to obtain relevant knowledge about ourselves as compared with the state, focussed on knowledge about desires rather than about opportunities and consequences.

71. Dennis Lowry, Tarn Ching, Josephine Nio, and Dennis Leitner, 'Setting the Public Fear Agenda: A Longitudinal Analysis of Network TV Crime Reporting, Public Perceptions of Crime and FBI Crime Statistics', *Journal of Communication*, 53 (2003), 61–73. See also Frank Bovenkerk, *Een gevoel van dreiging* (Amsterdam: Atlas Contact, 2011). See Robert Goodin and Frank Jackson, 'Freedom from Fear', *Philosophy and Public Affairs*, 35 (2007), 249–265, for an alternative route to linking freedom and fear.

72. Cf. Jihong Zhao, Biran Lawton, and Dennis Longmire, 'An Examination of the Micro-Level Crime–Fear of Crime Link', *Crime and Delinquency*, 61 (2015), 19–44, for evidence of a correlation between actual crime rates and degrees of fear of crime.

73. James Wilson and George Kelling, 'Broken Windows: The Police and Neighborhood Safety', *Atlantic* (March 1982), www.theatlantic.com/magazine/archive/1982/03/broken-windows/304465 [perma.cc/4FK5-F78E].

74. See Matthew Williams, Pete Burnap, and Luke Sloan, 'Crime Sensing with Big Data: The Affordances and Limitations of Using Open-Source Communications to Estimate Crime Patterns', *British Journal of Criminology*, 57 (2017), 320–340, for new evidence on the broken windows theory using big data. Cf. Bernard Harcourt and Jens Ludwig, 'Broken Windows: New Evidence from New York City and a Five-City Social Experiment', *University of Chicago Law Review*, 73 (2006), 271–320, who find no such evidence.

75. *Wisconsin* v. *Yoder* [1972] 406 US 205.

76. Russell Hardin, *How Do You Know? The Economics of Ordinary Knowledge* (Princeton: Princeton University Press, 2009), 201.

77. *Wisconsin* v. *Yoder* [1972] 406 US 205, at 235, the court writes that 'the Amish … have convincingly demonstrated … the hazards presented by the State's enforcement of a statute [of compulsory high-school education] generally valid as to others. Beyond this, they have [demonstrated] the adequacy of their alternative mode of continuing informal vocational education in terms of precisely those overall interests that the State advances in support of its program of compulsory high school education.'

78. Russell Hardin, *How Do You Know? The Economics of Ordinary Knowledge* (Princeton: Princeton University Press, 2009), 201.

79. See, e.g., Jonathan Kvanvig, *The Value of Knowledge and the Pursuit of Understanding* (Cambridge: Cambridge University Press, 2003), or Duncan Pritchard, Alan Millar, and Adrian Haddock, *The Nature and Value of Knowledge: Three Investigations* (Oxford: Oxford University Press, 2010). It may well be that the main issue with educational freedom is that people may disagree not so much about the purposes that might license or mandate the acquisition of knowledge, but rather about the sources of knowledge acquisition. While my position is that the arguments from desire satisfaction and responsibility show that everyone concerned with these two values should also be concerned with knowledge, I do not think this entails that it should be the state's task to generate such knowledge, at least not without further assumptions. See generally Carl Friedrich and Zbigniew Brzezinski, *Totalitarian Dictatorship and Autocracy* (Cambridge, MA: Harvard University Press, 1956), for the dangers of having a state monopoly on information and communication. The problem is both the (empirical) observation that in such circumstances the likelihood of being correctly informed decreases, and the (conceptual) observation that (even for the correct beliefs that citizens acquire) there will be a lack of epistemic justification: the totalitarian state is not a good source of testimonial knowledge. What is also important in relation to *Wisconsin* v. *Yoder* is that any educational programme has opportunity costs. The mandatory high-school education against which the Amish successfully appealed excludes the Amish 'alternative mode of continuing informal vocational education', (ibid. 235), and vice versa.

2
From Brainwashing to Neuromarketing

Freedom of Belief

If you assign value to freedom because of its contributions to desire satisfaction, responsibility, or self-realization, then you should a fortiori assign value to known freedom. What is valuable is not just that you expand your opportunity set. Rather, such an expansion is valuable only as long as it is accompanied by an appropriate increase in information. You should have information about the actions that are available to you, their consequences, and the likelihood of these consequences obtaining, otherwise you will not do much with your freedom. That is the main takeaway from the previous chapter.

I am not the first to link freedom with knowledge and information. Martin van Hees and Marcel Wissenburg, for instance, once started a paper with the very question: 'Does our knowledge of genetic engineering enlarge our freedom?'[1] Isaiah Berlin, for one, held that 'knowledge … tends to render us more effective and extend our liberty, which is liable to be curtailed by ignorance and the illusions, terrors and prejudices that it breeds'.[2] Matthew Kramer contends that ignorance 'will often be a straightforwardly disabling factor and will thus impair a person's overall liberty', which is to say that ignorance 'amounts to a freedom-curtailing condition in proportion to the difficulty of its being overcome'.[3] Ian Carter, taking a more radical perspective, even considers the effects of 'forcible hypnosis' and 'brainwashing' on a person's freedom:

> if I force you to think certain thoughts, then there are also likely to be many actions that I am preventing you from performing, so that it can at least be said that forcible hypnosis and brainwashing can entail great reductions in freedom.[4]

The Business of Liberty. Boudewijn de Bruin, Oxford University Press.
© Boudewijn de Bruin (2022). DOI: 10.1093/oso/9780198839675.003.0003

Not everyone agrees that false beliefs or lack of knowledge affect your free-dom (or what you can do with it).[5] John Rawls did not think that the 'inability to take advantage of one's rights and opportunities as a result of poverty and ignorance … is … among the constraints definitive of liberty'.[6] Rather, he said, 'I shall think of these things as affecting the worth of lib-erty, the value to individuals of [their] rights'.[7] Philip Pettit seems to adopt a similar view by drawing a distinction between factors that 'condition' peo-ple's freedom (such as 'handicap and poverty and ignorance') and those that genuinely 'compromise' freedom; and he argues that the state should 'promote people's effective freedom' not only by reducing what compro-mises freedom, but also by increasing 'the range and ease with which people enjoy' freedom'.[8] And on another occasion, Isaiah Berlin made a similar ob-servation (somewhat contradicting the earlier quotation), opining that it is 'important to discriminate between liberty and the conditions of its exer-cise'; for, if someone is 'too poor or too ignorant or too feeble to make use of his legal rights, the liberty that these rights confer upon him is nothing to him, but it is not thereby annihilated'.[9]

There is certainly merit to the views of both camps. Yet, in order to the-orize the concept of known freedom adequately, it is important to draw distinctions more rigorously than most of these authors have done. For instance, while the idea of ignorance 'conditioning' freedom sounds attrac-tive, ignorance conditions freedom in a very different way from poverty and disability, which both Rawls and Pettit mention in the same qualifying sentence. Poverty and disability make your opportunity set smaller—you cannot buy the house or travel by train without assistance. So they limit the degree of your freedom. Ignorance, by contrast, does not limit the de-gree of your freedom, I argue. It limits the degree of your known freedom. Similarly, while Carter is right to point to the significance of considering brainwashing and similar more 'real-life' techniques in the context of po-litical freedom, it is not, I argue, that such techniques decrease a person's freedom per se, but rather that they decrease a person's epistemic freedom, and thereby their known freedom.

Cases

Exploring the concept of epistemic freedom is a goal of this and the next chapter. I start by considering five illustrative cases that have been discussed in the literature, with the aim of paving the way for a more theoretically oriented discussion of epistemic freedom, and its relation to known freedom.

Brainwashed Beliefs

The first is a case of brainwashing.

> *Brainwash*. Olivia has brainwashed Oliver into believing that, if he were to leave the restaurant, he would be shot down by an armed person waiting outside. Then Olivia left. In reality, however, there is no one waiting outside, and Oliver can safely leave the restaurant.

To begin with, it is important to note that a case involving brainwashing may sound too sci-fi to be worth taking seriously. I discuss this worry later, and quote recent work in psychology, cognitive science, and neuroscience showing that brainwashing is a less remote possibility than some people might think. So here I focus on the main central question: why would you think that Oliver is unfree to leave the restaurant on account of him having been brainwashed?

Here is one argument. Olivia changed Oliver's beliefs in such a way that the action of leaving the restaurant is no longer 'supported' by his beliefs and desires. Not wanting to risk his life, and believing that he would die if he left, he decides against leaving the restaurant. Oliver lacks relevant known freedom; more than that, the brainwash has made it impossible for him to *acquire* the beliefs needed for known freedom. This is because, as Michael Smith phrases it, brainwashing affects the way that people deal with evidence. Even if Oliver were to look out of the window, the brainwash would either cause him 'to ignore that evidence or to reinterpret it, or in some other way [prevent] the evidence from playing its proper cognitive role'.[10] The extent of known freedom Oliver can hope for is affected by his irrational, brainwashed, belief formation policies.

False Beliefs

But you need not be brainwashed to suffer from a lack of known freedom. Consider the following case, taken from Matthew Kramer.[11]

Shed. Olivia has abducted Harry and put him in a shed. Then she left. She has not, however, locked the door of the shed. Yet Harry believes the door is locked and remains where he is.

Harry's predicament is similar to Oliver's: both have incorrect beliefs about relevant aspects of their choice situation, and both hold these beliefs irrationally. So both lack known freedom. In Kramer's construal of the case, however, Harry could have found out very easily about the escape route—for instance, by walking around the shed, or by trying to turn the door knob. Failing to do so, Kramer argues, Harry neglects 'to take advantage of an opportunity that has been present all the same', which is to say that evidence that is readily available to him has not played 'its proper cognitive role'.[12] So, unlike Oliver, who, due to the brainwash, was unable to deal with evidence in the right way, here it is Harry who forgoes the opportunity to increase his known freedom, all by himself.

Incomplete Beliefs

Harry's lack of known freedom is ultimately rooted in his having *false* beliefs, for he believes that the door is locked. But a lack of known freedom can also arise out of *incomplete* beliefs.[13] Consider another case, also taken from Matthew Kramer.[14]

Combination Lock. Olivia has put George in a cell with a massive door that opens and closes by means of a combination lock. George does not know the code. He can try out any six-digit combination, but he can do so only once, which he knows. If he succeeds, the door will open. If he does not succeed, he will have to remain in his cell.

George knows that he does not have the known freedom necessary to escape. He also knows that he has precious little space to gain known freedom, as there is only one in a million chance that, when he types a random six-digit number, it will turn out to be the right number. While Harry, in *Shed*, believed that there is no route to escape, George does believe that there is a route to escape. It is only that he does not know which one. Using scholastic terminology, you might say that George has a de dicto belief that is not de re.[15]

Rational Beliefs

It looks as though it is significantly easier for Harry than for George to overcome his ignorance. But the ease of overcoming ignorance cannot just be explained in terms of the probability that some action (walking around the shed, typing in some number) gives the required information. This is because, among other things, the decision maker's prior beliefs determine whether it makes sense (whether it is rational) to select such actions. This becomes clear if we consider a new case.

> *Hut*. Olivia has abducted Noah, put him in a hut, and asked for a ransom. Then she left. She has not locked the hut, and Noah could easily and safely leave. Noah recalls a recent newspaper article about a criminal who has kidnapped various people in the neighbourhood, brought them to a hut, and asked for ransom. Some of the abducted people have tried to escape, but they were shot by their kidnapper. All others have been released after ransom was paid to her.

Harry (in *Shed*), George (in *Combination Lock*), and Noah (in the *Hut*) lack known freedom. But all for different reasons. The newspaper article gives Noah sufficient reason to believe that leaving the hut will have fatal consequences, which is to say that he perceives the scope for investigation vis-à-vis escape options as very limited. He has no reason to doubt that he is sufficiently and adequately informed about his choice situation. So, unlike Harry, his lack of known freedom is not the result of epistemic irrationality, and, unlike George, his lack of knowledge is not something of which he is aware.

Probabilistic Beliefs

A final case shows that people may be in very similar situations as to the chances of satisfying their desires, even though they are very dissimilar in terms of their known freedom.

> *Lottery*. Olivia has abducted Jack and brought him to an uninhabited island. Then she left. Exploring the island, Jack finds a box with a ticket for the Lottery. He also finds a letter written by Olivia, explaining that,

if his ticket wins the top prize, she will come back to get the ticket, and take Jack back on her way home. If another ticket wins the prize, Jack will have to stay on the island. The chances that Jack has the winning ticket are one in a million.

Quite clearly, George (in *Combination Lock*) and Jack (in *Lottery* case) have a one in a million probability of escaping their predicament. Yet structurally these cases are different. *Combination Lock* is an epistemic predicament. George has one million actions at his disposal, exactly one of which leads to a sure escape. But he does not know which one, so he does not have complete information about his choice situation. George would consequently be helped by being informed about the correct six-digit number—an 'epistemic rescue operation', if you wish. That would give him the known freedom he needs to escape. Jack, by contrast, is not ignorant about his available actions, or about their likely consequence. He is fully informed about his choice situation, and hence an epistemic operation would be of no avail to him. Rather he needs someone to send for a rescue ship.[16]

Upshot

I started this chapter with a few quotations that, despite important differences, express the connection between freedom and knowledge. The subsequent cases were then meant to give some feel for the idea that this connection must be spelt out with more precision. I gestured towards an approach according to which, for instance, we should say that George (in *Combination Lock*) is free to leave the cell, that he does know de dicto that he is free, that he does not know that de re, and that is lack of de re knowledge is what explains why he will not leave.

Not everyone will be persuaded. Michael Garnett, for instance, finds such a reading unappealing, because, if George did in fact possess this freedom, his abductor would not have been very successful in locking him up.[17] Similarly, but with different arguments, Matthew Kramer finds that, if we were to describe George as free to leave his cell, 'we would be distorting his plight beyond recognition'.[18] He maintains that 'ignorance is itself a disabling factor', because, if we were to eliminate George's ignorance, this 'would change his status from currently unfree-to-leave-the-cell-at-*t* to currently free-to-leave-the-cell-at-*t*'.[19] My point is, however, that if we separate more clearly the epistemic and non-epistemic aspects of George's situation, we get a better, rather than a distorted, understanding of his plight and its causes. We can say that George is free to leave the cell, because he is free to type the correct six-digit code. He does not know, however, which code he has to type, and this is because his abductor has successfully diminished his room for investigation. Cell and lock were set up so as to ensure that George had no investigative actions at his disposal to determine the correct code. He can type in a code only once. His abductor, I want to suggest, has successfully interfered with his epistemic freedom, and that is what explains his unfortunate condition.

Gaining Knowledge

But what is epistemic freedom precisely? To answer that question, we need some account of epistemic agency.[20] That is what I turn to now. I need to settle some terminology first. When I speak about *knowledge* here, I use it in the way in which most philosophers use it. Knowledge, in that sense, comes with two success conditions: if you have gained knowledge about something, you have adopted a belief that is true; and, secondly, the evidence that you have for it *justifies* your adopting the belief, which means, roughly, that you are warranted or entitled to adopt the belief, or in other words that it is rational for you to do so, given the evidence you recruited. Philosophers disagree about the precise way to think of knowledge. Edmund Gettier has at least made it clear that we should resist equating knowledge with justified true belief only.[21] For my more practical purposes here, however, I use the word *justification* loosely to refer to the idea that, when people attempt to gain knowledge, their aspiration is to arrive at true beliefs that are in some way or another supported by the evidence that they recruit in their attempt; or, put alternatively, following Timothy Williamson's suggestion, that when people are engaged in inquiry their aspiration is to arrive at knowledge.[22]

Consider this. Asked for advice by a customer, a salesperson may recommend a particular over-the-counter drug, thinking it might help with the condition from which the customer suffers. But, if the salesperson's thinking is just a wild guess, they should not be said to have made the advice based on knowledge, because they do not have a rational justification for what they believe. For the salesperson to possess knowledge, they should, for instance, have read something about the drug, learned about it from a reliable and more experienced colleague, or otherwise have obtained information justifying the belief. This example shows that it is possible to have a *true but unjustified* belief. It is also possible to have a *false but justified* belief. The salesperson has read the drug's instruction for use, has talked to a senior colleague, and has come to believe on epistemically impeccable grounds that it will help the customer. But, unbeknownst to all, the customer has a condition in which taking the drug will have unpleasant side effects, not mentioned in the information sheet. Then the salesperson has no knowledge. Their belief is false, even though it was justified.

That knowledge satisfies the two success conditions of truth and justification has a paradoxical consequence for the concept of *epistemic action*, by which I mean an action that gains you knowledge. As we cannot always know that we have gained knowledge (the salesperson did not know they did not have knowledge about the drug), we cannot always know it when we perform an epistemic action. Still we do have a clear sense as to what in general the constitutive elements of epistemic actions should be: we need a belief, we need evidence, and we need some kind of justificatory link between evidence and belief. We get a belief by adopting a doxastic or belief-like stance (we believe a proposition, say). We get evidence through inquiry—that is, by performing one or more investigative actions. And we get the justificatory link by ensuring that the doxastic stance we adopt is justified by the outcome of our inquiry.[23] So we have a tripartite analysis of epistemic action, with the following three constituent elements: investigation, belief adoption, and justification. All three are key to the analysis of epistemic freedom and unfreedom, for epistemic unfreedom arises, I argue, as the result of interference with one or more of the three elements. I now consider these in more detail.

Investigation

It is instructive to distinguish two kinds of investigative actions. Some investigative actions aim at the acquisition of *primary knowledge*, obtained by perception, logical deduction, statistical inference, introspection, or rational intuition. Such actions lead to knowledge that, in a way, does not depend on other people, although, of course, others may have helped us improve our perception, logic, or statistics, or may have set things up in a way that enables perception. When, for instance, a supervisor gives a demonstration of how a particular tool or technique works, employees gain primary knowledge to the extent that they see what happens. Other investigative actions are aimed at gaining what philosophers generally call *testimonial knowledge*. The word *testimony* has a slightly awkward legal undertone, as if you need a witness to produce it. But testimonial knowledge is taken very broadly to include all knowledge relayed to us through other people. Next to showing how the tools work, the supervisor will, for instance, also talk about their own experiences with the machine, or speak about the experiences of other people. So testimonial knowledge arises in a host of diverse ways, involving not only speech, but also writing, gesturing (I tell you where to find the printer), demonstrating (my Chinese friends show my children how they hold their chopsticks), and so on. Obtaining primary knowledge often involves perceptual agency.[24] You have to open your eyes, turn them in the right direction, focus them, let your eyes adjust to darkness or brightness, follow a moving object. You have to listen, focus on certain sounds, follow their temporal development; and similarly for taste and touch and smell.

If these are the things you need to do to gain knowledge about something, then your freedom to gain knowledge will be restricted when your perception is hindered. This may involve simple things. Blindfolding blocks vision, earmuffing blocks hearing, but closing the curtains may do just as well. It may also involve more sophisticated methods. Medicines extracted from the common foxglove, for instance, are claimed to tint your vision yellowy, making it difficult or impossible to distinguish other colours. But, simple or sophisticated, theoretically it is all straightforward: you are barred from using your perceptual organs in one way or another. Obtaining testimonial knowledge requires a *source* of testimony (parents, teachers, scholars, experts, and what have you) as well as a *channel* through which it can be got (conversations, lectures, team meetings, books, websites, advertisements, and so on). Bars to gaining primary knowledge will often also bar obtaining testimonial knowledge. But epistemic unfreedom in this regard can more specifically arise in the following two ways: making the source or making the channel unavailable. One can kill the 'heretic', incarcerate them, silence them. One can burn their books, destroy their communications satellites, or filter the Internet. One can close schools, temples, and conference centres—and try out all other options one has to limit freedom of speech and expression, and freedom of assembly. And again, while these options to limit people's epistemic freedom in this regard are indefinite, they are theoretically all straightforward.

This is George's predicament in *Combination Lock*. By ensuring such things as that the lock's user's manual is not lying around in the cell, that George has no phone available, and that no one provides him with information about the code, his abductor has made it impossible for him to carry out any investigative actions that would give him testimonial knowledge about the six-digit combination. Moreover, he has no opportunities for gaining primary knowledge either. This point is a bit subtle. It might seem that George can perform precisely one investigative action that would yield primary knowledge about the code, since, if he types the correct code, he learns that it opens the door. But it is odd to call that a genuine *investigative action*. It would not reflect the fact that an investigative action often requires experimentation, and it would go against the intuition that we must have a reasonable expectation that an investigative action will eventually help us gain evidence concerning the proposition we want to gain knowledge about—yet of course without already entailing that we know whether it is true or false. Something of this sort would be the case if George could try all one million options, for only then could he know in advance that he will find the answer to his question. But he can try out only one number.

In sum, by having set up George's predicament in *Combination Lock* that way, Olivia has ensured that there is no way for George to gain relevant primary and testimonial knowledge. To explain why George does not leave the cell, some might want to say that it is because he lacks the freedom to leave the cell. But it would be vastly preferable to say, I believe, that he lacks the *known freedom* to leave, as describing his predicament that way shows that the reason he will not leave is that he lacks the epistemic freedom to find out how. His predicament is also one of epistemic unfreedom.

Belief Adoption

The techniques Olivia used in *Brainwash*, the case with which I started this chapter, were more fanciful than those in *Combination Lock*; for there she brainwashed her victim into believing that an armed person would kill him if he left the restaurant, and then she left. In reality, however, there is no one waiting outside, and Oliver could safely have left the restaurant. We ask ourselves the question whether Olivia has made Oliver unfree to leave the restaurant. The answer is negative if we use words the way I suggest we should use them. If Oliver tried to leave the restaurant, he would not be shot, because there is no armed person. Just like George in *Combination Lock*, Oliver has no known freedom in this respect, since he falsely believes that he cannot leave, and this lack of known freedom is again due to the fact that Olivia restricted her victim's epistemic freedom. This time, however, the interference targeted that part of epistemic agency that is to do with adopting a doxastic attitude, rather than investigation. Olivia brainwashed Oliver, and so forced him to adopt a specific belief about the armed person.

Philosophers often use brainwashing in thought experiments without spelling out the mechanisms supposedly causing it, which has led Sam Black and Jon Tweedale to reject such thought experiments as incoherent or unrealistic.[25] But philosophers are not alone in discussing brainwashing. Legal scholars and psychologists have taken an interest in brainwashing at least since the 1950s, when they observed how American prisoners of war returned from the Korean war—meek, numbed, and sometimes with virulently communist convictions, or, as many thought, brainwashed by Chinese forces assisting North Korea.[26]

As Kathleen Taylor shows, since then a wealth of psychology, cognitive science, and neuroscience research has laid bare the many mechanisms that explain what may have happened to them as well as to the many other documented cases.[27] Taylor gives many examples of how physical, chemical, psychological, and social techniques can be used to manipulate people's beliefs. Anecdotal are 'magic mushrooms' that induce the belief you can fly (and every now and then lead to newspaper reports of people jumping out of a window after consuming them).[28] Some are rigorously researched, as, for instance, the influence of consuming oxytocin on your estimates of another person's trustworthiness.[29] Some examples are quite subtle, such as the observation that exposing people to the smell of rotten eggs and cigarettes, while they are asleep, somewhat decreases their desire to smoke, a phenomenon called *sleep nudging*.[30] Research on hormone manipulation, moreover, shows that changing a person's brain hormones and neurotransmitters changes the way they look at luxury brands, or significantly impairs their long-term memory, to mention just two examples.[31] And, perhaps more heavy handed, transcranial magnetic stimulation can deactivate particular areas in the brain and affect the way that people think of consuming insects.[32] It works by holding an electromagnet close to a person's skull to activate or depress particular nerve cells.

Transcranial magnetic stimulation can also evoke the sensation of seeing a light flash, or even out-of-body experiences, where people report seeing themselves from above, lying in bed.[33] And, while surely this has somewhat of a sci-fi feel to it—or may remind you of *soma*, the state-provided drug creating social cohesion in *Brave New World*— given the military and commercial stakes, it is unsurprising that neurotechnology is rapidly developing.

This enumeration is also meant to provide (some) empirical ground to worry less about a related worry that is to do with the thesis of doxastic voluntarism. *Direct doxastic voluntarism* is the thesis that we can decide what to believe at will. But then, more elegantly put, this thesis sounds exceedingly odd. Anyone holding on to this thesis would then have to show how to believe, right now, that New York is the capital of the US. According to the weaker thesis of *indirect doxastic voluntarism*, we have indirect control over what we believe—for instance, by the way we recruit and screen our sources of information. The thought is that, if you know that some newspaper or website tends to present evidence in favour of the belief that you would like to adopt, then your strategy might be to expose yourself to information from that source only.

I do think that adopting beliefs is more like a regular action, more decisional, than many philosophers think, but for current purposes this is not so very relevant.[34] We are here in a position not unlike that of the political theorist vis-à-vis determinism. If determinism is true, then it might seem to make little sense to talk about political freedom, because our opportunity sets are, then, singletons anyway. But, even if they are, that does not necessarily mean that the conceptual work that goes into analysing freedom and its value thereby becomes invalidated. Moreover, even if we ourselves have little direct influence on the beliefs we form, others may still have considerable influence on our beliefs. Olivia has brainwashed Oliver into falsely believing that there is a gunman waiting outside the restaurant, and, to the extent that she has succeeded in making Oliver immune against counterevidence, she has had a very direct influence on his doxastic attitudes. I hope, however, that the main assumption that I make for present purposes is much less contentious than fully embracing doxastic voluntarism: that neurotechnology, if it works, may restrict a person's known freedom by directly affecting their doxastic attitudes. If there is a pill the consumption of which induces a belief that you have the ability to fly, then making a person swallow it decreases their known freedom, not by changing their opportunity set, but by changing their doxastic attitude—that is, their known freedom. That is the idea, not more, not less.

Justification

The upshot so far is that I have shown how known freedom can be decreased by interfering with a person's investigative activities, and by interfering with their adopting particular doxastic attitudes—that is, beliefs and disbeliefs. It is now time to turn to the third element of epistemic actions: justification.[35] To do that, suppose you want to know something about a certain topic. You want to know whether some statement is true or false. You recruit relevant evidence and adopt the belief that the statement is true. For this belief to count as knowledge, it has to be justified. Philosophers have given many different answers to the question of what justification should amount to, and what else is needed to make sure you end up with genuine knowledge. Plato's suggestion in the *Meno* was that, when we know things, we bind things to us through arguments, which is sometimes seen as the first statement of the view that knowledge is justified true belief.[36] Robert Nozick famously introduced an approach according to which knowledge has to satisfy a condition to the effect that if, counterfactually, the statement were false, you would not believe it.[37] Your belief formation practices 'track' the truth in the sense that if φ is true, you believe φ, and if φ is false, you disbelieve φ (so believe its negation). While Nozick's approach has the attractions of logical elegance, many other accounts of justification have been given, and my hope is that what I say here is compatible with most of the accounts of justification (or warrant, entitlement, rationality, understanding) on the market.

The main question is, then, how can one go about interfering with justification.[38] I should make one thing clear upfront. I do not mean to imply fancifully that justifying a belief is something an agent does. It is not an action. I rather adopt the standard view that justification is a requirement to be met for an agent's believing something to qualify as knowing it. The thought is then that one could hinder the satisfaction of that requirement in ways that are irreducible to, or independent of, the ways in which one hinders the performance of an investigative action or the adoption of a belief. I distinguish two such hindrances, one internal to the agent, the other external.

Internal Obstacles

In the case that started this chapter, Olivia brainwashed Oliver into believing there was an armed person waiting outside the restaurant. One way in which she may have accomplished that feat was, as we saw, by exercising influence on his brain to make it physically impossible for him to store the contrary belief. She interfered at the level of belief adoption.

Here is another way, to do with justification. First, Olivia ensures that Oliver will uncritically and unreasoningly take any seeming bit of evidence for a given proposition as actual evidence for it; that is, she makes him overly credulous. She may, for instance, give him a variant of *Credon*, David Owens's 'anti-doubt pill' that will 'lull your suspicions, [and] make you credit your partner's stories'.[39] Subsequently, she simply tells the story.

Interference with the justification requirement is different from the first two forms of interference (with investigative actions and belief adoption). Olivia does not prevent Oliver from carrying out any investigative action. He could ask, for instance, why the other guests do not leave the restaurant. Nor does Credon make it physically impossible to adopt the right belief; for, if Olivia had told Oliver that there is no gunman, Oliver would have believed *that*. But it would not have been knowledge in that case either, for, had there counterfactually been a gunman in that already counterfactual scenario, then Oliver would still have believed Olivia's false statement.[40]

Gullibility pills are still a philosopher's fancy. But neurotechnology makes progress. We have already encountered oxytocin, also known as the *love hormone* or *liquid trust*, which may go some way to making people less critical.[41] More importantly for now, however, people can be made overly credulous (or, conversely, overly sceptical) in other ways, with mechanisms including sleep deprivation or forced hypnosis, or by exposing them to unquestionable authority or terror, as witnessed in some religious and non-religious sects, 're-education' camps for political dissidents in authoritarian regimes, and so forth.[42] But credulity is also reinforced by insufficiently critical parents or educators, or when other role models or influencers show that they adopt beliefs for which they have insufficient evidence. If you grow up in an environment where YouTube forms the primary source of news, or you get the bulk of your education in a decidedly uncritical classroom climate, or where the question 'How do you know?' is never asked, or answered, you are less likely to require your beliefs to be supported by evidence. The converse is also true. Parents teaching their children to doubt everything make them unfree to gain knowledge just as much as those who imbue a sense of uncritically believing everything. Ernest Sosa, for instance, somewhere discusses

> the beliefs of a 'naïf' with a crude conception of what justification requires in a certain ambit, who acquires his beliefs in ways that he is convinced are methodologically sound, simply because he was raised in culture where such ways are instilled.[43]

Another illustration of this phenomenon is offered by Naomi Oreskes and Erik Conway, who demonstrate that creating a culture of doubting scientific findings makes it difficult for laypeople to gain knowledge about, for instance, the risks of smoking.[44]

This may sound like an extreme position. Am I really saying that one person's unjustifiedly adopting beliefs may interfere with another person's epistemic freedom? Of course, I do not mean to say that interference would here take the form of barring the person from performing an investigative action or adopting a particular belief. As justification here concerns the link between evidence and doxastic attitude, interference has a different structure. The model I have in mind here is more that, when someone becomes gullible, they no longer consider certain of their prior beliefs as evidence against some purported statement. Consequently, making someone gullible bars them from appreciating the plausibility of that purported statement, given what they already know. Gaining knowledge is more difficult for them, perhaps impossible.

External Obstacles

So far I have discussed obstacles to justification that affect the way in which the decision maker deals with the evidence. Even though the source of these obstacles (the gullibility pill, the overly sceptical climate) is outside the decision maker, I call them *internal* as they happen 'within' them. This is also to contrast them with a second type of obstacle that is *external*.[45] An illustrative example concerns contextual framing, a phenomenon that is studied widely by psychologists. It goes back at least as far as to the Russian film director Lev Kuleshov, who was working in the 1920s.[46] Kuleshov found that the way an audience perceives a shot of an actor's facial expressions depends on what scenes precede it. He showed one and the same shot of a man's face right after a scene of a funeral, and to a different audience right after a scene with a playing child. He observed that the viewers of the first clip believed they had seen a *sad* face, while those who had seen the second clip believed they had seen a *happy* face. How you use the evidence about the man's face to form a belief about his feelings depends, then, on what else you have seen. Your belief formation is sensitive to what psychologists call *contextual framing*.

Such framing effects are everywhere, and often for good reasons. Psychologists argue that the presence of context is essential to avoid making perceptual errors, and that, without such context, we would be incapable of perceiving many things. In Kuleshov's example, the context of a funeral helps you to see particular facial expressions as a signal of sorrow and grief. But contextual framing is not always conducive to gaining true and justified beliefs. You have watched a news show to learn about a recent wave of demonstrations somewhere in the country, and you have seen footage of a large crowd of what you believe are aggressive protestors. You are worried and consider supporting people calling for firmer police action. That you perceive these individuals as *aggressive* may, however, be due to the fact that this clip of the protestors was preceded in the news show by an interview with a clearly aggressive spokesperson, who was almost attacking the journalist. If the news-show editors had selected a different interview, with a peaceful middle-aged professorial-looking participant, you would have seen a peaceful crowd. And you would not have found more intense policy scrutiny necessary.

This is *short-term framing*. Here is an example of *long-term framing*. The historical context is the 2003 Iraq War, and, while my example is based on relevant media scholarship, the precise connection I make is speculative. I should also point out that more recent research on, for instance, Brexit and the US presidential elections is gradually coming forward, but, as at the time of writing the dust has not settled here, I am going back a bit more. The *casus belli* was, among others, the idea that Saddam Hussein, the then president of Iraq, was in possession of weapons of mass destruction. Such weapons were, however, never found. Yet, when the Iraq War started in 2003, about 30 per cent of Fox News viewers believed that American intelligence had actually found weapons of mass destruction in Iraq, about three times as much as NPR/PBS viewers.[47]

How is that possible? Fox News was quite outspoken in its pro-war attitude. But we need not assume that it ever stated a falsehood. Rather it may have exploited a general fact about human psychology. White House officials made statements about alleged evidence of the presence of weapons of mass destruction in Iraq. These statements had to be retracted, however, in all cases. But, as Stephan Lewandowsky, Werner Stritzke, Klaus Oberauer, and Michael Morales show, merely following up with a retraction is insufficient, as we have a tendency to stick to believing something even if confronted with a rejection.[48] One may sensibly hypothesize that this is particularly true if the retraction is presented with less emphasis than the original statement. When alleged evidence for weapons of mass destruction tends to appear in the opening of a news show, accompanied by vivid visual imagery, and White House withdrawals are deferred to the end of the show, only read out by the anchor, with no images, then viewers are likely to end up with mistaken beliefs.

Neuromarketing

I now turn to the topic of neuromarketing that I touched upon briefly earlier in this chapter.

A Buy-Button?

Neuromarketing and *consumer neuroscience* are umbrella terms for marketing research and marketing practice using theories and techniques from neuroscience. It is often thought by practitioners and consumers to enable marketers to brainwash people into buying things that otherwise they would not have bought—witness claims that neuroscientists have now found consumers' 'buy button'.[49] More modestly, it can be described as the application of neuroscientific insights to product design, branding, labelling, pricing, placement, promotion, and other elements of marketing. Campbell Soup, for instance, redesigned its packaging in the light of neuroscientific insights.[50] Some neuromarketing techniques attempt to scan the human brain, using electroencephalography (EEG), positron emission tomography (PET), or functional magnetic resonance imaging (fMRI), a technology that allows them to compare images of successive brain states of a person engaged in a task, such as a purchasing decision. Other techniques try to track physiological proxies of brain activity, such as heartbeat and respiration rate, skin conductivity, pupil dilation, eye tracking, or the tiny subtle movements of the muscles of your face. Some also measure hormone levels (testosterone, cortisol, oxytocin, and so on) and neurotransmitter levels (serotonin).

But how could such studies benefit marketers?[51] Here is one example. In a 2011 op-ed in the *New York Times*, Martin Lindstrom, a marketing consultant, argued that fMRI data had shown that people love their iPhones the way they love their romantic partners.[52] While a group of neuroscientists quickly responded that Lindstrom had been way too enthusiastic in his interpretation of the results, it is not hard to see the potential relevance to the likes of Apple of future neuroscientific findings about the way customers think of their phones.

A more rigorous illustrative study concerns the impact of brand names. Participants in an experiment carried out by Samuel McClure and colleagues were offered a choice from two cups, containing Coke and Pepsi, while lying in an fMRI machine.[53] Participants in the *brand-cued delivery* condition were made aware of the brand names; the others, in the *anonymous delivery* condition, were ignorant about the brands. Participants had to choose several times in a row. In the anonymous delivery condition, the only knowledge the participants gained (over the course of trying several times) concerned the taste of the drink. fMRI analysis showed that in this condition the behaviour of the participants could be predicted on the basis of activity in the ventromedial prefrontal cortex. In the brand-cued delivery condition, on the other hand, participants also knew the correct brand name of the drinks in the cups. Here the selection of Coke (but not Pepsi) was significantly associated with activity in the hippocampus, the dorsolateral prefrontal cortex, and midbrain.

Hilke Plassmann and colleagues conducted a study to examine the effect of knowing, not the brand name of a product, but its price.[54] Twenty participants were offered various wines with price tags. Unbeknownst to them, however, some of the wines were offered twice, once with an expensive tag ($90) and once with an inexpensive tag ($10). The researchers found that higher price is associated with higher subjective reports of what they call *flavour pleasantness*, and with increased activity in the medial orbitofrontal cortex, an area of the brain that is associated with pleasantness.

Another example of a study that gives a sense of what neuromarketing can do includes the following. EEG and fMRI techniques can help predict the preference for films and sales data of music clips, after watching/listening to a trailer/fragment, and the degree of accuracy of these predictions is much greater than that of traditional marketing methods such as customer surveys and focus groups.[55] And the relevance of all this is underscored by the fact that companies such as NBC, TimeWarner, Microsoft, Google, Amazon, and Facebook have set up their own in-house neuromarketing teams, as well as by the rise of neuromarketing companies such as NeuroFocus, and an increasing numbers of patents in this area.

Criticism

Some people are worried. Clive Hamilton and Richard Deniss, for instance, write that 'we have not so much been brainwashed into drinking Coca-Cola', which is more the traditional view of what marketing may do, but rather 'we have had our brains rewired to want it', and that is what makes neuromarketing so scary.[56] The impression one gets from the scholarly literature is, however, that business ethicists are not too worried. The thought seems to be that neuromarketing is old wine in new bottles, because the type of strategies that marketers develop on the basis of neuroscientific findings are not categorically different from those based on more traditional marketing research. Steven Stanton, Walter Sinnott–Armstrong, and Scott Huettel even go so far as to applaud, persuasively I believe, the potentially beneficial effects of neuromarketing, even though they do signal the possibility of neuromarketing creating *artificial wants* or *desires* for things that people do not need.[57] But that is an old ethical problem, already discussed by John Kenneth Galbraith.[58]

Neil Levy uses the Coke–Pepsi study to defend a similar position.[59] That consumers who are brand-cued with Coke and Pepsi experience their opportunity sets differently, and select different options, is something we do not need neuroscience for us to uncover. We know that already from behavioural observations. The fact that fMRI can demonstrate hippocampal activity while people make such choices does not tell us much in this respect. Levy notes that critics of consumer neuroscience seem to adhere to a view that distinguishes between two types of influence marketing could have. One type of influence is internal to the decision maker, exemplified by customer brains being directly stimulated, or when consumers are directly administered oxytocin. Another type of influence is external to the agent, so the shopping environment is manipulated, as, for instance, by the way products are placed in a grocery store. Levy thinks there is no good reason to make a fundamental distinction between internal and external influence, because 'both can result in changes in beliefs, and in the actions which express those beliefs'.[60]

I agree with Levy that there is some room to believe that more traditional methods of marketing may lead to results that are difficult to distinguish from neuromarketing. An example here is a famous case in which Target, the American retail company, sent advertisements for items related to pregnancy and babies to a woman who had not yet informed anyone about her pregnancy.[61] They simply used powerful data analysis. But, first, it is not only about changing beliefs, but also about changing desires. And, secondly, even when it is about changing beliefs, then different neuromarketing tools may change beliefs in different ways, and some ways may be more normatively problematic than others.

Changing Desires

So I do not fully agree with Levy. To show why, I return to freedom and known freedom. I start with desires. In the previous chapter we saw that, according to some conceptions of freedom, a person's freedom is dependent on their or other people's desires (or cognate world-to-mind attitudes): freedom is the ability to do what one desires to do (for Mill), what is socially desirable (for Green), or what one authentically desires and what helps one realize oneself (for Taylor). Now let us make a contrast here. For Mill it is unimportant (when we talk about freedom) what a person's desires are, and it is unimportant how they came about; their desires are just there and are not the object of further scrutiny when it comes to describing a person's freedom. For Green, by contrast, the *what* is important, for the person's desires should track such things as social progress or the common good, but it is unimportant how the person acquires these desires. For Taylor, by contrast, both the *what* and the *how* are important: the person's desires must be authentic—that is, they have to have their origin in the person's authority (answering the *how* question), and their content has to be such that they contribute to the person's self-realization (answering the *what* question).

As Taylor's is the most demanding conception of freedom, then, it is natural to ask whether neuromarketing might diminish—or perhaps enlarge?—a person's positive freedom à la Taylor. Perhaps it can. Take transcranial magnetic stimulation (TMS), which, as we saw, involves an electromagnet held close to the skull, thereby diminishing activity in particular parts of the brain. There is fairly widespread agreement among researchers that TMS can change the way we value food, and repetitive TMS has been tested as a treatment of bulimia nervosa and related eating disorders. To the extent that bulimic preferences are inauthentic, TMS might be heralded from the point of view of positive freedom. But one can also imagine other usages. Research by Moran Cerf, a consumer neuroscientist, is reported to have shown how TMS may change people's level of fear and disgust about insects, with the advertised goal of being able to make us more tolerant to eat insects, which are arguably an environmentally cost-effective source of protein.[62] This again may sound far-fetched, but advocates of a Taylorian version of positive freedom have much to worry about if such techniques are scaled up, and direct manipulation of customer brains becomes a reality. And they may: the erstwhile implausible idea that people *love* their iPhones the way they love their romantic partners seems to have obtained much stronger empirical support recently.[63]

Changing Beliefs

So far about changing desires. Let us move on to the thought that neuromarketing might change a person's beliefs. Borrowing from Levy again, imagine that a salesperson wants to increase their customer's trust.[64] They can administer oxytocin (imagine for the sake of argument that it is contained in coffee, or mixed through). Or they can 'have kittens around, or pictures of kittens', supposedly something that people are likely to take as evidence for the salesperson's trustworthiness.[65] Or they could simply apply some marketing trick, such as first telling the customer that the product they are looking at is unsuitable for them, thereby creating the impression that the salesperson is there to serve rather than to sell, which the customer might again take as evidence of their trustworthiness, and then turn to the next thing.

The hypothetical customer, we assume, changes their beliefs in all three cases. But such belief changes are to be judged differently if we look at the customer's epistemic freedom. Using oxytocin, in the first case, is clearly close to the case in which Olivia brainwashed Oliver into believing that he would die if he left the restaurant. Moreover, the salesperson's trick, in the third case, is similar to Harry's predicament in *Shed*. Harry believed he was unable to leave the shed, but he could easily have found out about a safe escape route. That he did not end up with knowledge of his choice situation was, in Matthew Kramer's words, because the available evidence had not played 'its proper cognitive role'.[66] Here, too, it requires very little common sense to suspect that a salesperson will use such and similar tricks to sell you something. Most people—certainly if you shop with children—know full well why marketers place candy bars near the checkout rather than in the vegetables section.

But what about the second case (the kittens)? Here the phenomenology may be subtle. Unlike in the third case, the customer may not have introspective access to the connection between the purported evidence (the pictures of the kitten) and their adopting a belief (that the salesperson is trustworthy). But, like the third case, if the customer made the connection, they would immediately revise their belief. And there is another point that I should stress. Suppose that the salesperson is, in fact, trustworthy. Then the customer's beliefs are true. The way the scenarios are set up, however, ensures that these true beliefs are not knowledge. The beliefs are true, but only accidentally. They are in no better position epistemically than a wild guess, because they have arisen in ways that have no bearing whatsoever with what they are about (in the first two cases) or are not justified by what they originate from. Oxytocin, a salesperson's kittens, or a salesperson's trick are not a good basis for your belief about their trustworthiness, even if the customer's belief may be true. More is needed, then. To show why more is needed—why knowledge is needed—is the topic of the Chapter 3.

Notes

1. Martin van Hees and Marcel Wissenburg, 'Freedom and Opportunity', *Political Studies*, 47 (1999), 67–82, at 67.
2. Isaiah Berlin, *Four Essays on Liberty* (London: Oxford University Press, 1969), 'Introduction', pp. xxxiv–xxxv.
3. Matthew Kramer, *The Quality of Freedom* (Oxford: Oxford University Press, 2003), 265, 266.

4. Ian Carter, *A Measure of Freedom* (Oxford: Oxford University Press, 1999), 206.

5. See Rik Peels, *Responsible Belief: A Theory in Ethics and Epistemology* (Oxford: Oxford University Press, 2017), for the question of whether such things as indoctrination excuses us, an issue that I set aside here.

6. John Rawls, *A Theory of Justice* (Cambridge, MA: Harvard University Press, 1971), 204.

7. Ibid.

8. Philip Pettit, *Republicanism: A Theory of Freedom and Government* (Oxford: Oxford University Press, 1997), 289.

9. Isaiah Berlin, *Four Essays on Liberty* (London: Oxford University Press, 1969), 'Introduction', p. liii.

10. Michael Smith, 'A Theory of Freedom and Responsibility', in Garrett Cullity (ed.), *Ethics and Practical Reason* (New York: Clarendon Press, 1996), 308. If what is wrong about undergoing a brainwash is only that it instils a number of false beliefs about your choice options, liberals would not have reason to lament brainwashing that results in correct beliefs, paternalistically, so to speak. See Alvin Goldman, 'Epistemic Paternalism: Communication Control in Law and Society', *Journal of Philosophy*, 88 (1991), 113–131, and Kristoffer Ahlstrom-Vij, *Epistemic Paternalism: A Defence* (London: Palgrave Macmillan, 2013). This does not only apply to factual beliefs, but also to normative beliefs. I may be brainwashed into believing (correctly as it turns out) that I have a duty to help a person, something that without the brainwashing I would not have believed. Ronald Dworkin, 'Foundations of Liberal Equality', in *Tanner Lectures on Human Values* (Salt Lake City: University of Utah Press, 1991), 50, cited in Gerald Dworkin, 'Autonomy', in Robert Goodin and Philip Pettit (eds), *A Companion to Contemporary Political Philosophy* (Malden: Blackwell, 1993), 359–365, at 363, has argued that 'no event or achievement can make a person's life better against his opinion that it does not'. The epistemic paternalist is in a different predicament, as they need to consider cases in which the 'event' includes changing the person's beliefs in such a way that *ex post* it will not be 'against his opinion'.

11. Matthew Kramer, *The Quality of Freedom* (Oxford: Oxford University Press, 2003), 265–266. Gerald Dworkin, *The Theory and Practice of Autonomy* (Cambridge: Cambridge University Press, 1988), 14 and 105, discusses a similar scenario.

12. Matthew Kramer, *The Quality of Freedom* (Oxford: Oxford University Press, 2003), 266.

13. People have incorrect beliefs if they disbelieve a true proposition, and they have incomplete beliefs if they neither believe nor disbelieve it (they have suspended belief). In standard doxastic logic, an incorrect belief about φ is one

where $\mathbf{B}\neg\varphi$ holds (while φ is true), whereas incomplete information with respect to φ happens when $\neg\mathbf{B}\varphi \land \neg\mathbf{B}\neg\varphi$ (and φ may be true or false). See Philip Nickel, 'Voluntary Belief on a Reasonable Basis, *Philosophy and Phenomenological Research*, 81 (2010), 312–334, locating voluntariness in situations allowing some suspension, and Nikolaj Nottelmann, 'The Varieties of Ignorance', in Rik Peels and Martijn Blaauw (eds), *The Epistemic Dimensions of Ignorance* (Cambridge: Cambridge University Press, 2016), 33–56, for the epistemology of ignorance.

14. Matthew Kramer, *The Quality of Freedom* (Oxford: Oxford University Press, 2003), 80–86, 265–267. See also Michael Garnett, 'Ignorance, Incompetence and the Concept of Liberty', *Journal of Political Philosophy*, 15 (2007), 428–446, at 438, and Gottfried Seebaß, 'Der Wert der Freiheit', *Deutsche Zeitschrift für Philosophie*, 44 (1996), 759–775, at 773.

15. I have de dicto knowledge that you have an email address (I know you have one), but I do not have de re knowledge of your email address (I do not know which one). It is the difference between $\exists x \mathbf{K} F(x)$ and $\mathbf{K}\exists x F(x)$. See generally Emar Maier, 'Presupposing Acquaintance: A Unified Semantics for *de dicto, de re* and *de se* Belief Reports', *Linguistics and Philosophy*, 32 (2009), 429–474. So Harry's belief state is $\mathbf{B}\neg\exists x Escape(x)$, while George's is $\mathbf{B}\exists x Escape(x) \land \neg\exists x \mathbf{B} Escape(x)$. See, e.g., Boudewijn de Bruin, 'Epistemic Logic and Epistemology', in Vincent Hendricks and Duncan Pritchard (eds), *New Waves in Epistemology* (Basingstoke: Palgrave Macmillan, 2008), 106–136, for further discussion of epistemic logic and epistemology.

16. See, e.g., Keith Dowding and Martin van Hees, 'The Construction of Rights', *American Political Science Review*, 97 (2003), 281–293, for how to deal with probabilities and freedom ascriptions, an issue I here set aside.

17. Michael Garnett, 'Ignorance, Incompetence and the Concept of Liberty', *Journal of Political Philosophy*, 15 (2007), 428–446, at 438.

18. Matthew Kramer, *The Quality of Freedom* (Oxford: Oxford University Press, 2003), 81.

19. Ibid. 83.

20. See, e.g., Conor McHugh, 'Exercising Doxastic Freedom', *Philosophy and Phenomenological Research*, 88 (2014), 1–37, Philip Pettit and Michael Smith, 'Freedom in Belief and Desire', *Journal of Philosophy*, 93 (1996), 429–449, Ernest Sosa, 'Epistemic Agency', *Journal of Philosophy*, 110 (2013), 585–605, and David Velleman, 'Epistemic Freedom', *Pacific Philosophical Quarterly*, 70 (1989), 73–97.

21. Edmund Gettier, 'Is Justified True Belief Knowledge?', *Analysis*, 23 (1963), 121–123. See Robert Shope, 'Conditions and Analyses of Knowledge', in Paul Moser (ed.), *The Oxford Handbook of Epistemology* (Oxford: Oxford University Press, 2002), 25–70, for a detailed overview.

22. Timothy Williamson, *Knowledge and Its Limits* (Oxford: Oxford University Press, 2000).

23. See Laurence Bonjour, 'Internalism and Externalism', in Paul Moser (ed.), *The Oxford Handbook of Epistemology* (Oxford: Oxford University Press, 2005), 234–260, for internalism and externalism about justification, which may be relevant for spelling out some repercussions of this idea.

24. See, e.g., Thomas Crowther, 'The Agential Profile of Perceptual Experience', *Proceedings of the Aristotelian Society*, 110 (2010), 219–240, and Eva Schürmann, *Sehen als Praxis: Ethisch-ästhetische Studien zum Verhältnis von Sicht und Einsicht* (Frankfurt am Main: Suhrkamp, 2008).

25. Sam Black and Jon Tweedale, 'Responsibility and Alternative Possibilities: The Use and Abuse of Examples', *Journal of Ethics*, 6 (2002), 281–303. Cf. generally, e.g., Richard Arneson, 'Freedom and Desires', *Canadian Journal of Philosophy*, 15 (1985), 425–448, Stephen Mumford and Rani Anjum, 'Powers, Non-Consent and Freedom', *Philosophy and Phenomenological Research*, 91 (2015), 136–152, and Chandra Sripada, 'What Makes a Manipulated Agent Unfree?', *Philosophy and Phenomenological Research*, 85 (2012), 563–593.

26. See, e.g., Anthony Dick and Thomas Robbins, 'Law, Social Science and the "Brainwashing" Exception to the First Amendment', *Behavioral Sciences and the Law*, 10 (1992), 5–29, and James Ogloff and Jeffrey Pfeifer, 'Cults and the Law: A Discussion of the Legality of Alleged Cult Activities', *Behavioral Sciences and the Law*, 10 (1992), 117–140.

27. Kathleen Taylor, *Brainwashing: The Science of Thought Control* (Oxford: Oxford University Press, 2004).

28. See, e.g., Toby Sterling, 'Ban on Magic Mushroom Sales Curbs Dutch Drug Policy', *Guardian*, 13 October 2007, theguardian.com/world/2007/oct/13/drugsandalcohol.uk [perma.cc/28GK-YXGC], and Joke Harte and Ingrid van Houwelingen, 'Het groeiende toerisme in Amsterdam en de aanzuigende werking op criminaliteit', *PROCES*, 96 (2017), 338–348, at 343 (after several deadly incidents with magic mushrooms among tourists, the Netherlands banned the sales of them, giving evidence of around ten intoxicated people drowning in the Amsterdam canals yearly (beverages and drugs)). To the extent that hallucinogenic or psychedelic substances induce religious experiences (or other experiences not obtainable by other means), banning them may be seen as also removing opportunities for adopting particular beliefs (namely, those that consuming these substances lead to). A notorious case that came before the US Supreme Court ruled the sacramental use of peyote, which is a core element of the Native American Church, is not protected by the Free Exercise clause of the First Amendment (that is, freedom of religion). *Employment*

Division, Department of Human Resources of Oregon v. *Smith* [1990] 494 US 872. It is hard to say how the tension between religious and recreational use should be resolved. A complicating issue is that most of these beliefs will not constitute fully-fledged knowledge. See, e.g., Walter Clark, 'Religious Aspects of Psychedelic Drugs', *California Law Review*, 56 (1968), 86–99.

29. Michael Kosfeld, Markus Heinrichs, Paul Zak, Urs Fischbacher, and Ernst Fehr, 'Oxytocin Increases Trust in Humans', *Nature*, 435 (2005), 673–676.

30. Anat Arzi, Yael Holtzman, Perry Samnon, Neetai Eshel, Edo Harel, and Noam Sobel, 'Olfactory Aversive Conditioning during Sleep Reduces Cigarette-Smoking Behavior', *Journal of Neuroscience*, 34 (2014), 15382–15393.

31. See Anke Sambeth, Wim Riedel, D. Tillie, Arjan Blokland, Albert Postma, and Jeroen Schmitt, 'Memory Impairments in Humans after Acute Tryptophan Depletion Using a Novel Gelatin-Based Protein Drink', *Journal of Psychopharmacology*, 23 (2009), 56–64.

32. Carmelo Vicario, Robert Rafal, Sara Borgomaneri, Riccardo Paracampo, Ada Kritikos, and Alessio Avenanti, 'Pictures of Disgusting Foods and Disgusted Facial Expressions Suppress the Tongue Motor Cortex', *Social Cognitive and Affective Neuroscience*, 12 (2017), 352–362.

33. Olaf Blanke, Christine Mohr, Christoph Michel, Alvaro Pascual-Leone, Peter Brugger, Margitta Seeck, Theodor Landis, and Gregor Thut, 'Linking Out-of-Body Experience and Self Processing to Mental Own-Body Imagery at the Temporoparietal Junction', *Journal of Neuroscience*, 25 (2003), 550–557.

34. With more logical precision, the doxastic attitudes you can adopt towards a proposition φ are **B**φ (belief) and **B**¬φ (disbelief), or in predicate logic, $\mathbf{B}\exists x\varphi(x)$, $\mathbf{B}\neg\exists x\varphi(x)$, $\exists x\mathbf{B}\varphi(x)$. Note that $\neg\exists x\mathbf{B}\varphi(x)$ is not a belief, and $\mathbf{B}\exists x\neg\varphi(x)$ and $\exists x\mathbf{B}\neg\varphi(x)$ are not really beliefs about φ. Suspension of belief is of the form $\neg\mathbf{B}\varphi(x)\wedge\neg\mathbf{B}\neg\varphi(x)$. Believing φ may come down to giving full credence to φ, but it may also mean accepting φ (rather than its negation) for the sake of argument or for the sake of practical deliberation. What is important, however, is the logical makeup of the various doxastic states.

35. It is not my purpose here to defend a view of what justification is. Briefly, however, I think the following would be methodologically attractive: imagine an agent who acts on the basis of beliefs and desires (an expected utility maximizer). How should the agent's belief formation processes be optimally designed? Probably they would be largely automatic for a fairly large class of simple beliefs, with a reliable process underlying it, and quite voluntary and internal to the agent for a smaller class of more complex beliefs the acquisition of which requires real labour. The conditions such a system should satisfy coincide (or entail) the conditions of what makes a belief justified.

36. Plato, *Meno* 98a3–4 (own translation). Of course this has to be linked to other discussions, particularly in the *Theaetetus*.

37. Robert Nozick, *Philosophical Explanations* (Cambridge, MA: Harvard University Press, 1981), 172–185.

38. I am not saying that only by interfering with justification one prevents knowledge, but I do not separately discuss ways to interfere with what sits in between knowledge and justified true belief, if anything.

39. David Owens, 'Disenchantment', in Louise Antony (ed.), *Philosophers Without Gods: Meditations on Atheism and the Secular Life* (Oxford: Oxford University Press, 2007), 175.

40. It may matter here whether you adopt an internalist or an externalist view of justification. What Credon does could, for the internalist, be described as something that interferes with Oliver's reasons, because he can do all he wants to do, but he cannot do it anymore for certain reasons. On an externalist reading of the case, perhaps Credon should be seen as interfering with the reliability of Oliver's cognitive powers.

41. See, e.g., Antonio Damasio, 'Brain Trust', *Nature*, 435 (2005), 571–572, and Michael Kosfeld, Markus Heinrichs, Paul Zak, Urs Fischbacher, and Ernst Fehr, 'Oxytocin Increases Trust in Humans', *Nature*, 435 (2005), 673–676. Cf. Moïra Mikolajczak, James Gross, Anthony Lane, Olivier Corneille, Philippe de Timary, and Olivier Luminet, 'Oxytocin Makes People Less Trusting, Not Gullible', *Psychological Science*, 21 (2010), 1072–1074.

42. See, e.g., Kathleen Taylor, *Brainwashing: The Science of Thought Control* (Oxford: Oxford University Press, 2004), and Solomon Schimmel, *The Tenacity of Unreasonable Beliefs: Fundamentalism and the Fear of Truth* (Oxford: Oxford University Press, 2008). See Sven Ove Hansson, 'Science Denial as a Form of Pseudoscience', *Studies in History and Philosophy of Science Part A*, 63 (2017), 39–47, on cherry-picking evidence among climate deniers. To the extent that memory offers justification, making people forget may also be an example of interference.

43. Ernest Sosa, 'Plantinga on Epistemic Internalism', in Jonathan Kvanvig (ed.), *Warrant in Contemporary Epistemology: Essays in Honor of Plantinga's Theory of Knowledge* (Lanham: Rowman and Littlefield, 1996), 73–87, at 82.

44. Naomi Oreskes and Erik Conway, *Merchants of Doubt: How a Handful of Scientists Obscured the Truth on Issues from Tobacco Smoke to Global Warming* (New York: Bloomsbury, 2010).

45. See also Helen Longino, *Science as Social Knowledge: Values and Objectivity in Scientific Inquiry* (Princeton: Princeton University Press, 1990), for the relevance of social context to epistemic justification, and Stephen Stich, *The Fragmentation of Reason: Preface to a Pragmatic Theory of Cognitive Evaluation*

(Cambridge, MA: MIT Press, 1990), for the cultural acquisition of the concept of justification.

46. Dean Mobbs, Nikolaus Weiskopf, Hakwan Lau, Eric Featherstone, Ray Dolan, and Chris Frith, 'The Kuleshov Effect: The Influence of Contextual Framing on Emotional Attributions', *Social Cognitive and Affective Neuroscience*, 1 (2006), 95–106.

47. Steven Kull, Clay Ramsay, and Evan Lewis, 'Misperceptions, the Media, and the Iraq War', *Political Science Quarterly*, 118 (2003), 569–598, at 584.

48. Stephan Lewandowsky, Werner Stritzke, Klaus Oberauer, and Michael Morales, 'Memory for Fact, Fiction, and Misinformation: The Iraq War 2003', *Psychological Science*, 16 (2011), 190–195.

49. See, e.g., a blog on the website of Hill + Knowlton, an international public relations company, 'Buy Button: Neuro-Marketing: It's All in your Head', Hill + Knowlton Strategies, 17 July 2017, www.hkstrategies.com/magnify-neuromarketing-its-all-in-your-head [perma.cc/5YSJ-N436].

50. Scott Huettel, interviewed by Ania Wieckowski, 'When Neuromarketing Crosses the Line: Three Leading Researchers Weigh In', *Harvard Business Review* (January 2019), 76.

51. See, generally, Eben Harrell, 'Neuromarketing: What You Need to Know', *Harvard Business Review* (January 2019), 64–70.

52. Martin Lindstrom, 'You Love Your iPhone: Literally', *New York Times*, 30 September 2011, www.nytimes.com/2011/10/01/opinion/you-love-your-iphone-literally.html [perma.cc/24UY-B82N].

53. Samuel McClure, Jian Li, Damon Tomlin, Kim Cypert, Latané Montague, and Read Montague, 'Neural Correlates of Behavioral Preference for Culturally Familiar Drinks', *Neuron*, 44 (2004), 379–387.

54. Hilke Plassmann, John O'Doherty, Baba Shiv, and Antonio Rangel, 'Marketing Actions can Modulate Neural Representations of Experienced Pleasantness', *PNAS* 105 (2008), 1050–1054.

55. See Gregory Berns and Sara Moore, 'A Neural Predictor of Cultural Popularity', *Journal of Consumer Psychology*, 22 (2011), 154–160, and Maarten Boksem and Ale Smidts, 'Brain Responses to Movietrailers Predict Individual Preferences for Movies and their Population-Wide Commercial Success', *Journal of Marketing Research*, 52 (2015), 482–492.

56. Clive Hamilton and Richard Deniss, *Affluenza: When Too Much Is Never Enough* (Crows Nest: Allen & Unwin, 2005), 42.

57. Steven Stanton, Walter Sinnott–Armstrong, and Scott Huettel, 'Neuromarketing: Ethical Implications of its Use and Potential Misuse', *Journal of Business Ethics*, 144 (2017), 799–811.

58. John Kenneth Galbraith, *The Affluent Society* (Boston: Houghton Mifflin Company, 1958).

59. Neil Levy, 'Neuromarketing: Ethical and Political Challenges', *Etica & Politica/Ethics and Politics*, 11 (2009), 10–17.

60. Ibid. 16.

61. Charles Duhigg, 'How Companies Learn Your Secrets', *New York Times*, 16 February 2012, www.nytimes.com/2012/02/19/magazine/shopping-habits.html [perma.cc/G795-RBSZ].

62. Eben Harrell, 'Neuromarketing: What You Need to Know', *Harvard Business Review* (January 2019), 64–70, at 70.

63. Ibid. 66.

64. Neil Levy, 'Neuromarketing: Ethical and Political Challenges', *Etica & Politica/Ethics and Politics*, 11 (2009), 10–17, at 11.

65. Ibid.

66. Matthew Kramer, *The Quality of Freedom* (Oxford: Oxford University Press, 2003), 266.

3

From the Value of Knowledge to Skills and Stereotypes

The Individual Ideal of Known Freedom

People possess known freedom to the extent that they have knowledge concerning their choice situation. They have to know which actions are available, and which ones not. So they have to know what their opportunity set looks like, and what actions are not in the opportunity set. In addition, they have to know what the possible consequences are of performing these actions, and they have to know with what distinct probabilities these consequences arise. This has to be de re rather than de dicto knowledge: the degree of one's known freedom to travel increases if a vague awareness of the existence of as yet unspecific travel options is updated and revised into knowledge *of* specific travel options being available.

Known freedom has value because freedom has value. That is how the concept of known freedom was set up in the first place: if desire satisfaction, moral responsibility, or self-realization gives freedom value, then a fortiori they give value to known freedom. Yet some of the value that known freedom generates comes from the value that knowledge generates, rather independently of freedom: in particular, the value that knowledge (with its justification, warrant, rationality, and what have you) has over and above the value of mere true belief.

This may sound implausible at first, for what could knowledge add to a true belief? If what makes known freedom better than freedom is that it allows people actually to seize the opportunities they have because with known freedom they are aware of them, then why would that awareness need to be knowledge? The answer is subtle: I develop the view in this chapter that, while ultimately the awareness need not be knowledge in all cases, generating knowledge is the best way to make the awareness most stable. You may have true beliefs about various investment

The Business of Liberty. Boudewijn de Bruin, Oxford University Press.
© Boudewijn de Bruin (2022). DOI: 10.1093/oso/9780198839675.003.0004

opportunities as well as about their risks and expected returns. But, if you have knowledge, and know, for instance, what the evidence is on the basis of which these risks and returns are calculated, and how strong such evidence is, then you are less likely to lose your true beliefs if your opportunity set undergoes changes that are due to financial market developments.

Known Freedom

Imagine you are contemplating retirement planning options. You could save all your money in a bank account. You could invest the money on the stock market. You have the opportunity to participate in a *defined benefit* investment scheme set up by your employer that guarantees a fixed monthly payout when you have reached retirement age, or in a *defined contribution* scheme where the size of the instalments that you will ultimately receive is dependent on the success of the scheme's investments. Most people hardly ever attain anything close to known freedom with respect to retirement planning. They may be unaware of the difference between defined benefit and defined contribution schemes. They may fail to grasp the risks of putting large amounts of money in a bank account (banks may go bust) or overestimate their abilities to select a decent portfolio meeting their ends. They may also fail to see that, even if a defined benefit scheme is said to *guarantee* a fixed monthly payout, the scheme may no longer exist when they need it—for even pension funds can go bankrupt in some jurisdictions, voiding the guarantee.

Known freedom grows in several ways. It grows when a person's freedom grows: the number of retirement planning options may increase when, for instance, some financial services provider starts offering a new retirement product with different possible consequences and probabilities—that is, with different risks and expected returns, with a different composition of underlying assets, or with anything else that might appeal to the decision maker. Known freedom also grows when knowledge grows: the change is then that the decision maker obtains better beliefs about availability or unavailability of actions, about the consequences of these actions, and the probabilities attached to them. A person learning about the time value of money, about portfolio diversification, about the corporate governance of pension schemes (and the fact that they do sometimes wind down), or about the fact that the fund invests only in firms meeting particular sustainability requirements gains known freedom: they get a more accurate view of their retirement planning options.

Retreat in the Inner Citadel?

The move to known freedom I promote here may look like the error Isaiah Berlin uncovered in conceptions of freedom that make the extent of a person's freedom depend on their desires. Take such a conception, say, John Stuart Mill's, according to which I am free to the extent that I can satisfy my desires. Now consider two worlds. In both worlds I have a small set of opportunities each of which generates limited expected utility. In one world my opportunity set expands, allowing me to select an action with greater expected utility. For Mill, this counts as an increase of freedom. In the other world, there is no change in my opportunity. But I change my desires. I extinguish my current desires and substitute them by desires that my current opportunity allows me maximally to satisfy. And so I reach a level of freedom equal to the level I have in the first world, at least if we adopt Mill's definition.

Berlin uses the suggestive term of the *retreat to the inner citadel,* which he associates with Epictetus, the Hellenistic stoic philosopher and liberated slave.[1] The supposed unattractiveness of this retreat is for Berlin the prime reason to reject the most prominent desire-dependent conception of freedom, the one promoted in *On Liberty.* I doubt whether Berlin's extrapolation of the stoic notion of freedom to nineteenth-century British political thought is warranted.[2] Apart from that, however, he seems right on systematic grounds to be worried about a political conception of freedom that allows one to say that someone's freedom has increased on account of their having changed their desires.[3] And, indeed, granting Berlin that point does not seem to bode well for a conception of freedom that makes it dependent on belief (or knowledge), for that is just as much a mental state as desire. Moreover, as we saw, Berlin was clearly sceptical about such a conception:

> Knowledge liberates not by offering us more open possibilities amongst which we can make our choice, but by preserving us from the frustration of attempting the impossible.[4]

So, is the ideal of known freedom vulnerable to the same attack? Should we not say that, if beliefs can change a person's freedom, then also desires can change a person's freedom?

I do not think so. It is true that, as beliefs and desires are both mental states, the extent of your known freedom is dependent on some of your mental states. But these are states with opposite direction of fit. Desires have a *world-to-mind* direction of fit: they express how one would like the world to be, and a typical response in case of a mismatch between mind and world is to change the world, or at least to attempt it. Beliefs have a *mind-to-world* direction of fit, as they express how one thinks the world actually is. The standard way to resolve a mismatch between mind and world here is a change of mind: you update or revise your beliefs. What Epictetus recommends to us, according to Berlin (that is, the retreat to the inner citadel), is an atypical response to a mismatch between desires and world.[5] What known freedom recommends is, by contrast, the standard response to a mismatch between beliefs and world: update or revise them. So one gains known freedom by changing beliefs in an epistemically entirely impeccable and unproblematic manner. No retreat to the inner citadel is needed.

Fasten Your Beliefs

But why do our beliefs have to be knowledge? Is it not sufficient if our beliefs about our opportunities be true? We derived known freedom using the logic of the arguments from desire satisfaction, moral responsibility, and self-realization. If we value these things, and if we assume that they grow when freedom grows, then they grow even more when known freedom grows. The key observation driving this conclusion was that only if you are aware of some opportunities will you use them to satisfy your desires, assume responsibility, and realize yourself.

It may seem, however, that these good things would happen equally if you possessed, not knowledge, but mere true beliefs. Consider this. I consult an astrologist for investment advice. They tell me that XYZ is undervalued at the moment, and that is why I buy shares in the company. A week later, XYZ announces it has made a major step forward in developing a vaccine for some global disease. XYZ shares go up by about 20 per cent. I sell them, pocket the gains, and use them to satisfy my desire of buying a Steinway. My beliefs became better after talking to the astrologists. But surely I did not gain any knowledge about the consequences of buying XYZ shares. Yet that lack of epistemic status has not had any influence on my ability to satisfy my desires.

The question about the difference between knowledge and belief goes back at least as far as to a discussion towards the end of Plato's *Meno*. Socrates first suggests to Meno that, for practical purposes, knowledge and true belief have equal utility.[6] To argue this point, he asks Meno to consider a person merely believing the way to the town of Larisa, and another who possesses genuine knowledge about the way. Would the former be a worse guide than the latter if it were your aim to visit Larisa? Socrates thinks not, and Meno agrees. Yet Meno remains puzzled. He wonders why, if that is the case, knowledge is still seen as more valued or 'honoured' than true belief. In answer to that question, Socrates introduces the view that we briefly encountered in Chapter 2. The idea is that the difference between knowledge and belief is that knowledge has a 'binding' and comes with 'chains', that knowledge is 'fastened', and that the chains make knowledge more likely to stay, just as Socrates thought that the statues of Daedalus had to be tied down lest they would run away.[7] You could say, then, that a thing that is believed (and true) is more easily lost than a thing that is known.

But should that not also have practical repercussions? Is there not a risk that the true-belief guide might lose the beliefs about the way to Larisa if these beliefs are insufficiently fastened, and that therefore a knowing guide is a better bet than a true-belief guide, if you want to visit Larisa?

A recent take on this issue is provided by Timothy Williamson.[8] Here is my slightly adapted version of an illustrative example he gives.[9] Suppose a burglar is ransacking a house all night, and suppose you are offered two alternative explanations. One is that the burglar possessed knowledge that there was a diamond in the house. The other is that the burglar had only a true belief to that effect. Williamson suggests that the explanation for the event of the burglar's ransacking the house all night in terms of mere true belief is not as good as an explanation in terms of knowledge. This seems to me intuitively plausible. The true-belief burglar's beliefs (if they are not knowledge) are less secure, more easily lost, than those of the knowing burglar, and so it is considerably less likely that the true-belief burglar remains in the house if he does not, after a few attempts, succeed in locating the diamond. A sequence of unsuccessful attempts will lead the true-belief burglar to give up on his beliefs and conclude there is no diamond in the house in the end. If this is right, then Meno should have given a different answer to

Socrates's question about the guide to Larisa; for it does make a difference whether the guide possesses knowledge or only true belief of the road to Larisa. A knowing guide is more likely to help you realize your goal of visiting the town than a guide with merely true beliefs, because the true-belief guide may lose beliefs more easily and turn back.[10]

Back to known freedom. With this excursion to Williamson's take on the value of knowledge, we now seem to have an answer to the question with which we started—namely, whether the arguments for freedom's value are really arguments for known freedom, or for 'truly believed' freedom. The idea is that the burglar or the tourist guide is better off with knowledge than with true belief, when it comes to desire satisfaction, say. As a result, the argument from desire satisfaction is really an argument for full-dress known freedom.

Belief Revision

As soon as we fill in some of the details of the cases, things may appear differently, though. Williamson's burglar with knowledge must have recruited some evidence for his belief about the diamond in the house. So let us assume he has seen it there on an earlier occasion. (He had to flee without the diamond, but then the owners came back unexpectedly.) The true-belief burglar, by contrast, does not have such evidence, for otherwise he would have knowledge. This means he is in one of the following situations. First: his true belief about the fact that there is a diamond in the house may be an entirely wild guess, not based on any other belief, so he has no further beliefs about the diamond besides this one. Secondly: his true belief may be based on some bit of evidence, but on less evidence than the knowing burglar possesses, as a result of which the true-belief burglar has fewer true beliefs about further relevant details about the diamond than the knowing burglar. Or thirdly: his belief about the diamond may be based on false beliefs, so he has more false beliefs about it, as compared with the knowing burglar. And surely the last two cases can occur simultaneously.[11]

If this analysis is right, then another way to describe the difference between the knowing burglar (or tourist guide for Larisa) and the true-belief burglar (or tourist guide) is as follows: when it comes to desire satisfaction, what drives the knower's relative advantage is not the mere possession of knowledge, but rather the possession of more accurate *belief revision policies*. When the knowing tourist guide sees that the road is turning back again, they know this is not a sign that they are on the wrong track, but rather that this is simply a curvy road. The true-belief guide, by contrast, might take it as an indication that they had made an error, which may make them return. The knower would not need to revise their beliefs, or only marginally, whereas the believer would revise their beliefs, and in the wrong way.

So, in the end, what explains the difference between the two burglars (or between the two tourist guides) is not the epistemic status of their beliefs, but rather their belief revision policies. If the true-belief burglar had overheard a conversation in which, besides the bed, also the cabinet, the grand piano, and a drawer were mentioned in connection with the diamond, his belief revision policy would have led him to stay longer, even though it might well be based on false premises. (We may imagine that it was a conversation not between the two house owners, but between two entirely unrelated people, whom the burglar mistook for the house owners.) But these false premises may have led the burglar to adopt a belief revision policy that turned out to make him stay in the house just as long as the knowing burglar, and helped him to satisfy his desire of finding the diamond.

Lotteries

If this is right, we must conclude that Williamson's approach to the value of knowledge cannot be applied to show that knowledge is needed for desire satisfaction. What you need is good belief revision policies, but whether these beliefs and policies are grounded in evidence, or are only accidentally accurate, is unimportant. Where Williamson argues in favour of a 'knowledge-first' epistemology, we seem not to be too far away from concluding that a 'knowledge-free' epistemology is all we need here.

Before we proceed, it is only right to consider another attempt to demonstrate the primacy of knowledge, this one from John Hawthorne.[12] To show why knowledge rather than true belief is what drives our practical reasoning, Hawthorne imagines that you have bought a $1 ticket in a lottery with ten thousand tickets and a $5,000 first price. You deliberate selling your ticket to someone who has offered to buy it from you for one cent. Should you sell? You reason that you will lose the lottery anyway, and that, if you keep the ticket, you will get nothing. If you sell the ticket, you reason, you will gain a cent, so you conclude you should sell the ticket to the buyer. Now if you reasoned like this, Hawthorne claims, you would engage in an 'intuitively awful piece of practical reasoning', and he has the argument partly riding on the assumption that you agree with him.[13]

Next Hawthorne considers another scenario.[14] You have bought a $1 ticket in the same lottery again. There is no willing buyer involved here, and, rather than contemplating selling the ticket, you are musing about your upcoming holiday. You are, Hawthorne assumes, in a bookshop and want to buy a travel guide, and you deliberate about whether you should buy a book about an exotic destination, or about a destination closer to home. Since your funds are limited, whether you can afford to go to an exotic destination depends on whether you win the lottery. The chances of that event being dim, you reason that you will not be able to afford to go to an exotic destination, and that, if you buy a faraway destination book, you will not read it. On the other hand, you reason that, if you buy a local destination guide, you will use it. Hence you conclude you ought to buy the local guide. Here Hawthorne does not claim your reasoning is dubious.

There is something initially plausible to evaluating the two scenarios the way Hawthorne suggests. It is pretty difficult to make sense of what happens in the first scenario, whereas the second is easily understood and seen as reasonable. Yet, if the first scenario were an intuitively awful piece of reasoning, it would seem that the second should be in the same boat, for in both cases a one in ten thousand probability is rounded off to a zero probability. If nevertheless we concur with Hawthorne that the two cases are different, then we face a theoretical challenge to explain the difference. And it is while meeting this challenge that we get back to the question we started with, about the value of knowledge. So, in the end, Hawthorne seems to think along the following lines. The scenario in which you decided to sell your ticket at a cent had as its initial premiss that you would lose the lottery. But in that context, the thought is, that is not something you know. In the second scenario, the initial premiss is that you will not be able to afford to go to an expensive exotic destination, and that is something that you in fact do know in that context. Whether you know something depends, for Hawthorne, on the practical context in which knowing the thing might become operative, and that is why he claims that, as long as a belief is not knowledge, practical reasoning that involves beliefs rather than knowledge will be intuitively awful. This is immediately relevant to our concerns; for, if Hawthorne's line of approach works, an argument for freedom (at least the argument from desire satisfaction) is an argument for known freedom, not for truly believed freedom.

Yet looking at Hawthorne's argument from the perspective of economics (decision theory) leads to different conclusions. The reason is that Hawthorne does not specify the desires (utility function) guiding the decision maker—no economist would leave them out—and, as soon as we include them, we see that it is desires rather than beliefs that make the reasoning 'intuitively awful' in Hawthorne's first case.[15] The idea is this. In the first scenario, you can get one cent for sure, or take a risk of one in ten thousand of getting the lottery prize. Now your utility function must be rather oddly construed if it assigns higher utility to the first option than to the second: a cent is worth almost nothing, so why not take the chance of earning five hundred thousand times as much. This has nothing to do with the fact that you may or may not have genuine knowledge about the risky option. It is simply the observation that a utility function will be pretty intuitively awful indeed if a ten-thousandth of the utility of earning five thousand dollars is strictly less than the utility of earning a cent.

The advantage of considering the matter in terms of utilities is that it allows us to see that there may still be circumstances in which the reasoning of the first scenario is in fact totally acceptable. Suppose you are stranded in the desert, thirsting, and someone is offering you water for $2. You have only $1.99 plus the lottery ticket, and the water-seller tells you they would be happy to buy the ticket for a cent. Then you would die if you did not, so it should not be intuitively awful to reason like this if circumstances change.

Let me take stock. I have discussed Williamson and Hawthorne at some length because they offer strong and widely discussed philosophical arguments that might have helped me to show that the ideal of known freedom must be phrased in terms of genuine knowledge rather than mere true belief. If they had worked, then I could safely have left the matter there. But they do not work. I do not want to be taken to believe that this observation extends to the larger theoretical background framework that Williamson and Hawthorne introduce. An application for present purposes, however, does no good. Quite to the contrary, the argument developed here strongly suggests that what people need to satisfy their desires, assume responsibility, or realize themselves is primarily accurate and adequate belief revision policies. No genuine knowledge seems to be needed. Socrates seems right that, for practical purposes, there is no difference between knowledge and true belief.[16]

Before proceeding with some potential modifications of this view, let me point out the political relevance of this. Various studies point out that a significant number of US and European citizens do not assume the benefits of the state support they are entitled to (housing programmes, programmes for the disabled, state health insurance, childcare subsidies, jobseeker's allowance, and so on).[17] Naturally, the individual reasons are diverse, ranging from judging the support to be unnecessary, or having insufficient time to search, to the idea that participating in social programmes leads to social stigma. Interestingly, however, there are also a significant number of people who point out either that they know nothing at all about the relevant programme, or that they believe that the programme does not apply to them (while in reality they are eligible to the programme).[18] Clearly if such people had adequate beliefs, they would be able to obtain higher levels of desire satisfaction. But is *knowledge* needed? I could inform a person unaware of some programme that surfing a particular website, filling out a certain form, and carrying out a few other actions should result in their receiving €100 extra a month. But, if the website's address has changed, or if more than one form has to be filled out, they will not succeed, because they will not know how to revise their beliefs. They will still not enjoy their freedom. A different way to go about this would be to explain the programme more fully. They would learn a few things that they do not immediately need to get the monetary gain, but these things would enable them to deal, for instance, with slight changes in the programme, changes in the eligibility rules, changes in the application procedures, and so on.

The Value of False Beliefs

If this is seen as weakening my claim about the importance of known freedom, then perhaps a more acute problem arises when we consider another strand of work in psychology and epistemology that might seem to support the view that sometimes even *false* beliefs are good to have, and consequently knowledge or true beliefs should be avoided. We seem to be even further from home.

Duncan Pritchard introduces ravine jumping to illustrate this.[19] You have to jump a ravine, for reasons unimportant, but you know about the

risks, and hesitate. In such a case, Pritchard writes, 'it seems that a false belief in one's abilities would be better than a true belief'.[20] Pritchard does
not go much further to bolster his assertion, but his idea seems to be
that, if you deflated your assessment of the risks, you would be able to approach the predicament more confidently and assure yourself of a higher
probability of making a successful jump. Similar evidence can be gained
from social science research. Research from psychology and behavioural
economics presents us with many examples of cognitive biases that lead
us to adopt overly rosy pictures of our abilities and to set aside evidence
that might support a more unflattering view of ourselves, indicating how
these biases seem to be quite essential to human well-being. They make
us faster and more efficient, boost our self-esteem, and may be essential
to engage in longer-term projects.[21] William James even went so far as
to defend the position that sometimes we have the 'right'—sometimes the
'obligation'—to adopt a belief contrary to evidence.[22] While his prime motivation was religious belief or worldview, among his examples also figure
such proleptic forms of trust through which parents or prospective friends
openly anticipate, and thereby partly induce, their children's or friends'
trustworthiness.

The ravine-jumper case and its cognates seem to suggest that the values
that drive my argument for known freedom (desire satisfaction, responsibility, self-realization) are sometimes better served by false beliefs than by
true beliefs or knowledge. If that is true, this threatens the ideal of known
freedom. But, as we shall see, it is not so clear that false beliefs have this
type of value (or true beliefs the corresponding type of disvalue) if we look
at these conceptual and empirical findings from the point of view of desire
satisfaction or moral responsibility. I use the ravine jumper to show this.
While it is highly artificial, it is also a case with a very clear structure that
lends itself nicely to extrapolation to the real world.

So let us make that case more precise. Suppose that the world in which
you have an accurate assessment of the risk of ravine jumping is one in
which the probability of a successful jump is 70 per cent. That is, you know
that there is a 30 per cent chance of failure, and hence you do not jump. To
imagine a world in which you have deflated the risk of jumping, you have
to imagine another possible world in which, first, the probability of failure
is less than 30 per cent, and, secondly, your belief is false. So suppose, then,
that you manoeuvred yourself into believing that the success rate is 90 per
cent, and that the actual success rate is 80 per cent.

Do the resulting false beliefs boost your desire satisfaction? That depends. If you compare your chances of success with the world without false beliefs, then they are ten percentage points greater, which may seem a gain. But it is not clear that in the world with false beliefs you would satisfy your desires better. This is because if, in that world, you planned your life around what you believe the success rate is (that is, 90 per cent), then you might be worse off than in the world with the true beliefs (and where the chances of success are 70 per cent). Percentages are typically best understood by considering iterated decision-making. So, assume that you jump ravines more regularly, for the fun and thrill of it, and assume that, while you fall sometimes, you know you never hurt yourself too much. At most, you pay a rescue team to get you out of the gully, and so the key concerns here are your budget constraints, as you can pay only so many operations a year.

That is exactly where false beliefs may come into conflict with desire satisfaction. You believe that you have to pay for one out of ten jumps, on average, because you believe that your success rate is 90 per cent, and you have accordingly set aside some money. But, because your beliefs are false (it is 80 per cent, as we assumed), you will actually have to pay in one out of five jumps. It will cost you more money, and the case is easily so construed that this decreases your desire satisfaction. The same argument shows how false beliefs negatively affect personal responsibility. In the 70 per cent world, where you are accurately informed about the risks of ravine jumping, you know that iterated jumping will make you responsible for calling, on average, three rescue operations in ten attempts. In the false-belief world, however, you foresee failure only in one in ten attempts, but will be confronted with failure twice as often. For which failures are you responsible? It is not my aim here fully to discuss this case. Indeed, we cannot immediately say that you are also responsible for the failures you did not foresee, because generally one cannot be held responsible when knowledge of one's choice situation is lacking. But, if we manufacture our beliefs ourselves, and more or less consciously allow false beliefs to arise and to stick, then we might plausibly suspect this to lead to culpable or wilful forms of ignorance.[23]

This line of reasoning seems to apply both to the Kantian view of responsibility and to the consequentialist view. According to the consequentialist view, the practice of holding people responsible is meant to create incentives for people to act in particular ways, where the incentives are the anticipated praise or blame they may get after performing certain actions. If, however, decision makers misconstrue the consequences of their actions, there will be cases where they select a course of action in the expectation of obtaining praise and be surprised to receive blame. Where the mismatch between the anticipation of praise and the reception of blame persist, incentives will, however, lose their force in the long run.

The Kantian view leads to more complex reflections, and I do not have the space here to discuss this in detail. But one may gain some feel for this by imagining a case of emergency. Suppose someone assists by performing some technique on a victim (say, the Heimlich manoeuvre) that is entirely inappropriate to perform, with potentially lethal consequences in these circumstances, but by sheer luck results in the victim's survival in this particular case. The person, one could imagine, had seen the Heimlich demonstrated once, but had forgotten what it was meant for. We could ask if they merit praise for saving a life. Clearly, they did save a life, and it was their intention to do so. But the action they selected was one that *decreased* the probability of the intention being fulfilled, and that was something that they should and could have known. I find it odd to say that someone in such circumstances can merit praise, and note that, at the very least, from a consequentialist point of view, such a conclusion is crystal clear: if we praise this person, and the anticipated praise creates incentives in them as well as in people witnessing their behaviour who see they get praised for it, then we should expect that the number of surviving victims will *decrease*.

Back to the main line of my argument. I started with known freedom as a normative ideal. Then I connected this to a prominent discussion in epistemology on the value of known freedom but I argued that this did not ultimately endow known freedom with extra value. I subsequently looked into a related epistemological discussion on the value of false belief and showed that it is unlikely that false beliefs will do any good to desire satisfaction, moral responsibility, or self-realization—at least in such a way and to such an extent that the concept of known freedom should be revisited. It seems, then, that what the arguments from desire satisfaction, moral responsibility, and self-realization support is first and foremost that the decision maker possesses adequate belief revision policies concerning their choice situation, rather than known freedom in its full epistemological sense.

This is not the end of knowledge, though. To begin with, known freedom is an ideal, and, if we extrapolate adequate belief formation policies, then in the limit we may find knowledge. Casting the ideal in terms of knowledge also seems to make it less vulnerable to the type of cases we met in Chapter 2: one can be brainwashed into believing something that is true, but one cannot be brainwashed into knowing it, because brainwashing excludes justification. But at least for now most importantly: very often the best belief revision policies arise when people are endowed with knowledge. This becomes clear when we consider forms of knowledge that are particularly relevant to human agency: know-how, skills, competencies, and so on. It is the business of the remainder of this chapter to examine them further.

Skills and Know-How

Know-how is traditionally considered a form of non-propositional knowledge, ever so different from propositional knowledge or *know-that*. The intuitions that lie behind this contrast, and that were articulated most famously by Gilbert Ryle, are that manual skills and many other human competences and proficiencies do not seem to involve adopting a doxastic or epistemic stance towards particular propositions.[24] My knowing *how* to ride a bike, for instance, does not seem to entail—and neither to ensue from—my knowing *that* pedalling makes the chain wheel rotate and ultimately moves the bike. I can ride my bike, play the piano, and kick a ball without any propositional knowledge about mechanics, acoustics, or kinetics.

It is, without fail, crucial to pay due attention to know-how and know-that if we want to describe the extent of an agent's freedom, and the influences their beliefs have thereon. If I have a bike, but I do not know how to ride a bike, should we say that bike-riding is in my opportunity set? Or should we rather say that access to the bike is in that set? The latter, it seems. Beliefs appear once the set of available actions has already been determined; beliefs do not help constituting this set. As a result, there is no place for know-how. To put it bluntly, my opportunity set contains access to a bike, a piano, and a ball; that I need to know how to ride, play, and kick has to go unmentioned. Or so it may seem.

Knowing Ways to Do Things

To shed light on these matters, I am going to apply an insight contributed to the literature on know-how by Jason Stanley and Timothy Williamson.[25]

Defending the position that know-how is a form of propositional knowledge after all, they equate my know-how to ride, say, with the existence of a way w of which I know that w is a way to ride my bike. That is, I know how to ride a bike if, and only if, there is some way w of which I have de re knowledge that it constitutes bike-riding for me.[26] As it stands, this is not too informative, as obviously the authors' proposal presupposes a theory of what kind of things *ways* exactly are. For current purposes, I suggest interpreting ways as actions, which may or may not be in the decision maker's opportunity set. So let us see how to describe my predicament of *not* knowing how to drive a car. All individual actions constituting driving a car to my holiday destination are available to me. No one would block my attempts to put the key in the keyhole, start the car, push the clutch pedal, put the car into gear, and so on. And also, if I succeeded in genuinely making the car move, there would not be any road blockages on my way.

Yet I will not get there. For, although these actions are available, I do not have overly many correct de re beliefs about them. I may know de re that I can open the car by putting the key in the door and turning it, and I may also know that I can start it by putting the key in the ignition. But, since I have never learned to drive a car, I only have de dicto beliefs about changing gears, and the like. I just do not know *exactly* when to put down the clutch, move the gear lever, and release the clutch, and, in like fashion, I do not have de re beliefs about particular reference points making it easier to align the car when I want to park, and to work out the right angle for reversing. That I do not know how to change gears, to park, to drive round corners, and overtake other cars is expressed by the fact that I do not have the appropriate de re beliefs.

We are not yet there, though. Interestingly, I may have de re beliefs about every single action I can perform with respect to car driving, and still lack the know-how to drive. In fact, anyone spending some time investigating a car, trying to push pedals and move levers, will in a sense gather correct de re beliefs of the things one can do with a car. If I do this, I will come to know that I can push and release a particular pedal, move a lever, turn the wheel, and so on, and I may even get some idea of what this is all for, as I have seen so many other people drive cars. So, if that is the case, I have correct de re beliefs about the availability of all actions I would have to perform to drive a car.

But something essential is missing. What is missing are de re beliefs about the precise consequences of these actions. I have gathered some knowledge that I can move a lever, and I may assume that this will have *some* effects, but I do not know de re that I will successfully change gears only if I simultaneously put down the clutch in some specific way. I do not know, that is, *how* to change gears. Similarly, I know that I can turn the wheel, but I do not know de re what consequences a particular instance of turning the wheel will have in a specific situation. The lack of correct de re beliefs about consequences comes distinctly to the fore when we consider what happens if one makes a mistsake. A person who knows how to drive a car has de re knowledge about the sounds the car engine makes when they attempt to move the gear lever without pushing in the clutch. They know what to expect when they change down gears at too high a speed or try to turn the wheel. Besides that, they have correct de re beliefs about which actions would be available after making a mistake, and which ones would not be, and also about the likely consequence of these subsequent actions. Such a person would, in other words, know how to correct errors, or to avert their worst consequences. By contrast, the novice (if they have any correct de re beliefs about the individual actions they can perform after a mistake) lacks de re beliefs about consequences to the largest extent.

This elaborate example paves the way for showing that skills are in a very real sense the place where freedom and knowledge meet. Skills have a clear knowledge component, for to possess the skill to drive a car is to have appropriate de re knowledge, as we have seen. But skills also have a clear freedom component, or so I argue now. Consider the following example. A car does not mean much to a person stranded in a remote village if they do not know how to drive it. Does the person lack the freedom to leave the village? No one would obstruct them if they left by car. Moreover, all actions that are necessary to perform for driving the car are available. All the same, leaving the place by car is not a viable option. This decision maker's predicament is difficult to understand purely in terms of available actions or interfering third parties. Rather, that they will not leave the town is because they lack the know-how: they lack knowledge about available actions (but, as we have seen, that is remedied fairly quickly), and they lack knowledge about the consequences of performing particular actions (to remedy which requires such things as driving lessons). That is, the person stranded in the remote village lacks the known freedom to leave. Lack of skill is lack of known freedom, and gaining skills is gaining known freedom.[27]

Institutional Support for Skills

We can foster and frustrate the acquisition of skills in many ways. Let me, first, consider an example of how skills and know-how can be fostered. The example comes from economics. A starting point of the literature on skills is Gary Becker's seminal work on human capital, which put skills on the research agenda of economists.[28] It has inspired a large swathe of subsequent literature that has attempted to understand the relation between the level of skills in a given population, on the one hand, and the productivity, wages, well-being, economic success, and other outcome variables, on the other. In this literature, skills are often identified with levels of education. This is natural. Education increases a person's skills. Qualifications and certifications give access to certain occupations. And the skills exercised in these occupations—in the workplace—are what drive the increased productivity. This view emphasizes the straightforward role of education to foster skills. But it is a fairly static view of human capital 'possessed' by the individual, largely abstracting from social and economic institutions.[29]

Intriguing work in economic history, by contrast, focuses on the dynamic and institutional aspects of skill development and maintenance. David de la Croix, Mattias Doepke, and Joel Mokyr, for instance, investigate the characteristics of Western Europe's preindustrial economy, how this economy contrasts with those of China, India, and the Middle East, and how its characteristics might have planted the seeds for the Industrial Revolution.[30] Their view: skills were fostered by four institutions: the family, the clan, the guild, and the market. Each of them engendered a specific way of apprenticeship, which was responsible for the transmission of skills from one generation to the next and created incentives to improve skills and to develop and gain new ones. De la Croix and colleagues found that guilds and markets stimulated the growth and dissemination of skills and know-how to a larger degree than families and clans. Whereas within families and clans one is likely to be taught skills by people who have all received their training from one or a few common sources (ancestors), guilds and markets link apprentices with a sequence of masters who learned *their* skills from a larger variety of masters. This creates greater freedom—namely, a greater diversity of taught techniques, with productivity (and, one may assume, desire satisfaction) growing as a result. Skills—that is, known freedom—flourish with increased freedom.

Stereotypes Threatening Skills

The market fosters the development and exercise of skills. Can we say something about what frustrates these things? The literature on human development and social mobility offers a case in point to do with the impact of parenting on skills development. James Heckman and Stefano Mosso show that what explains why on average children growing up in socioeconomically disadvantaged environments develop lower levels of cognitive and noncognitive skills is not mere household finance, but rather the ways in which children are mentored, supported, and stimulated, as well as the degree of parental attachment they enjoy.[31] This can be linked to such straightforward variables as the time a parent spends with their children or the sort of educational stimulus, or more generally their living environment.[32]

But know-how can also be affected in other ways. The key term here is *stereotype threat*.[33] A representative example is found in an experiment conducted by Karla Hoff and Priyanka Pandey.[34] Indian children were asked to solve maze puzzles, with children from the high and low end of the Indian caste spectrum. In the treatment group, Hoff and Pandey publicly announced the name and caste of each child. In the control group, they did not. In the control group, no statistically significant differences in performance between low-caste and high-caste children were found, but, in the group in which caste was publicly announced, there was a 20 per cent decrease of the average number of mazes correctly solved—among low-caste children, that is. Similar effects have been demonstrated concerning a host of further tasks and social groups including women, Asians, Afro-Americans, elderly people, disabled people, but also white males, US soldiers, and French college students.[35] This is all subsumed under the idea that, in the presence of a widespread and common stereotype concerning some group G and some domain of know-how D, when a person's membership of G is made salient, they perform less on D-tasks as compared with a situation in which the stereotype is not salient.[36] These tasks are not only cognitive, as the maze problem, but include a variety of activities such as athletic performance, singing—and indeed also driving a car.[37]

It is a matter of considerable debate to what extent the experiments demonstrating the effects of stereotype threat can be replicated, whether they generalize, and whether these effects have any sizeable economic or social effects. It seems, however, beyond sensible dispute to claim that, in important cases such as education and hiring, stereotype threat is constantly lurking. Moreover, to the extent that stereotype threat is a contributing factor in gender inequalities in the labour market, as some economists seem to suggest, there is good reason for normative analysis.[38] Clearly, a good normative analysis must be sensitive to the causal mechanism of the phenomenon, and there does not seem to be a consensus view available yet. Claude Steele has argued that, when a stereotype about the (supposedly low) performance of D-tasks by G-members is salient in a member of G, then they perform less well on a D-task out of fear for confirming the stereotype.[39] Perhaps the resources (cognitive or otherwise) that they have at their disposal for performing the task are partly consumed by worrying about the stereotype, with the result that they cannot focus as intensely on the task as individuals unhindered by the fear. Steele writes that in some cases stereotype threat is enough to 'raise your blood pressure, dramatically increase ruminative thinking, interfere with working memory, and deteriorate performance on challenging tasks'.[40] So stereotype threat leads to self-doubt, to distraction, to stress, to anxiety. In some neuroscience experiments, stereotype threat 'dampened down activity in the part of the brain we use to do mathematics and increased activity in the part of the brain associated with vigilance to one's social context and to emotion'.[41]

What is important from a normative perspective is whether the performance-lowering effects of making a stereotype salient are such that individuals can be held responsible for them. It seems they cannot. The effects may, for instance, happen to us without us noticing them.[42] But, to the extent we cannot be held responsible for them, we should, I submit here, think of the act of making a stereotype salient as constituting interference with a person's known freedom: the number of actions typically related to a particular skill is decreased.

Consider a study by Sabine Koch, Stefan Konigorski, and Monica Sieverding.[43] They activated the stereotype that women perform less in maths tests in a simulated job interview among a group of participants by way of an actor playing the role of a 'sexist' interviewer. In the control group, the same actor conducted interviews in a 'neutral' manner. After the interview, participants engaged in standardized maths and language-related tests. The treatment group performed significantly less well than the control group in maths, but not in the language test. Both groups were mixed (male, female). For male participants there was no statistically significant difference between scores at all. The effects of stereotype threat were restricted to female participants. It is still out in the open whether this type of phenomenon generalizes to real-world job interviews. But, to the extent it does, we have here a case in which an interviewer interferes with a potential female candidate's performance of particular tasks. The interviewer performs particular actions (those that constitute 'sexist' behaviour), which bar the interviewee from engaging in particular puzzle-solving activities at a later point in time. Using the terminology from Chapter 2, this could be described as decreasing her epistemic freedom. Publicly acknowledging people's capacities might remedy this. The corresponding normative ideal of acknowledged freedom is the topic of the next chapter.

Notes

1. Isaiah Berlin, 'Two Concepts of Liberty', in Berlin, Four Essays on Liberty (London: Oxford University Press, 1969), 24.
2. Berlin's potentially exaggerated worries may have to be understood against the background of the cold war. Berlin held his BBC lectures, on six anti-liberal thinkers, in 1952, and delivered his inaugural lecture, on two concepts of liberty, in 1958—that is, in a decade that witnessed the Korean War, the formation of the Warsaw Pact, the violently suppressed Hungarian uprising, and the Suez crisis. See generally Alan Ryan, 'ISAIAH BERLIN: Political Theory and Liberal Culture', Annual Review of Political Science, 2 (1999), 345–362. It is also somewhat unclear (to me) whether Berlin understood Epictetus.
3. Whether you actually experience an increase of freedom as a result of contracting your desires the way Epictetus (according to Berlin) suggests depends on the concept of freedom you use in your assessment of your choice situation. If that is a desire-dependent one, you may in fact undergo a feeling of increased freedom, but if, like Berlin, you favour a concept of freedom that is entirely independent of desires, you will feel no inch more free after changing your desires, even though you will feel that the number of possibilities of desire satisfaction has grown. Berlin's dictator–liberator should therefore change not only their subject's desires, but also their conception of freedom to make the argument plausible.
4. Isaiah Berlin, 'Two Concepts of Liberty', in Berlin, Four Essays on Liberty (London: Oxford University Press, 1969), 24.
5. Whether a response is atypical depends very much on the historical context of course.
6. Plato, Meno 97c.

7. See ibid. 98a, for difference between knowledge and belief, and 97d for the remark about the Daedalus statues.

8. Timothy Williamson, *Knowledge and its Limits* (Oxford: Oxford University Press, 2000).

9. Ibid. 62 ff.

10. See, e.g., Duncan Pritchard, 'Recent Work on Epistemic Value', *American Philosophical Quarterly*, 44 (2007), 85–110, at 86, on this point.

11. P. D. Magnus and Jonathan Cohen, 'Williamson on Knowledge and Psychological Explanation', *Philosophical Studies*, 116 (2003), 37–52, construe a similar argument in terms of Bayesian updating. It seems to me, however, that lexicographic beliefs may be more helpful to describe the fundamental distinction between the two burglars than the approach these authors put forward. Instead of one single probability distribution, each burglar's beliefs are then modelled by means of a hierarchy of probability distributions to represent subsequent stages in the process of belief revision. Both burglars start out from identical initial beliefs to the effect that $P_1(\text{bed}) = 1$, as they are both absolutely sure that the diamond is under the bed. Nevertheless, they can ponder how they would revise their beliefs if their initial belief turned out wrong, which is the key difference with traditional probabilistic beliefs. One burglar's belief revision is represented by $P_2(\text{cabinet}|\neg\text{bed}) = 1$—that is, when he does not find the diamond under the bed, he assigns probability one to the diamond being in the cabinet, and similarly with third-degree belief revision to the effect that $P_3(\text{piano}|\neg\text{bed} \wedge \neg\text{cabinet}) = 1$. The other burglar revises differently. His second-degree belief is something like $P_2(\neg\text{house}|\neg\text{bed}) = 1$—that is, if the diamond is not in the bed, then it is not in the house. For him, it is rational to leave the house immediately. The *locus classicus* of a formal treatment of lexicographic probabilities is Lawrence Blume, Adam Brandenburger, and Eddie Dekel, 'Lexicographic Probabilities and Choice under Uncertainty', *Econometrica*, 59 (1991), 61–79.

12. John Hawthorne, *Knowledge and Lotteries* (Oxford: Oxford University Press, 2004).

13. Ibid. 174.

14. Ibid. 177.

15. Charity Anderson and John Hawthorne, 'Knowledge, Practical Adequacy, and Stakes', in Tamar Szabó Gendler and John Hawthorne (eds), *Oxford Studies in Epistemology: Volume 6* (Oxford: Oxford University Press, 2019), 234–258, may go some way to addressing these issues, even though it is unclear (to me) that this can be made consistent with neoclassical economic orthodoxy in a straightforward sense.

16. Plato, *Meno* 97c. This position may incidentally lead one to adopt a view of justification more along the lines of economics: as something that increases

expected utility maximization. Where it does not, justification cannot be rationally required, and is perhaps irrational to acquire. This approach would suggest that desires are primary. We need beliefs to the extent that we have desires. For an expected utility maximizer, the mere possession of beliefs (true or false ones) is uninteresting.

17. See, e.g, Albertjan Tollenaar, 'Sociaal zekerheidsrecht: recht realiseren in de sociale zekerheid', in Catrien Bijleveld, Arno Akkermans, Marijke Malsch, Bert Marseille, and Monika Smit (eds), *Nederlandse Encyclopedie Empirical Legal Studies* (Meppel: Boom Juridische Uitgevers), 589–610.

18. Caren Tempelman, Aenneli Houkes, and Jurriaan Prins, *Niet-gebruik inkomensondersteunende maatregelen: Eindrapport* (Amsterdam: SEO Economisch Onderzoek, 2011), *Kamerstukken I*, 2011/12, 33024, nr B, zoek. officielebekendmakingen.nl/blg-157674.pdf [perma.cc/ZT22-JRM6].

19. Duncan Pritchard, 'Recent Work on Epistemic Value', *American Philosophical Quarterly*, 44 (2007), 85–110, at 102.

20. Ibid.

21. See, e.g., Roland Bénabou and Jean Tirole, 'Mindful Economics: The Production, Consumption, and Value of Beliefs', *Journal of Economic Perspectives*, 30 (2016), 141–164.

22. William James, 'The Will to Believe', *New World*, 5 (1896), 327–347. See also Nikolaj Nottelmann and Boudewijn de Bruin, 'Impermissible Self-Rationalizing Pessimism: In Defence of a Pragmatic Ethics of Belief', *Erkenntnis*, 86 (2021), 257–274.

23. See Douglas Husak and Craig Callender, 'Willful Ignorance, Knowledge, and the "Equal Culpability" Thesis: A Study of the Deeper Significance of the Principle of Legality', *Wisconsin Law Review*, (1994), 29–70, Kevin Lynch, 'Willful Ignorance and Self-Deception', *Philosophical Studies*, 173 (2016), 505–523, and James Montmarquet, 'Culpable Ignorance and Excuses', *Philosophical Studies*, 80 (1995), 41–49, for legal and philosophical accounts of culpable and wilful ignorance.

24. Gilbert Ryle, *The Concept of Mind* (London: Hutchinson, 1949), 25 ff.

25. Jason Stanley and Timothy Williamson, 'Knowing How', *Journal of Philosophy*, 98 (2001), 411–444. See also Jason Stanley and Timothy Williamson, 'Skills', Noûs, 51 (2017), 713–726. See Nico Stehr, 'Le savoir en tant que pouvoir d'action', *Sociologies et sociétés*, 32 (2000), 157–170, for a sociological approach to this issue, and James Wong, 'Can Power Produce Knowledge? Reconsidering the Relationship of Power to Knowledge', *Southern Journal of Philosophy*, 41 (2003), 105–123, for an account using the works of Michel Foucault.

26. Jason Stanley and Timothy Williamson, 'Knowing How', *Journal of Philosophy*, 98 (2001), 411–444, at 430.

27. I have somewhat ignored the question of whether belief in one's more general capacities fosters successful decision-making. There is some evidence it does. See, e.g., Tim Bogg and Elizabeth Millad, 'Demographic, Personality, and Social Cognition Correlates of Coronavirus Guideline Adherence in a US Sample', *Health Psychology*, 39 (2020), 1026–1036, for evidence that self-efficacy contributes to adherence to Covid-19 recommendations, and Camelia Kuhnen and Brian Melzer, 'Noncognitive Abilities and Financial Delinquency: The Role of Self-Efficacy in Avoiding Financial Distress', *Journal of Finance*, 73 (2018), 2837–2869, showing that self-efficacy (belief that your actions influence the future) is correlated with taking measures to mitigate financial risks.

28. Gary Becker, *Human Capital: A Theoretical and Empirical Analysis, with Special Reference to Education* (New York: Columbia University Press, 1964).

29. Ibid. 40.

30. David de la Croix, Mattias Doepke, and Joel Mokyr, 'Clans, Guilds, and Markets: Apprenticeship Institutions and Growth in the Preindustrial Economy', *Quarterly Journal of Economics*, 133 (2018), 1–70.

31. James Heckman and Stefano Mosso, 'The Economics of Human Development and Social Mobility', *Annual Review of Economics*, 6 (2014), 689–733.

32. James Heckman, Rodrigo Pinto, and Peter Savelyev, 'Understanding the Mechanisms through which an Influential Early Childhood Program Boosted Adult Outcomes', *American Economic Review*, 103 (2013), 2052–2086.

33. See, generally, Claude Steele, *Whistling Vivaldi: How Stereotypes Affect Us and What We Can Do* (New York: Norton, 2010).

34. Karla Hoff and Priyanka Pandey, 'Discrimination, Social Identity, and Durable Inequalities', *American Economic Review*, 96 (2006), 206–211.

35. Claude Steele, *Whistling Vivaldi: How Stereotypes Affect Us and What We Can Do* (New York: Norton, 2010), 97.

36. See, generally, ibid.

37. See Angelica Moè, Mara Cadinu, and Anne Maass, 'Women Drive Better if not Stereotyped', *Accident Analysis and Prevention*, 85 (2015), 199–206, Jeff Stone, Christian Lynch, Mike Sjomeling, and John Darley, 'Stereotype Threat Effects on Black and White Athletic Performance', *Journal of Personality and Social Psychology*, 77 (1999), 1213–1227, and Penelope Watson, Christine Margaret Rubie-Davies, and John Allan Hattie, 'Stereotype Threat, Gender-Role Conformity, and New Zealand Adolescent Males in Choirs', *Research Studies in Music Education*, 39 (2017), 226–246. See Claude Steele, *Whistling Vivaldi: How Stereotypes Affect Us and What We Can Do* (New York: Norton, 2010), 97, for further examples.

38. See, e.g., Uri Gneezy, Muriel Niederle, and Aldo Rustichini, 'Performance in Competitive Environments: Gender Differences', *Quarterly Journal of*

Economics, 118 (2003), 1049–1074, and Muriel Niederle and Lise Vester-lund, 'Do Women Shy Away from Competition? Do Men Compete Too Much?', *Quarterly Journal of Economics*, 122 (2007), 1067–1101. See, generally, Francine Blau and Lawrence Kahn, 'The Gender Wage Gap: Extent, Trends, and Explanations', *Journal of Economic Literature*, 55 (2017), 789–865.

39. Claude Steele, 'A Threat in the Air: How Stereotypes Shape the Intellectual Identities and Performance of Women and African Americans', *American Psychologist*, 52 (1997), 613–629.

40. Claude Steele, *Whistling Vivaldi: How Stereotypes Affect Us and What We Can Do* (New York: Norton, 2010), 132.

41. Ibid. 125. See Anne Krendl, Jennifer Richeson, William Kelley, and Todd Heatherton, 'The Negative Consequences of Threat: A Functional Magnetic Resonance Imaging Investigation of the Neural Mechanisms Underlying Women's Underperformance in Math', *Psychological Science*, 19 (2008), 168–175, for further neuroscientific evidence.

42. Claude Steele, *Whistling Vivaldi: How Stereotypes Affect Us and What We Can Do* (New York: Norton, 2010), 126.

43. Sabine Koch, Stefan Konigorski, and Monica Sieverding, 'Sexist Behavior Undermines Women's Performance in a Job Application Situation', *Sex Roles*, 70 (2014), 79–87.

4
From Common Knowledge to the Ethics of Communication

The Social Ideal of Acknowledged Freedom

The choice situation facing a decision maker is made up of the following three components: their opportunity set—that is, the options they have to their disposal; for each of these options, the possible consequences of selecting it; and, thirdly, the probabilities with which these consequences would arise, were the decision maker to select a specific option.

The main claim defended in the previous three chapters is that a decision maker will be better placed to extract value as embodied in the arguments from desire satisfaction, responsibility, and self-realization, to the extent that, other things being equal, their opportunity set grows and the knowledge they possess about their choice situation deepens. We also saw that perhaps full-blown knowledge is strictly speaking not necessary, as accurate and sufficiently detailed belief revision policies can do the job. Yet the most stable and straightforward ideal is still best described in terms of knowledge rather than true belief.

Facilitating Known Freedom

How do people gain knowledge about their choice situations? One distinction that is useful here is that between parametric and strategic choice, because, depending on which of the two you are in, you will be reasoning differently. Another distinction is between strategic interaction and coordination and collaboration. These distinctions help us to use the concept of common knowledge, which is central in this chapter, and which, I argue, facilitates and protects known freedom. After discussing these two benefits of common knowledge, I conclude with observations about the

The Business of Liberty. Boudewijn de Bruin, Oxford University Press.
© Boudewijn de Bruin (2022). DOI: 10.1093/oso/9780198839675.003.0005

model of informed consent for shareholders and the responsibilities of lenders and borrowers.

Strategic Interaction

A choice situation is *strategic* if the possible consequences of the available actions (or the probabilities attached to them) depend on the actions other people choose to perform. A *parametric* choice situation, by contrast, is one in which the possible consequences and probabilities do not depend on other people, but only, as the jargon has it, on what 'nature' does. Whether or not you experience any side effects from taking a particular drug, for instance, is independent of the behaviour of other people. It is just the result of the way your body responds to the drug, and so, when you reason about whether to take it, you represent your predicament as parametric.

A great deal of economic and business behaviour is, however, strategic. Whether I succeed in buying vegetables on the market, and if so, at which price, depends on how many buyers attempt to do the same thing before me, and what they pay for it—as well as of course on what the seller asks, and so forth. So, with more precision, a decision maker faces a strategic choice situation if they think of it as involving other decision makers whose behaviour is led by *their* preferences (utility functions). By contrast, if a decision maker thinks the consequences of their available actions do not depend on the behaviour of other decision makers (with utility functions), then they see the situation as parametric. To see that this distinction bears on the way a decision maker gains information about their choice situation, suppose that you ponder whether or not to bring an umbrella. This is very naturally seen as a parametric choice, and that is why you try and gain relevant information from a rainfall radar website or consult weather forecasts. More generally, in a parametric situation, you try to find relevant statistical information, and use it to gain a better understanding of your choice situation, thereby increasing your known freedom.

Selecting Team Mates

But, as said, most decision-making in the economic realm involves strategic choice. Here is an example from a business context. Suppose that you and a colleague are setting up a team to work on a particular task. Both of you will be able to select one additional team member. You can select A or B, while your colleague can select S or T. For you, the most preferable team includes A and T; the second-best team includes B and S; the other two teams are ranked lower. You realize, moreover, that your colleague has a different ranking (preference ordering, utility function) and thinks that it is always better to have S on a team than T. And now you reason as follows: if I choose A, then we end up with a team with A and S. If I choose B, then we have a team with B and S. Since I prefer the latter team over the former, it is best for me to choose B, even though A figures in my most preferred team.

Seeing a situation as strategic leads you to place yourself in the perspective of other decision makers, and to reason about what they will do. This is so very common. It happens all the time and can get pretty complicated. In the previous example, you put yourself in the position of your colleague, and reasoned that they would select S no matter what. But for your colleague to make up their mind it was unnecessary to put themselves in *your* perspective. Now suppose, however, that each of you gets one additional option: C for you, U for your colleague. In the matrix shown here, the preferences for the possible teams are represented, with larger numbers indicating more preferred teams, with the number before the comma representing your preferences (you can select A, B, or C), and the number after it the preferences of your colleague (who can select S, T, or U).

	S	T	U
A	(1, 3)	(3, 2)	(3, 1)
B	(2, 3)	(1, 2)	(2, 1)
C	(0, 0)	(1, 1)	(1, 0)

How should you decide? Again you put yourself in the perspective of your colleague, and reason that they will not select U, as your colleague considers a team with U as undesirable, no matter whom you select (U is *strictly dominated* by T, for your colleague). So you *delete* U from the matrix, so to speak, and turn to the next question of whether your colleague will select S or T.

To take that next step, however, you must not just put yourself in your colleague's position. More than that, you must imagine yourself to be in your colleague's position when they are imagining *themselves* to be in *your* position. Why? You have excluded your colleague from playing U, and want to know now whether your colleague will select S or T. You realize that they prefer S over T, unless C becomes a team member. But your colleague can reason that you will never select C, because they see that, for you, C is strictly dominated by A: you do not want C on the team. Now, moreover, *you* can see that your colleague will reason thus about you. So you reason that, just as you deleted U from the matrix, your colleague will do that with C. And once you have gone through those steps, you can reason as in the first case.

Let us approach this a bit more abstractly. What is the information that you used in your reasoning? To begin with, information about your colleague's preferences. That was sufficient to delete U. But then, in addition to that, information about your colleague's possessing information about *your* preferences. That was what allowed you to see that your colleague would eliminate C from the matrix, and therefore to see that they would choose S. But also, and perhaps a bit trivially: information about your colleague's rationality—that is, the fact that they maximize expected utility; for otherwise you could not have been sure that they would act according to their preferences. So what is ultimately needed is common knowledge of rationality, and common knowledge of the decision situation, the game; that is, information about the decision makers' opportunity sets, consequences of available actions, and preferences.[1] And things may become more complex. There may be more colleagues involved in making a choice, so you would have to have information about the preference orderings of more than one person. Or the number of options might be larger. But the general idea remains the same: you will proceed on the basis of information about the other decision makers' preferences, and about the beliefs they have about each other (including you).

Common Knowledge and Common Belief

Formally this can be grasped by the concepts of common belief and common knowledge. A proposition φ is *common belief* among two people A and B whenever the following conditions hold (with *knows* instead of *believes* for common knowledge):

A believes that φ;
B believes that φ;

A believes that B believes that φ;
B believes that A believes that φ;
A believes that B believes that A believes that φ;
B believes that A believes that B believes that φ;
and so on.

There are infinitely many clauses. But that is rather more an artefact of the way we use logic and language than that it suggests something deep about the space common belief or knowledge would have to occupy in our brains or minds. The finitary representation is only logically more challenging, and that is why I stick to the infinitary representation.[2]

Common belief and knowledge may fail to hold. It is great if traffic rules (plus the intention to abide by them) are commonly known among traffic participants, as this allows you to predict what others will do. But sometimes people do not know the rules, or do not want to follow them, and, if you believe the driver approaching you is a case in point, you would do well to adjust your beliefs correspondingly. Yet, whenever common belief or knowledge exists, it allows people to fill in the details of their choice situation in ways that would have been unavailable to them had they thought of their predicament as parametric. Exploiting the strategic aspects of a choice situation helps them to get a better view of their opportunities and probable consequences, and consequently it boosts their known freedom. The way I describe this is to say that common knowledge is a *provider of known freedom in strategic contexts*.[3]

Coordination and Cooperation

The utility functions from the earlier team selection example show that you and your colleague have somewhat opposed preferences. Such types of strategic interaction (with zero-sum games as the limit) can be contrasted with another type of situation, in which the agent's utility functions allow for coordination. There, too, common knowledge plays the role of a provider of known freedom, but in an interestingly different way from the previous one. In the examples about team formation, common knowledge was entirely endogenous vis-à-vis the choice situation: it involved the structure of the situation (actions, consequences, utilities), but no elements outside of it. An example from Michael Chwe shows, however, how common knowledge may arise as the result of events external to the situation, and how it then helps people to coordinate behaviour.[4]

The example is set in 1984. You wish to buy a computer, and you can choose a regular personal computer, or an entirely new brand, an Apple Macintosh. You know that the new brand is not compatible with the regular personal computers, so you are facing a coordination problem. Buying an Apple Macintosh computer then will satisfy your desires only if large numbers of people buy them, because only then will a sufficiently wide range of software be developed for it. But, similarly, buying a regular computer makes sense only if sufficiently large numbers of people decide to stick to buying them and do not switch to the contestant.

Apple was acutely aware that consumers would experience this predicament. Their solution: the Super Bowl, the television programme attracting the largest number of viewers every year in the United States, which some have described as the 'the convening of American men, women and children, who gather around the sets to participate in an annual ritual'.[5] Apple bought sixty seconds of time during the programme to broadcast an eye-catching commercial launching their computer. As Chwe suggests, if these people watch a particular advertisement about a new computer during the Super Bowl, they not only learn about the computer, but they also learn that a great many other American men, women, and children learn about it, that many Americans learn that many Americans learn about it, and so on, with the end result of generating common knowledge, exogenously. So next to being a provider of knowledge in strategic contexts, common knowledge is a *provider of knowledge in coordination contexts*.[6]

Clearly watching just any arbitrary advertisement will not do it, because for all I know only a few people may watch it. And, even if I know many others watch it too, I may still not be moved to buy the new brand of computer as long as I think that these other viewers are *not* aware of the fact that many others have seen the advertisement. (To see this, imagine you are a foreigner in the US, ignorant about the Super Bowl's status.) With a bit more precision, let us call *unconditional buyers* those gadget-happy early adopters who do not care much about compatibility and software, just go with the fad, and decide to buy a new computer simply because they have watched the commercial. Next come what could be called *conditional buyers* who do care about connectivity and software, and they come in different degrees. Some are satisfied already if a relatively small group of other individuals joins in buying an Apple computer, but others require more. An

n-conditional buyer would be a conditional buyer who buys when they are convinced that at least n per cent of the population buys a Mac. Unconditional buyers and small percentage conditional buyers, that is, are trend setters or *lighthouse consumers*; the others are followers.[7]

In the Super Bowl scenario, a consumer knows that the number of people watching the commercial is gigantic, and that as a result the number of unconditional buyers is substantial. But, since it is common knowledge among US consumers that the Super Bowl attracts very large numbers of viewers each year, they also know that the small percentage conditional buyers will find sufficient reason in the commercial to buy a new computer (for it is common knowledge that these small percentage conditional buyers know there is a large group of unconditional buyers, and so have sufficient reason to buy). Now surely this is fairly impressionistic, and it is unlikely that any consumer will have a clear sense of the ultimate share of viewers deciding to buy a Mac. The main point of this example is, however, to show that advertisements or other exogenous events may generate common knowledge that allows decision makers to coordinate.

Here, as in the example about team formation, common knowledge generates known freedom. It creates a clearer sense of the possible repercussions of buying a Mac, the likelihood of being able to buy relevant software, and to connect to, or exchange data with, other people. Before they watched the advertisement, most people may have known that they could buy a Mac; having watched the commercial, consumers also knew what to expect from buying it. Knowledge about the probabilistic consequences of buying has grown (and, potentially complicating things, the probabilities themselves may have changed).

Common knowledge contributes known freedom, allowing people to co-ordinate their actions in many different ways, as is witnessed by the many and various examples that economists have studied in this regard, including wage bargaining, social changes and revolutions, speculative bubbles, the efficiency of decentralization, discrimination, the propagation of news in markets, and trust and reciprocity, to name just a few key applications.[8] These applications need not be solely economic.[9] Take language and communication. For a speaker to use a particular term successfully in communication with a particular hearer, there has to be common knowledge among them about the meaning of the term. If I consider it possible that you will interpret my use of the word *library* as referring to a bookshop (for instance, because I think you, a French speaker beginning to speak

English, may be misguided by the French word for bookshop, *librairie*), it is irrational for me without further qualifications to use *library* if I want to talk about a library with you.[10]

Before we proceed, it is important to realize that the relevant forms of common knowledge may arise in various ways—that is, in other words: exogenous common knowledge of the choice situation may have different origins, which may roughly be distinguished as involving either coordination or cooperation. The Mac buyers can be said to *coordinate* behaviour in the sense that their individual choices result in an outcome all find desirable, but it would be odd to say that they *cooperate*. Unlike such cases as a work team, a symphony orchestra, or a hiring committee, it is here not the case that the Mac buyers perform some action *jointly*, so to speak.

It is, however, difficult to describe the difference between an orchestra and the Mac buyers if we take an external and synchronic point of view: for all we know, the Mac buyers might be cooperating. Once we look into how they got their beliefs—so once we see what gave them common knowledge—it becomes clear that saying that they *cooperate* is inappropriate. To see this, suppose a bridge crosses a river, and trading boats have to wait until the bridge-tender opens it. Opening the bridge causes congestion on a busy road, so the bridge-tender opens the bridge only when there is a minimum of ten ships waiting. Skippers want to minimize waiting time, and as a result face a coordination problem much along the lines of the prospective Apple buyers. The best time to arrive at the bridge is, of course, when at least nine others have arrived there as well. So, to minimize costly waiting time, it would be good if skippers established a convention, such as to sail to the bridge on the hour.

Now we may imagine two ways in which such a convention might arise.[11] First, skippers may meet and talk to each other and agree on a specific time, say ten o'clock in the morning, or a shipping company may give its skippers (at least ten of them) such instruction. But, secondly, a convention may also develop more slowly and gradually. Some vessels may be furnished with cargo in the morning, and then sail off, and find themselves near the bridge between 9.30 and 10.30 a.m. The perceived salience of the whole hour may lead all of them—without communication with each other—to plan to arrive at 10 a.m.[12]

In both cases there is common knowledge among some group of skippers about the consequences of arriving at the bridge at ten o'clock, and, if all goes well, this shortens waiting times for them. But only in the first case should we say that they perform a genuine joint action. Only there do they act together. This in underscored by the fact that, if a skipper arrives later than 10 a.m, only in the first case are the other skippers justified in blaming the tenth skipper for not showing up earlier—for the tenth skipper did not follow a rule that they or the shipowner imposed on them. In the second case, by contrast, the first nine skippers are at most justified in voicing their frustration about being unlucky.

Phenomena like these are plentiful. In many countries, there is a typical go-to place for news and job advertisements in higher education. Some journals specialize in the topic, as the *Times Higher Education*, but not all. If you are interested in an academic position in Germany, the national weekly newspaper *Die Zeit* is the salient point to start.

To conclude, consider an observation made by Michael Alvarez and Jonathan Nagler concerning the 2000 US presidential elections.[13] Individuals with a preference for Ralph Nader over Al Gore, and a preference for Al Gore over George Bush, could have predicted that, given the fact that Gore and Bush were running a neck-to-neck race, a vote for Nader would effectively support their least preferred presidential candidate. The authors observe that quite a few voters did not make use of such information at all, or did not even seem to be aware of it. An increase in known freedom would here have helped to improve (the chances of) desire satisfaction. Beliefs about the political preferences of other voters would have allowed such Nader supporters to predict the outcomes of their available actions, which they might have used in their deliberation about which action to select. Knowing that their most preferred outcome would never be reached, the best thing to do would arguably have been to vote for Gore; for that would have increased the chances of reaching their second-best outcome.

Protecting Known Freedom

The argument developed so far is to the effect that common knowledge is a source of known freedom in the sense that establishing common knowledge in strategic choice situations increases known freedom in the decision makers involved. Perhaps somewhat loosely, I call this *acknowledged freedom*. The reason is that, in a typical condition of common knowledge, agents acknowledge and recognize their own freedoms and those of the other decision makers. This acknowledgement may be forced upon them, as in the case where the skippers were mandated by the shipowner to sail to the bridge at a specific time. But the acknowledgement may also arise spontaneously, for reasons of salience, for instance. So one could say that acknowledged freedom *facilitates* the establishment of known freedom.

But there is a second and perhaps more obvious sense in which acknowledged freedom is an ideal to strive for: it not only facilitates, but also *protects*, known freedom. This idea is quite prominently present in republican thought as well as in work on recognition and respect.[14] It is, however, not necessary to adopt any of these views to appreciate this value of acknowledged, commonly known, freedom. How would common knowledge of freedom help protect stakeholders? Here is an example to begin with. A team manager grants one of the team members a temporary reduction of their workload and justifies this to the team by referring to specific challenging personal circumstances—say, illness in the family. The privilege (which may or may not follow from a legal right to short-term compassionate leave) and its justificatory grounds are, that is, common knowledge among the team members. A few months later, another team member is in a very similar situation and asks for the same privilege. The thought now is that it is much harder for the manager to refuse the request as compared to a situation without common knowledge. It is much more difficult to say no, and to find a motivation that the team will accept.

More generally the mechanism is the following. Suppose that it is common knowledge among A and B that B has asserted some proposition φ at some earlier occasion, and that now B asserts $\neg\varphi$, not-φ, the negation of φ. What should or could A do?

To begin with, A could ignore the new assertion, and maintain the belief that B actually backs φ. In that case, A has to assume that A has misunderstood B's assertion that $\neg\varphi$, or that B has made an error when they stated $\neg\varphi$, or that B is deceptive in implying that they believe $\neg\varphi$, and so on. A second way out for A would be to revise their belief that B believes that φ is the case and change it into a belief that B does not believe φ to be true. A may reason that they have misunderstood B's earlier statement that φ, or that the statement that φ was erroneous, or that B was lying when they said that φ is the case, or that B has genuinely changed their mind about φ. Thirdly, A could suspend beliefs, reasoning that, in the light of equally strong evidence for and against it, they have no decisive reason to adopt one rather than another doxastic attitude. These three things are the most straightforward things A could do. But one thing is clear: it is impossible simply to adopt the belief that B does not believe that φ, without further ado, because A cannot avoid noticing the contradiction between the earlier statement (φ) and later assertion ($\neg\varphi$). Simply adopting the belief that B does not believe φ is only then possible for A provided B has not made a prior statement concerning φ.

But that is only part of the story. To see this, return to the story of the team manager. If the manager rejects the second team member's request for a short-term compassionate leave or more relaxed working conditions, all team members see that this is incompatible with the way the manager responded to the first request. Since granting the first request and the reasons for granting it were publicly communicated (and became common knowledge among the team as a result thereof), the manager knows that each team member will notice the incompatibility. Manager and team members anticipate all this, because of common knowledge.

If it is common knowledge among A and B that B has asserted φ at some point in time, then, for A to adopt the belief that B does *not* believe φ, A needs more evidence (more information) as compared to a situation in which this statement is *not* preceded by such common knowledge. B can easily see such a thing by placing themselves in A's position. B will anticipate that their denial of φ will be met with one or more of a range of responses, including surprise, disbelief, suspicion, and distrust. B will anticipate that further questions are likely to be asked: 'Have you changed your mind about φ, and if so, why?', or: 'Were you honest when you first asserted that φ?', and if not: 'Can I be sure that you are honest about $\neg\varphi$ now?' It is, in sum, more difficult for B to persuade A to believe that B does not believe φ, in the second scenario.

In the abstract, the core element of the argument is purely epistemic, concerning as it does A's belief formation policies in the light of B's appearing inconsistent over time. But, in the workplace, the dynamic that follows upon the sensed inconsistency is likely to be decidedly practical. The manager rejecting the second employee's request for a reduced workload in times of family illness will not only have to answer questions—'Why? Have you changed your mind?'—and meet surprise, disbelief, suspicion, or distrust. They will also, perhaps primarily, meet resistance, opposition, hostility, and contempt; and the anticipation of such reactions may sway the manager's decision. This is a third benefit of acknowledged freedom. Next to being a provider of known freedom in strategic and coordination contexts, acknowledged freedom is a *guardian of known freedom*.

No Trade with Common Knowledge?

When we considered the argument from desire satisfaction in Chapter 1, we saw that it may be questioned on logical and psychological grounds (such as the steak-and-salmon example, *embarras de choix*, anticipatory regret). In Chapter 3, we considered arguments against knowledge, attempting to demonstrate that it is sometimes good to have false beliefs (such as the ravine-jumper example). The question that we need to address now is: Does common knowledge have similar downsides?

It seems so. To begin with, there is the so-called *no-trade theorem*, a result that comes from Paul Milgrom and Nancy Stokey, showing that, under particular conditions of common belief, trade may come to a standstill.[15] Very roughly, the idea is as follows. Suppose that we have an initial allocation of goods that is commonly known to be Pareto optimal, and that it is also common knowledge that further standard economic conditions hold, such as that all decision makers are rational, risk-averse, with identical prior beliefs. Then a simple *reductio* shows that, if a salesperson offers something for sale to a prospective customer, then the customer should reason as follows: because they are in a Pareto optimal world, one of them will lose out on the deal, and since it is reasonable to believe that sellers take the initiative only when they have gained some private information showing that they will gain from the trade, the buyer concludes that they will lose, and consequently rejects the offer. Yet, while the no-trade theorem may sometimes explain some stock market behaviour, it has little to say when I buy vegetables from the market; for, even though the greengrocer does have private information (about the price they paid, the quality, and future demand), I am happy to trade because I clearly foresee an improvement in my situation. Despite its fame, in many contexts the no-trade theorem is of no consequence. We can, I believe, safely set it aside here.

Perspective Change

A second argument against common knowledge is to do with perspective change. In an argument about freedom and privacy, Stanley Benn claimed that privacy invasions do not in general constitute genuine forms of interference. In defence of that claim, he asked us to imagine a case in which a man is beating a donkey. One way to make him stop doing that would be to take away the stick. But he may also stop upon being watched, and, if he does so, then 'being observed affects his action ... by changing his own perception of it'; for Benn argues that the man then sees the action of beating the donkey 'in a different light, through the eyes, as it were, of the observer'.[16]

For perspective change to happen, the beating does not need to be common knowledge among beater and observer. It is sufficient that the beater knows that the observer knows about the beating. But, whenever there is common knowledge, there will be perspective change. For the donkey this is good news, and in this case perhaps also for the beater, but, to the extent that we have a desire or an interest to protect our privacy, and to avoid adopting an observer's perspective towards our own action, we have an interest to avoid making things common knowledge. Workplace privacy comes to mind easily. In a business set up as a Benthamite panopticon, employees will continuously be forced to adopt the perspective of the manager—the warden—with increased productivity sometimes, but also with a decreased sense of autonomy.[17]

For our purposes, however, the main issue is whether a perspective change might negatively affect a decision maker's known freedom. To begin with, Benn's case depends for much of its plausibility on the assumption that the perspective the beater adopts after he has witnessed the observer has a particular moral content: that beating a donkey is bad. A donkey-beater will not care much as long as they think that the observer does not find beating a donkey reproachable. For compare: if the person in Benn's example were mending their garden, taking an observer's perspective would not have made them stop. In fact, if in circumstances that are perhaps more difficult to imagine the beater knew the observer were *praising* them for beating, then the very fact that the beating had become common knowledge might have led the beater to carry on with extra vigour.

What happens to your choice situation if you think the observer approves or disapproves of what you are doing? Clearly no actions are added to, or taken away from, your opportunity set. Moreover, as long as the observer does not perform any further actions, and the only thing happening is the perspective change, there is no change in the consequences of your actions. At most, what can happen as the result of a perspective change is that you change your utility function. The desire to continue beating the donkey suddenly disappears.

This is not to say that making things common knowledge cannot change a choice situation. But to see that, we need to imagine a different case from Benn's. A pianist may perform at a very high level at home, undisturbed, but as soon as they realize someone is listening, they get desperately nervous: hands start to tremble uncontrollably, heartbeat increases, memory fails, fingers become cold and stiff. The perspective change has made some actions unavailable. The pianist's opportunity set is temporarily changed. Or, with the same aim, consider an example from business: workplace surveillance in the form of email monitoring, which about half of all employers may engage in.[18] The perspective change that is happening here is that the employee knows that what they write may be read (or will be read) by some supervisor. Employers establish such form of surveillance for legal reasons as well as in the hope of boosting performance. This may make good sense if employees are likely to spend significant parts of their time on private emails, or to write too many emails, or if unmonitored email creates too many opportunities for illegal behaviour, for instance. But, as William Smith and Filiz Tabak observe, email monitoring may also depress employee creativity, create a culture of distrust, lead to a negative attitude towards work, weaken employee morale, and increase job-related stress.[19] These authors ask us to imagine what the most extreme case of surveillance, keystroke monitoring, would amount to:

> If, in the heat of the moment, an employee types a comment such as 'the boss is an idiot', but changes his or her mind, backspaces and deletes 'an idiot', and types 'mistaken' (or something more diplomatic), even if there is no e-mail sent or received, keystroke monitoring will record the original 'idiot' entry.[20]

Nor is the full force of common knowledge needed here. It suffices that the pianist or worker knows someone knows they are playing, or typing the word *idiot*.

So, indeed, common knowledge may hamper freedom. Yet how forceful is this as an argument qualifying the ideal of acknowledged freedom? I do not think it has enormous force, even though the phenomena described above are very real. It is important to see, however, that these things may also play out in the other direction. The pianist might be an audience-loving performer, who needs people around them to play. And there is no reason to ignore the fact that many workers are just simply more productive when supervisors monitor their work. While common knowledge—particularly of the panopticon type—may have deleterious effects in some cases, these cases do not generalize.

Common Knowledge in Republican Thought

Before proceeding, let me add one last observation about the value of common knowledge. It is derived from republican political thought but has broader applicability. As we saw in Chapter 1, the republican conception of freedom equates it with non-domination. A person is free in that sense in so far as no one has the capacity to interfere with them on an arbitrary basis. Republican freedom has value in part because it contributes to desire satisfaction, responsibility, and self-realization. But, as Philip Pettit claims, it engenders additional benefits that other conceptions of freedom do not have. Among these benefits, Pettit mentions the idea that, in a republic, citizens can 'look each other in the eyes' (more than in other worlds); that citizens 'do not have to bow and scrape' in order to satisfy their desires; and that citizens in republics are better informed than in other worlds about the likelihood of facing interference.[21]

A key element here is common knowledge, both in that it delivers information about interference, and in that it constitutes mutual recognition and respect. The idea is best grasped in two propositions. First, a theoretical claim to the effect that, since republican freedom is about diminishing the opportunity for arbitrary interference, republican freedom is largely a matter of establishing *resource equality*; for it is resource differentials that enable people to wield arbitrary power over others. Secondly, an empirical claim that people are generally well informed about the allocation of relevant resources. Pettit writes:

> Such resources tend to be prominent and detectable by those to whose disadvantage they may be deployed, and … this helps ensure that where one person has any dominating power over another, in virtue of an inequality of resources, it is a matter of common knowledge that this is so.[22]

We can ignore some details of the argument; what is important here is that common knowledge of resource equality—an ideal that is close to acknowledged freedom—is exactly what generates these additional benefits of republican freedom.[23] The thought is that, whenever resource equality is common knowledge among agents, they will 'look each other in the eye', or, as one could say, that they mutually recognize and respect each other.[24] And, while it is not undisputed that we need a republic to realize that ideal, this line of argument does suggest that one reason to support the ideal of acknowledged freedom is that it may contribute such forms of mutual recognition.[25]

Fostering the Ideal

What can we do to come closer to acknowledged freedom?[26] To answer that question, it is instructive first to consider how establishing and sustaining common knowledge can be supported, or frustrated. For common knowledge of some proposition φ to arise among a group of people, there has to be a kind of openness that allows group members to see each other (to see each other in the eye, if you wish), and to see that they can see each other, and so forth. Think of national assemblies, often with a circular or semi-circular, amphitheatrical line-up. Think of round or oval boardroom tables. Or think of how online conversations often do not lead to common knowledge: for if I suspect that one of the team members has not been listening, or that there was a glitch in the video-conferencing connection, common knowledge breaks down.

Making it impossible for group members to notice each other, or, more extremely, barring the formation of a group, or dismantling it, are, then, ways to interfere with the establishment of common knowledge. In political terms, you might say that, if there is a specific human right protecting common knowledge, then it should be the right to freedom of assembly and association. But often it is more subtle than that: merely distracting a colleague when a purported public announcement is made in the workplace is sufficient to obstruct common knowledge.

I have elsewhere used the word *interlucency* to describe what I think are the prime contributors to common knowledge.[27] A worker informs the team about the mechanical malfunctioning of a certain system with which they are working, telling them about something odd that happened earlier this day. For this to become common knowledge in the team, it is not enough that every team member singly processes and stores the information. Two things have to happen. First, the worker has actively to make sure to *track understanding*—that is, to see whether the co-workers receive the information, pay attention, and actually understand the information. Secondly, the co-workers have to make sure that they *acknowledge receipt* of the information.

To establish common knowledge, senders and recipients have to contribute both. Tracking and acknowledging together make the situation interlucent. One could also say that interlucent communicators ensure that they track and acknowledge. Interlucency is, I believe, arguably the most important driver of acknowledged freedom in most stakeholder interactions. Illustrating this is what I do in the remainder of this chapter. It will bring us in contact with a concept from medical ethics that some have argued should be taken more seriously in other branches of applied ethics as well: informed consent.

Informed Consent in Business

As John Hardwig aptly observes, *informed consent* has become the 'byword' of today's bioethics.[28] Informed consent guides the interactions between doctors and patients, as well as between medical researchers and research subjects, and is often defended by recourse to the normative ideal of autonomous decision-making. Informed consent typically involves the provision of information about the benefits, harms, and risks of a medical procedure, after which the patient signs, or verbally gives, consent.

Consenting Shareholders

Hardwig advocates the use of the informed-consent model in business, and in particular the interactions between corporate management and the owners of equity in the firm, its shareholders. He believes that the informed-consent model has raised awareness among bioethicists and medical professionals of the fact that patients have values other than health that might be important when they make decisions about medication, lifestyle changes, and surgical procedures, and that, as a result, doctors are now more sensitive to patients who do not want to get the medically maximal treatment. He thinks that a similar move should force us to see that shareholders may have different concerns other than the sole preoccupation with the maximization of their wealth.

Sven Ove Hansson has put forward similar suggestions.[29] While he would disagree with Hardwig's argument about shareholders (Hansson thinks that informed consent has little merit when it comes to guiding management's dealings with collectives), he does stand up for informed consent as a normative ideal for salespeople to provide customers with a decent amount of reliable information about the products or services they offer to them.

If we extend Hardwig's and Hansson's views to other stakeholders, such as employees and suppliers, we obtain a theory of informed consent in business (or the beginnings thereof). While I believe there is some merit in applying the informed-consent model to business interaction—for instance, for the reason that fostering informed consent will typically foster known freedom—it is important to warn against a tendency in medical ethics to cast the requirements of informed consent only in terms of the *provision* of information, instead of, as Neil Manson and Onora O'Neill think is better, as something that a doctor *communicates* to a patient.[30] One of their examples is the following.[31] Two people, *A* and *B*, are given information to the effect that they are about to participate in a medical research project about the psychological effects of a drug. *A* is told the drug is called *lysergic acid diethylamide*, while *B* learns that it is *LSD*. Since only a few people know that these names refer to the same substance, it is likely that *A* and *B* come to think of the experiment in different ways. Manson and O'Neill write that the researcher, while speaking truthfully to both, may '*pragmatically* ... mislead[s]' them when they use the lesser-known term.[32]

Ethics of Communication

It is not hard to come up with similar examples in business. As we saw in Chapter 3, the Financial Services Authority told UK citizens that a so-called *defined-benefit* pension scheme 'guarantees' a fixed monthly retirement payout. But they failed to tell them there was no guarantee against the scheme going bust.[33] Just as in the case of research on LSD, it is reasonable to side with critics accusing the FSA of 'misleading' UK citizens, as Ros Altmann, a British pension expert did.[34] Similarly, banks sold 'interest-only' mortgages to clients, who took that literally and were very surprised to learn later that they had to repay the capital.[35] Or what about a 'LIBOR-based rollover mortgage' arrangement? So, when Manson and O'Neill claim that we have to rethink informed consent and replace the transactional information-provision model with what is effectively an ethics of communication, this has great plausibility for business ethics too.

The way I have set up things is that such ethics of communication contributes to acknowledged freedom. What goes wrong when things are explained using words such as *lysergic acid diethylamide*, *guarantee*, or *interest-only mortgage* is that patient and doctor, citizen and regulator, or client and banker fail to establish common knowledge of the terms of the procedure or contract.

This lack of common knowledge is often due to a lack of interlucency on the part of the sender. When the FSA explains a defined-benefit plan in a leaflet, they should realize that, trivially, the typical addressee of that information is someone who does not know what such a plan is. That is the reason why such a person reads the FSA leaflet. And the FSA should realize that a person who does not know what such a plan is cannot be reasonably assumed to have an understanding of the insolvency risks that come with particular retirement products. If you cannot tell a defined-benefit and a defined-contribution mortgage apart, then it is unlikely you know the bankruptcy laws applying to pension funds. So, in the FSA case, there is a clear failure to track understanding. Similarly, calling a mortgage *interest-only* is misleading for clients with minimal financial literacy (a significant proportion of people). A mortgage typically has two components you need to pay: interest and capital. Calling a mortgage *interest-only* strongly suggests that the second component is absent in this type of mortgage. That such a thing makes no economic sense is something we cannot expect everyone to appreciate.

The case of the 'LIBOR-based rollover mortgage' has to be analysed a bit differently, though. If a salesperson mentions this type of mortgage to a customer, the customer will immediately notice it, if they do not understand what type of mortgage that is: the word *LIBOR* has no meaning besides finance. So in this case it is reasonable to expect that the customer would ask for clarification, signalling their lack of understanding to the salesperson. A salesperson using such a term does not therefore mislead the customer, not even pragmatically.

This suggests a rule of thumb: it is, first, primarily the task of the recipient (patient, customer) to notify the sender (doctor, salesperson, adviser) when they do not understand technical terms; and it is, secondly, primarily the task of the sender to notify the recipient when non-technical terms are used in non-standard jargonal ways.

Responsible Lending

What I advocate here is a model in which contracting parties ensure informed consent, grounded in common knowledge about the characteristics of the contract (which, for me, ultimately reduce to information about the likely consequences of the available actions).[36] This is not, however, the approach that legislators have so far chosen when it comes to protecting the interests of consumers in financial markets. It is instructive to see how recent legislation deviates from this idea. My example here is the 2008 Consumer Credit Directive, the centrepiece EU legislation in this domain, and I argue that such legislation is inferior as compared with what an approach based on informed consent and common knowledge would sponsor.[37] The Consumer Credit Directive is intended to instigate Member States to take measures to promote 'responsible practices during all phases of the credit relationship', including such things as 'the provision of information to, and the education of, consumers, including warnings about the risks attaching to default on payment and to over-indebtedness'.[38] Moreover, 'it is important that creditors should not engage in irresponsible lending or give out credit without prior assessment of creditworthiness'.[39]

Various commentators have argued that the requirements embedded in the Consumer Credit Directive are a far cry from the ideal of responsible lending.[40] Earlier proposals for EU regulation had included proposals to the effect that lenders should 'take into account the consumer borrowers' interests and needs throughout the relationship in order to prevent consumer detriment'.[41] The Consumer Credit Directive, however, requires only a test of the borrower's creditworthiness and the provision of information.

I agree with the commentators that a more substantial reading of *responsible lending* is preferable, but I do not think it can reasonably be expected of a lender that their actions are always tailored to the best interests of their clients. What I suggest is that the concept of responsibility should be taken as central, and that a lender should simply see what conditions should satisfy responsible lending. These conditions include by now straightforward things: both parties to the contract should have knowledge about their opportunity sets. In the case at hand, that entails in particular that the borrowers possess knowledge, including of the finer details of the contract. But, I suggest, it also includes common knowledge. For a lender responsibly to extend credit to a particular borrower, the lender should have knowledge of the fact that the borrower understands the contract. Taking John Hardwig's and Sven Ove Hansson's suggestions seriously, what should be required is no less than requiring that the borrower has given their informed consent.

The Average Consumer

This is a more radical suggestion than it may seem. To appreciate this, it is instructive to pay some attention to the model of the *average consumer* that current legislation adopts.[42] The idea is that such regulation 'takes as a benchmark the average consumer, who is reasonably well-informed and reasonably observant and circumspect'.[43] Yet clearly a large number of consumers are less than average. The way they recruit, process, interpret, and use information will not lead to 'reasonably observant and circumspect' behaviour. They may be prone to a host of behavioural biases, or lack the required reading and financial competence. As a result, their beliefs about the characteristics of particular credit arrangements (and about the consequences of taking out such credit arrangements on their household finances eventually) may be highly inaccurate. This is exacerbated by the fact that, when banks are obligated to target their information provision at average consumers, they have an incentive to develop products that exploit the lack of knowledge of the sizeable proportion of consumers who are less than average consumers.

In Chapter 1 we encountered consumer obfuscation or naïveté-based discrimination in the context of phone plans designed to profit from our tendency to underestimate our phone-call minutes.[44] Oren Bar-Gill has demonstrated, however, that there is evidence that consumer contracts in finance similarly exploit the behavioural and cognitive weaknesses of consumers.[45] And similar things hold true of professional finance as well, as

Steven McNamara has argued in the context of credit rating and structured finance.[46]

For consent to be a good ground for responsible decision-making, the consenting party has to understand what they consent to. While some provision of information may be sufficient to place the average consumer in such epistemic conditions, much more is likely to be needed for consumers with lower than average background knowledge and capabilities—and, again, there are many of them. Once we shape the contractual relations between lenders and borrowers along the lines of informed consent as we know it from medical decision-making, the average consumer immediately drops out of the picture. It makes no sense and would plainly be unjustifiable to require physicians to provide patients with explanations targeted at the average patient. Every patient is different. Some will know that *LSD* and *lysergic acid diethylamide* are one and the same thing. Others will not. The ethics of communication that should support informed consent therefore naturally requires that the physician adjusts their explanation to the specific patient, so as to arrive at what in the model I am proposing here is common knowledge.

A second key element that distinguishes the model I propose here from current legislation is that it requires not only the provision of information, but also the tracking of understanding. The lender has to make sure, not only that the specific prospective borrower they are dealing with understands the offer on the table; they also have to make sure that they, the lender, know that the borrower understands. To that end, relevant feedback from the prospective borrower will have to be solicited. The borrower should be encouraged to acknowledge receipt.[47]

Clearly, this model diverges widely from the suggestions of other commentators, who believe that genuine responsible lending involves lenders making sure that they sell only what is in the best interests of their clients. I do not think that such paternalism is justifiable. If we give up the notion that people can ultimately decide, on their own, what is best for themselves, then a *very* different model of consumer contracts should be developed.[48] The advantage of the model I present here is that it keeps both parties in full control of their responsibility, but at the same time requires that mechanisms are in place that ensure that both parties possess the known freedom necessary to assume responsibility. That this ultimately requires more from the service provider than more paternalistic views sponsor is something we have to live with.

Notes

1. See, generally, Adam Brandenburger, 'Knowledge and Equilibrium in Games', *Journal of Economic Perspectives*, 6 (1992), 83–101, and Larry Samuelson, 'Modelling Knowledge in Economic Analysis', *Journal of Economic Literature*, 42 (2004), 367–403.
2. See Jon Barwise, 'Three Views of Common Knowledge', in Moshe Vardi (ed.), *Proceedings of the Second Conference on Theoretical Aspects of Reasoning about Knowledge* (San Francisco: Morgan Kaufman, 1988), 365–379. These logical observations are sufficient to discredit the argument that common knowledge is impossible to possess because of its infinitary character, as John Searle, *Mind, Language, and Society: Philosophy in the Real World* (New York: Basic Books, 1998), 191, did ('I don't think my head is big enough to accommodate so many beliefs'). He seems to have revised his view in John Searle, *Making the Social World: The Structure of Human Civilization* (New York: Oxford University Press, 2010), 49. See, e.g., Dirk Bergemann and Stephen Morris, 'Robust Mechanism Design', *Econometrica*, 73 (2006), 1771–1813, and Ariel Rubinstein, 'The Electronic Mail Game: Strategic Behavior under "Almost Common Knowledge"', *American Economic Review*, 79 (1989), 385–391, for relaxing the common knowledge assumption. Early work on common knowledge and coordination includes Morris Friedell, 'On the Structure of Shared Awareness', *Behavioral Science*, 14 (1969), 28–39, John Harsanyi, 'On the Rationality Postulates Underlying the Theory of Cooperative Games', *Journal of Conflict Resolution*, 5 (1961), 179–196, Paul-Hassan Maucorps and René Bassoul, 'Jeux miroirs et sociologie de la connaissance d'autrui', *Cahiers internationaux de sociologie*, 32 (1962), 43–60, and Thomas Schelling, 'Bargaining, Communication, and Limited War', *Conflict Resolution*, 1 (1957), 19–36. On Schelling, see also Daniel Klein, *Knowledge and Coordination: A Liberal Interpretation* (New York: Oxford University Press, 2012).
3. See Elliot Lipnowski and Evan Sadler, 'Peer-Confirming Equilibrium', *Econometrica*, 87 (2019), 567–591, for the impact of social networks on strategic knowledge.
4. Michael Chwe, *Rational Ritual: Culture, Coordination, and Common Knowledge* (Princeton: Princeton University Press, 2001), 11, 44 ff.
5. Thomas Ellrod, interviewed by Michael Lev, 'Super Bowl 25: The Football Hoopla Yields to Hype', *New York Times*, 6 January 1991, www.nytimes.com/1991/01/06/business/super-bowl-25-the-football-hoopla-yields-to-hype.html [perma.cc/KG8N-7Y9V]. Cf. Chwe, *Rational Ritual*, 11.
6. See Sylvain Chassang, 'Fear of Miscoordination and the Robustness of Cooperation in Dynamic Global Games with Exit', *Econometrica*, 78 (2010), 973–1006, for a model of the deleterious effects on coordination of fear of

miscommunication. Relatedly one may ask whether common knowledge of freedom, the ideal defended in this chapter, is a public good, something non-rival in consumption and non-excludable, such as public sanitation, national defence, environmental protection, which is unlikely to arise through markets, as is the content of Paul Samuelson, 'The Pure Theory of Public Expenditure', *Review of Economics and Statistics*, 36 (1954), 387–389. If it is, then liberals will find it less difficult to accept the potentially more far-reaching policy consequences of my approach.

7. There is a subtlety here. Compare two cases: I announce φ to my friends sitting around a table, or I announce φ on an email list. In both cases there is common knowledge (but cf. Ariel Rubinstein, 'The Electronic Mail Game: Strategic Behavior under "Almost Common Knowledge"', *American Economic Review*, 79 (1989), 385–391), but of different types. The friends know of each other that they know φ, and so on. But the members of the email list may not know who else is on the list. So for them there is a sort of conditional form of common knowledge: if it is common knowledge among some people that they are members of this list, then it is common knowledge among them that φ. This observation arose out of various discussions with Barteld Kooi. See Barteld Kooi, 'Expressivity and Completeness for Public Logics via Reduction Axioms', *Journal of Applied Non-Classical Logics*, 17 (2008), 231–253.

8. See, e.g., Patrick Bolton and Joseph Farrell, 'Decentralization, Duplication, and Delay', *Journal of Political Economy*, 98 (1990), 803–826, on the efficiency of decentralized economies, Carolina Castilla, 'Trust and Reciprocity between Spouses in India', *American Economic Review*, 105 (2015), 621–624, on trust and reciprocity, Christophe Chamley, 'Coordinating Regime Switches', *Quarterly Journal of Economics*, 114 (1999), 869–905, on social change and revolutions, Bradford Cornell and Ivo Welch, 'Culture, Information, and Screening Discrimination', *Journal of Political Economy*, 104 (1996), 542–571, on discrimination, Martin Evans and Richard Lyons, 'How Is Macro News Transmitted to Exchange Rates?', *Journal of Financial Economics*, 88 (2008), 26–50, on news in markets, Armin Falk, Ernst Fehr, and Christian Zehnder, 'Fairness Perceptions and Reservation Wages: The Behavioral Effects of Minimum Wage Laws', *Quarterly Journal of Economics*, 121 (2006), 1347–1381, on minimum wages, and Bryan Lim, 'Short-Sale Constraints and Price Bubbles', *Journal of Banking and Finance*, 35 (2011), 2443–2453, on bubbles. Cf. Vivian Lei, Charles Noussair, and Charles Plott, 'Nonspeculative Bubbles in Experimental Asset Markets: Lack of Common Knowledge of Rationality vs. Actual Irrationality', *Econometrica*, 69 (2001), 831–859, on bubbles. See also Jean Hampton, *Political Philosophy* (New York: Routledge, 1997), 105, on the role communication devices played in the collapse of European communism.

9. Herbert Hart, 'Acts of Will and Responsibility', in Hart, *Punishment and Responsibility: Essays in the Philosophy of Law* (Oxford: Clarendon Press, 1968), 90–112, *passim*, discusses the value of 'knowledge of circumstances or foresight of consequences' as part of the requirements of responsibility in criminal law. A related observation is made by Lon Fuller, *The Morality of Law* (New Haven: Yale University Press, 1964), 46–91, requiring promulgation of laws as one of the principles of legality. That is, laws have to be made known to the people to whom they are supposed to apply. The requirements of clarity and non-contradiction are also somewhat epistemic. What Hart, and to a greater extent Fuller, miss here is the requirement of common knowledge. Friedrich von Hayek, *The Constitution of Liberty* (Chicago: University of Chicago Press, 1959), 153, thought that '[t]here is little difference between the knowledge that if [a man] builds a bonfire on the floor of his living room his house will burn down, and the knowledge that if he sets his neighbour's house on fire he will find himself in jail. Like the laws of nature, the laws of the state provide fixed features in the environment in which he has to move.' Hayek overlooks the fact that the type of justifying evidence gained in a game against nature is of a different kind from that in a strategic game. See also John Rawls, *A Theory of Justice* (Cambridge, MA: Harvard University Press, 1971), 236 ('one legal order is more justly administered than another if it more perfectly fulfills the precepts of the rule of law. It will provide a more secure basis for liberty and a more effective means for organizing cooperative schemes').

10. See Boudewijn de Bruin, *Ethics and the Global Financial Crisis: Why Incompetence Is Worse than Greed* (Cambridge: Cambridge University Press, 2015), 160 ff., for an example involving stock recommendation bias, where it is common knowledge among professional investors (but not naive investors) and analysts that a recommendation to *hold* a piece of stock is really a recommendation to *sell* it. Ideas underlying this go back to David Lewis, *Convention: A Philosophical Study* (Cambridge, MA: Harvard University Press, 1969), and Stephen Schiffer, *Meaning* (Oxford: Oxford University Press, 1972). See also Robert Stalnaker, 'Common Ground', *Linguistics and Philosophy*, 25 (2002), 701–721.

11. See Peyton Young, 'The Evolution of Conventions', *Econometrica*, 61 (1993), 57–84, for how conventions can arise without common knowledge.

12. Thomas Schelling, *The Strategy of Conflict* (Cambridge, MA: Harvard University Press, 1960), is the *locus classicus* for salience. Cf. Vincent Crawford, Uri Gneezy, and Yuval Rottenstreich, 'The Power of Focal Points Is Limited: Even Minute Payoff Asymmetry May Yield Large Coordination Failures', *American Economic Review*, 98 (2008), 1443–1458.

13. Michael Alvarez and Jonathan Nagler, 'Should I Stay or Should I Go? Sincere and Strategic Crossover Voting in California Assembly Races', in Bruce Cain

and Elisabeth Gerber (eds), *California's Blanket Primary* (Berkeley and Los Angeles: University of California Press, 2002), 107–123.

14. See, generally, Axel Honneth, *Kampf um Anerkennung: Zur moralischen Grammatik sozialer Konflikte* (Frankfurt am Main: Suhrkamp, 1992). See Axel Honneth, 'Invisibility: On the Epistemology of "Recognition"', *Aristotelian Society Supplementary Volume*, 75 (2001), 111–126, for an epistemological account of recognition, partly inspired by an intriguing reading of Hegel's early work and insights from social psychology. See Philip Pettit, *Republicanism: A Theory of Freedom and Government* (Oxford: Oxford University Press, 1997), 60 ff., for a discussion of how common knowledge fosters mutual respect, from a republican point of view. Lisa Herzog, *Inventing the Market: Smith, Hegel, and Political Theory* (Oxford: Oxford University Press, 2013), 102 ff., shows that Smith thought that markets foster mutual recognition and respect, whereas Hegel thought markets frustrate this. See also Ulrich Steinvorth, 'Positive und negative Freiheit: Der richtige Mix?', in Thomas Meyer and Udo Vorholt (eds), *Positive und negative Freiheit* (Bochum: Projekt, 2007), 54–68, at 58–61, and Christopher Bennett, 'Liberalism, Autonomy and Conjugal Love', *Res Publica*, 9 (2003), 285–301.

15. Paul Milgrom and Nancy Stokey, 'Information, Trade and Common Knowledge', *Journal of Economic Theory*, 26 (1982), 17–27.

16. Stanley Benn, *A Theory of Freedom* (Cambridge: Cambridge University Press, 1988), 272

17. See, e.g., Michael Chwe, *Rational Ritual: Culture, Coordination, and Common Knowledge* (Princeton: Princeton University Press, 2001), 66 ff., on the panopticon and common knowledge, and Taryn Stanko and Christine Beckman, 'Watching You Watching Me: Boundary Control and Capturing Attention in the Context of Ubiquitous Technology Use', *Academy of Management Journal*, 58 (2015), 712–738, on manifestations of this phenomenon in business organizations.

18. American Management Association, 'The Latest on Workplace Monitoring and Surveillance', 8 April 2019, www.amanet.org/articles/the-latest-on-workplace-monitoring-and-surveillance/ [perma.cc/5NPN-JZF2].

19. William Smith and Filiz Tabak, 'Monitoring Employee E-mails: Is There Any Room for Privacy?', *Academy of Management Perspectives*, 23 (2009), 33–48. See also Matthew Hoye and Jeffrey Monaghan, 'Surveillance, Freedom, and the Republic', *European Journal for Political Theory*, 17 (2018), 343–363, for a republican argument about surveillance, and Titus Stahl, 'Indiscriminate Mass Surveillance and the Public Sphere', *Ethics and Information Technology*, 18 (2016), 33–39, and Titus Stahl, 'Privacy in Public: A Democratic Defense', *Moral Philosophy and Politics*, 7 (2020), 73–96, for arguments about governmental surveillance and democracy.

20. William Smith and Filiz Tabak, 'Monitoring Employee E-mails: Is There Any Room for Privacy?', *Academy of Management Perspectives*, 23 (2009), 39.
21. Philip Pettit, *Republicanism: A Theory of Freedom and Government* (Oxford: Oxford University Press, 1997), 87.
22. Ibid. 60.
23. Relations of domination and non-domination are as a result completely open and transparent to the agents involved, according to the republican. The empirical fact that any instance of domination, captured by proposition φ, is common knowledge, captured by $\mathbf{C}\varphi$, is represented by $\varphi \rightarrow \mathbf{C}\varphi$. If we assume that this empirical fact is common knowledge, that is, $\mathbf{C}(\varphi \rightarrow \mathbf{C}\varphi)$, then, modulo some further assumptions, it follows that any instance of non-domination is common knowledge, $\neg\varphi \rightarrow \mathbf{C}\neg\varphi$. As knowledge is veridical, common knowledge is veridical, and so we find that $\neg\varphi \rightarrow \neg\mathbf{C}\varphi$ (1). Negative introspection (the condition that, if one does not know that φ, then one knows that one does not know that φ) for common knowledge yields $\neg\mathbf{C}\varphi \rightarrow \mathbf{C}\neg\mathbf{C}\varphi$ (2). The assumed $\mathbf{C}(\varphi \rightarrow \mathbf{C}\varphi)$ moreover entails $\mathbf{C}\neg\mathbf{C}\varphi \rightarrow \mathbf{C}\neg\varphi$ (3). Combining (1)–(3) yields $\neg\varphi \rightarrow \mathbf{C}\neg\varphi$: if there is no domination, it is common knowledge that there is no domination.
24 Philip Pettit, *Republicanism: A Theory of Freedom and Government* (Oxford: Oxford University Press, 1997), 87. See generally Axel Honneth, 'Invisibility: On the Epistemology of "Recognition"', *Aristotelian Society Supplementary Volume*, 75 (2001), 111–126, for misrecognition and perception.
25. John Rawls, *A Theory of Justice* (Cambridge, MA: Harvard University Press, 1971), 133, discusses publicity of the principles of justice. He claims that this follows from a contractarian perspective, and that it is entailed by Kant's concept of moral law. He even mentions David Lewis, *Convention: A Philosophical Study* (Cambridge, MA: Harvard University Press, 1969), on common knowledge. The value of principles of justice being common knowledge is, for Rawls, that, 'when the basic structure of society is publicly known to satisfy its principles for an extended period of time, those subject to these arrangements tend to develop a desire to act in accordance with these principles and to do their part in institutions which exemplify them' (*A Theory of Justice* (Cambridge, MA: Harvard University Press, 1971), 177). This is one advantage. The second advantage is that 'the public recognition of the two principles gives greater support to men's self-respect' (ibid. 178). So there is reason to assume that 'the parties would accept the natural duty of mutual respect which asks them to treat one another civilly and to be willing to explain the grounds of their actions, especially when the claims of others are overruled' (ibid. 178–179). Rawls also seems to believe that respect breeds self-respect in that 'one may assume that those who respect themselves are more likely to respect each other and conversely' (ibid. 179).

26. Josiah Ober, *Democracy and Knowledge: Innovation and Learning in Classical Athens* (Princeton: Princeton University Press, 2008), discusses how developments in architecture, law, and social life contributed to the spread of common knowledge, fostering democracy in classical Athens. In particular, Ober notes that codification (standardization of weights, rules, etc.) ensured that the citizens of Athens possessed some knowledge about the fact that transactions costs were low (contracting, etc.), and that therefore they can engage in mutually beneficial business. Ibid. 211–263. But, in terms of knowledge about freedom, codification is important too, for, if there is unclarity about regulations (e.g., governing weights), or if there is a large diversity and complexity of regulations (e.g., governing subsidies or other governmental policies), then individuals will be less likely to possess full knowledge of their freedoms. Where there is one place where you can go to for any government document (driver's licence, passport, birth certificate, etc.), that registers more easily in your mind then when you get these documents in various different places. Similarly, Philip Pettit, *Republicanism: A Theory of Freedom and Government* (Oxford: Oxford University Press, 1997), 165–170, argues for a certain form of public space, which would counter the development, in American cities, of the middle class retreating to suburbs in houses protected by private security companies shielding them from the violence in city centres (where the offices are isolated from the houses), and from the rest of the activities that are going on in the neighbourhood. Pettit laments this development, because for him the public space is an important, perhaps primary, provider of common knowledge of non-domination, and hence a precondition for the benefits of non-domination to take effect. It is important to realize that my argument is neutral with respect to the particular political ideology, as far as possible. If it is the responsibility of some person or institution to establish common knowledge (which I think it is in certain circumstances), then this responsibility should not be seen as arising out of the communitarian project of stimulating communities to develop their conception of the good; for here the communitarian thought that individuals would not otherwise be able to exercise autonomy is rejected. Fully realizing the formal ideal I put forward here might entail establishing surprisingly sizeable institutions, but will always be entirely compatible with what Philip Pettit, *The Common Mind: An Essay on Psychology, Society, and Politics* (New York: Oxford University Press, 1996), 166, has disparagingly called 'social atomism', even though such atomism is not of course required. For an exchange of ideas, see Charles Taylor, 'Irreducibly Social Goods', in Geoffrey Brennan and Cliff Walsh (eds), *Rationality, Individualism, and Public Policy* (Canberra: Centre for Research on Federal Financial Relations, Australian National University, 1990) (defending a communitarian view), 45–63, and Robert Goodin, 'Irreducibly Social Goods: Comment

I', in Geoffrey Brennan and Cliff Walsh (eds), *Rationality, Individualism, and Public Policy* (Canberra: Centre for Research on Federal Financial Relations, Australian National University, 1990), 64–79 (criticizing the view). Miranda Fricker, *Epistemic Injustice: Power and the Ethics of Knowing* (Oxford: Oxford University Press, 2007), 147–175 (on hermeneutical injustice), can be interpreted as providing additional reasons to be sceptical about whether we can assume to possess shared linguistic resources required for realizing such social goods.

27. Boudewijn de Bruin, *Ethics and the Global Financial Crisis: Why Incompetence Is Worse than Greed* (Cambridge: Cambridge University Press, 2015), 161 ff.

28. John Hardwig, 'The Stockholder: A Lesson for Business Ethics from Bioethics?', *Journal of Business Ethics*, 91 (2010), 329–341, at 330.

29. Sven Ove Hansson, 'Informed Consent Out of Context', *Journal of Business Ethics*, 63 (2006), 149–154.

30. Neil Manson and Onora O'Neill, *Rethinking Informed Consent in Bioethics* (Cambridge: Cambridge University Press, 2007). See also Onora O'Neill, 'Ethics for Communication?', *European Journal of Philosophy*, 17 (2009), 167–180, for a discussion of disclosure of personal data and freedom of expression. In Onora O'Neill, *Constructing Authorities: Reason, Politics and Interpretation in Kant's Philosophy* (Cambridge: Cambridge University Press, 2015), 142, the author tempers expectations concerning the potential of novel communications technologies to contribute to democratic decision-making: 'Where standards for effective communication are ignored, the dissemination of speech content amounts only to quasi-communication'; and elsewhere: 'This is often apparent in company reports, promotional literature, press releases, as well as the "creative" use of small print, league tables, opinion polling, and much more' (ibid. 150).

31. Neil Manson and Onora O'Neill, *Rethinking Informed Consent in Bioethics* (Cambridge: Cambridge University Press, 2007), 13 ff.

32. Ibid. (emphasis in original).

33. Alistair Osborne, 'Pension Victims Accuse Government of Hypocrisy', *Daily Telegraph*, 19 September 2007, advance.lexis.com/api/document?collection=news&id=urn:contentItem:4PPF-00J0-TX33-70GP-00000-00.

34. See Norma Cohen, 'FSA Turns Down Plea on Pension Plan Losses', *Financial Times*, 4 August 2004, advance.lexis.com/api/document?collection=news&id=urn:contentItem:4D13-FRP0-TW84-P1TW-00000-00

35. Personal communication compliance officer ABN AMRO bank N.V.

36. See, generally, C. B. Bhattacharya, Sankar Sen, and Daniel Korschun, *Leveraging Corporate Responsibility: The Stakeholder Route to Maximizing Business and Social Value* (Cambridge: Cambridge University Press, 2011), for a discussion of the way corporations communicate CSR strategies with their stakeholders,

and see Jette Steen Knudsen and Jeremy Moon, *Visible Hands: Government Regulation and International Business Responsibility* (Cambridge: Cambridge University Press, 2017), for a methodology to analyse the responsibilities states and regulators have for shaping corporate social responsibility (CSR) policies.

37. Directive 2008/48/EC of the European Parliament and of the Council of 23 April 2008 on credit agreements for consumers and repealing Council Directive 87/102/EEC, 2008, *Official Journal of the European Union*, L 133/66.

38. Ibid. recital 26.

39. Ibid.

40. See, e.g., Olha Cherednychenko and Jesse Meindertsma, 'Irresponsible Lending in the Post-Crisis Era: Is the EU Consumer Credit Directive Fit for its Purpose?', *Journal of Consumer Policy*, 42 (2019), 483–519, and Vanessa Mak and Jurgen Braspenning, '*Errare humanum est*: Financial Literacy in European Consumer Credit Law', *Journal of Consumer Policy*, 35 (2012), 307–332.

41. Olha Cherednychenko and Jesse Meindertsma, 'Irresponsible Lending in the Post-Crisis Era: Is the EU Consumer Credit Directive Fit for Its Purpose?', *Journal of Consumer Policy*, 42 (2019), 483–519, at 486–487. See Proposal for a Directive of the European Parliament and of the Council on the harmonisation of the laws, regulations, and administrative provisions of the Member States concerning credit for consumers, COM(2002), 443 final, article 9.

42. See, e.g., Olha Cherednychenko and Jesse Meindertsma, 'Irresponsible Lending in the Post-Crisis Era: Is the EU Consumer Credit Directive Fit for its Purpose?', *Journal of Consumer Policy*, 42 (2019), 483–519, and Vanessa Mak and Jurgen Braspenning, 'Errare humanum est: Financial Literacy in European Consumer Credit Law', *Journal of Consumer Policy*, 35 (2012), 307–332.

43. Directive 2005/29/EC of the European Parliament and of the Council of 11 May 2005 concerning unfair business-to-consumer commercial practices in the internal market and amending Council Directive 84/450/EEC, Directives 97/7/EC, 98/27/EC, and 2002/65/EC of the European Parliament and of the Council and Regulation (EC) No. 2006/2004 of the European Parliament and of the Council, 2005, *Official Journal of the European Union*, L 149/22, recital 18.

44. Paul Heidhues and Botond Kőszegi, 'Naïveté-Based Discrimination', *Quarterly Journal of Economics*, 132 (2017), 1019–1054.

45. Oren Bar-Gill, 'The Behavioral Economics of Consumer Contracts', *Minnesota Law Review*, 92 (2008), 749–802.

46. Steven McNamara, 'Informational Failures in Structured Finance and Dodd–Frank's Improvements to the Regulation of Credit Rating Agencies', *Fordham Journal of Corporate and Financial Law*, 17 (2012), 665–749.

47. Art. 80e Besluit Gedragstoezicht financiële ondernemingen Wft in conjunction with art. 4:24 Wet op het financieel toezicht (Wft) require financial services

providers in the Netherlands to ascertain that the knowledge and expertise of a given consumer are sufficient for the consumer to understand the risks of the product, as well as that the respective product is suitable for the consumer. This may go some way to realizing the ideal of acknowledged freedom. See, generally, Jurgen Braspenning and Vanessa Mak, 'Nieuwe regels voor hypothecaire kredietverstrekking aan consumenten: over leren en bezweren', *Tijdschrift voor Consumentenrecht en handelspraktijken*, 2 (2015), 73–81, and Hélène Vletter-van Dort, 'Het belang van een goede balans tussen verantwoording en verantwoordelijkheid', in Danny Busch and Marco Nieuwe Weme (eds), *Christels Koers: Liber Amicorum Prof. mr. drs. C.M. Grundmann-van de Krol* (Deventer: Kluwer, 2013), 747–762, at 759–761. Yet the way in which banks implement this measure is still too generic to contribute to generating informed consent. Also: the requirement to ascertain the suitability of the product is more than what I argue for here.

48. Note that this does not apply to situations where there is a professional relation between a client and, say, a fund manager owing fiduciary duties to the client (principal). If I am managing funds you have entrusted to me, then of course I need to act in your best interests.

5

Sustainable Finance and Responsible Investors

Socially responsible investment (SRI) is a booming business. A poll among research analysts a while ago delivered the following top list of socially responsible companies: Dell, Gap, General Mills, Hewlett–Packard, Intel, Southwest Airlines, Starbucks, Timberland.[1] But the following bleak glosses could easily be added: Dell (fined $100 million for an accounting scandal), Gap (accused of sourcing from child sweatshops), General Mills (seems scandal free recently), Hewlett–Packard (CEO resigned on charges of sexual harassment), Intel (fined a record $1.44 billion for monopoly abuse), Southwest Airlines (serious issue about safety of more than one hundred planes), Starbucks (water waste scandal), Timberland (seems scandal free for now).

How social and how responsible is socially responsible investment really? Investment funds are not governments. But when they decide to limit consumer freedom of choice by eliminating assets that they deem unethical, they interfere. And when many of them interfere—or when citizens are forced into particular investment schemes because of the way retirement planning is organized—we should expect the arguments for such forms of interference to be high calibre. What arguments do responsible investors have? And how good are they? The answer is that their arguments are often not very good. In this chapter I give an overview of some of the reasoning behind SRI and look into two cases: the alcohol industry (to illustrate some of the claims defended here) and climate-change risks (and ways for firms to provide information about them).

Socially Responsible Investment

To get some feel for the matter, let us first consider some of the strategies SRI professionals deploy. A quick overview of the phenomenon of *shareholder*

The Business of Liberty. Boudewijn de Bruin, Oxford University Press.
© Boudewijn de Bruin (2022). DOI: 10.1093/oso/9780198839675.003.0006

democracy gives us the background information about responsible investing that we need before we can proceed. This term is used to denote the ideal that individuals and institutions holding equity in a corporation should participate in corporate decision-making.[2]

How far shareholder democracy extends is largely a matter of the rights and duties that come with the status of shareholder. Shareholders are often depicted as the 'owners' of the corporation. But, unlike ownership of a house, ownership of equity is extremely fragmented. Most firms are owned by a great many different shareholders. As shares are generally easily transferable, corporate ownership changes continuously. Unlike a house, a firm is controlled by a board of directors to which the shareholders have delegated management. The owners themselves are involved in decision-making only from a great distance. As a result, the rights of shareholders are a far cry from what most people think of when they think of ownership rights. This truncated form of ownership does not entail that shareholders have to sit idly. As a shareholder, you have, among other things, the right to vote in the general meeting, the right to obtain information from the company, and the right to file lawsuits against management.[3]

Shareholders sometimes exercise these rights with quite a bit of vigour. *Activist shareholders* may actively try to influence corporate decision-making by discussing issues with management, by getting shareholder resolutions accepted, and by starting legal action against managers. Such activists come in many stripes, as Russell Sparkes notes.[4] For, while some of these activists are motivated only by financial concerns—think of Gordon Gekko's notorious 'Greed is Good' speech in Oliver Stone's *Wall Street*—others want to use their rights to voice concerns about environmental and social issues. It is here that socially responsible investment starts. It includes such things as advocacy campaigning, engagement, and dialogue with management, which all seem to make a lot of sense to begin with.[5] If something is amiss with the firm you (partly) own, then why not exercise your right to influence policy?

Yet the more common SRI model is different. It involves investors putting so-called *negative screens* on companies—that is, to divest from them, or not to invest in them in the first place.[6] Almost all large American social investors, for instance, have a negative screen on tobacco, and many screen against alcohol.[7] In the finance literature, screens involving the alcohol, gambling, and tobacco industries are most often considered, but other negative screens can be found excluding the sex industry, defence, firms with abortion and birth-control issues, or with animal-rights issues, firms that rely on child labour somewhere in their supply chain, firms that struggle with environmental hazards, or are involved in production or sales of nuclear power, or firms that have employee rights issues.[8] Next to negative screens, SRI investors use *positive screens*, aimed at selecting firms that are progressive with respect to social and environmental criteria such as green technology, gender and ethnic diversity, workplace democracy, and so on.

An alternative technique used by SRI investors is that of *relative selection*.[9] Rather than excluding firms or entire sectors upfront, a 'best-in-class' approach is used, according to which firms are selected that score best among their sector competitors on the relevant criteria. The well-known Dow Jones Sustainability Index uses such an approach and is based on work by SAM Sustainability Investing, now part of S&P Global.[10] The technique of relative selection does not use negative screening, witness some of the Sustainability Leaders of 2020: Thai Beverage (alcohol), Las Vegas Sands (casino & gaming), and British American Tobacco (tobacco).

Effects of Social Responsibility

Practitioners sometimes believe there are reasons other than moral ones to identify SRI funds. They claim that in the long run SRI funds fare better than regular funds. In an insightful handbook chapter, Lloyd Kurtz casts doubt on this claim.[11] He observes that, for an SRI fund to do better than regular funds, it would have to satisfy two conditions. First, the higher levels of corporate social responsibility of a company selected by the fund would have to add significant economic value to the company over time. Secondly, financial markets would largely have to fail to perceive this added value. Kurtz claims that, even if the first condition holds—there is evidence it does—it is unlikely that the second condition also holds. Financial markets already expect above average growth from companies selected by SRI funds, which has the consequence that the added economic value is already reflected in the price of the shares. SRI funds are just as good financially speaking as regular funds.

Before we proceed, it is instructive to consider the mirror image of SRI funds: *vice funds* and *sin stocks*, including alcohol, tobacco, gambling, defence, nuclear power, and others. But the question of whether such funds do better has not received much scholarly attention to date. In an influential article, Harrison Hong and Marvin Kacpercsyk provide evidence that for the years 1965–2006 sin stocks had higher expected returns than comparable regular shares; they outperformed comparable shares by 29 basis points per month.[12] Plainly put, and combining their findings with those of Kurtz, the conclusion seems to be warranted that one may not so much lose by investing in SRI funds, but that one may gain by singling out shares that are the opposite of SRI.

Alcohol Industry

This chapter considers one of these sin stocks: the alcohol industry. One reason for this focus is that, when it comes to this industry, the strategies and arguments that SRI funds and SRI professionals put forward come farthest apart from how, from a liberal point of view, one should hope investors to assume their personal social responsibilities.

Alcohol shares are widely considered in SRI quarters as a sin stock par excellence, as one of the 'Triumvirate of Sin', alongside gambling and tobacco. In fact, alcohol is arguably the first industry to have felt the rebuke of SRI investors. The first SRI investors *avant la lettre* were the Methodists. Around 1750, John Wesley, the founder of the Wesleyan–Methodist Society, composed a sermon entitled 'The Use of Money'.[13] Wesley started from the assumption that there is nothing inherently wrong with gaining money, but only potentially with the way money is used. Wesley described money as 'an excellent gift of God' and encouraged his flock to 'gain all you can'.[14] Importantly, however, he introduced further principles qualifying this maxim: make sure that your money-making does not endanger your own life (and health and mind), nor the life (health and mind) of another. Wesley makes abundantly clear that investing in alcohol is, according to him, fully incompatible with Methodist preaching, for producers and sellers of alcohol 'murder his Majesty's subjects' and 'drive them to hell, like sheep'.[15] For Wesley, there is consequently no engagement or dialogue with the alcohol industry, no advocacy campaigning, but simply a plain negative screen.

A quick scan of the coverage by the *Financial Times* and the *Wall Street Journal* of the ten largest beer companies and the ten largest spirits companies over the period from 2001 to 2020 reveals that, about 270 years later, ethically motivated shareholder activism in the alcohol industry is still rare. A large number of SRI investors completely exclude the alcohol indus-try, irrespective of the particular company, kind of beverage, approach to marketing, or the company's environmental, social, or governance record, and irrespective of whether the company is involved in alcohol manu-facturing, licensing, retailing, or in the manufacturing of products that are a prerequisite for the production of alcoholic beverages, or whether the company owns an alcohol company, or whether it is being owned (as a company) by an alcohol company. Any company reeking of alcohol will rather be shunned. While shareholder activism in the alcohol indus-try addresses the common themes of executive remuneration, corporate strategy, mergers and acquisitions, and ineffective competition, genuine shareholder activism addressing environmental and social issues is almost entirely absent.

Investors

When it comes to defending negative screens, many SRI funds and in-vestors adopt a decidedly syncretic approach: a mix of private, public, utilitarian, virtue theoretical, and religious opinions and intuitions, not without a steady concern for financial profitability. Often they boil down to a concern either for common goods or for religious values, and hence I distinguish two arguments below: an argument from common goods and an argument from religious values. Before considering the merit of these arguments, let me give two reasons why it is important to do so. Both have to do with investor freedom.

First, many people invest parts of their wealth privately on the stock mar-ket (or in other assets). Most of us lack the time and skills to select portfolios ourselves, and so we use investment funds run by professionals. If we are indifferent vis-à-vis SRI, then any fund will do, and our only consideration will be financial. But, if we want our money to be invested in line with our principles, we need to find a fund that invests according to these princi-ples. If funds select assets based on flawed arguments—as I am going to show below—then it may become difficult or impossible to find an optimal investment fund.

The force of the point I am making here may not seem very strong if ultimately what SRI funds want to offer should be left to them to decide. A liberal cannot complain that their preferred ice-cream flavour is not

sold. A second and independent reason why arguments for specific negative screens should be examined more closely is, however, that, when
they are used by institutional investors, consumers may no longer have so
much freedom to move their money elsewhere. In many countries people
have little or no influence on how their retirement planning contributions
are invested (or what banks do with their deposits, or insurance companies with the premiums). As pension funds, commercial banks, insurance
companies—and even the European Central Bank—are increasingly embracing SRI principles, they are effectively forcing their views about what it
is right to invest in on members, clients, and citizens.[16]

Underscoring this, Hong and Kacperczyk found decisive evidence that
pension funds, university endowments, foundations, religious organizations, banks, insurance companies, and other investors with relatively high
public exposure and scrutiny invest less in sin stocks than investors such
as mutual and hedge funds that operate more in the margins. Even though
the authors are cautious enough not to attribute their findings to the influence of SRI explicitly, they do take their data to show that investors with
high public visibility are more constrained by norms than others.[17] I am
not saying that avoiding sin stocks never makes sense. A pension fund for
doctors divesting from the tobacco industry may be praiseworthy. But we
should tread with great care here, knowing that opinions about ethics can
come widely apart.

Argument from Common Goods

Here is a first argument investors use for SRI, the argument from common
goods. In abstract terms it can be found in the writings of such authors as
Lloyd Kurtz and Steven Lydenberg.[18] Following Kurtz's presentation, the
starting point of this argument is the so-called *Adam Smith problem* or
dilemma.[19]

One horn of the dilemma is formed by the morality of Smith's time,
which emphasized the importance of altruism, benevolence, and other
moral norms and values, and was allegedly propounded in *The Theory of
Moral Sentiments*. The other horn is inspired by the views of writers such
as Bernard Mandeville and Thomas Hobbes and amounts to the view that
it is egoism and self-interest that motivate our actions, a view also (and
caricaturally) associated with *The Wealth of Nations*. Applied to SRI, the

Adam Smith dilemma is: should we be egoists and seek the highest expected returns (given some level of risk we are willing to accept), or should we be altruists and forgo some expected payoffs for the sake of the common good?

You might think that Smith's invisible hand offers a way out. Echoing Mandeville's maxim that private vices lead to public benefits, Smith's idea was that markets work best when egoistic individuals act in their own interests, as then an invisible hand will ensure the most efficient production of common goods. But this solution to the Adam Smith problem comes with a cost for the SRI investor. Critics of SRI typically allege that, if the invisible hand is working well, there is no need for SRI in the first place, because the actual market outcome is then already the best possible world. Exit SRI.

Steven Lydenberg, co-founder of KLD Research & Analytics, an important player in the SRI industry, agrees in principle. But he thinks that the invisible hand needs a bit of help from investors and consumers. Slightly hyperbolically, he claims that it is these stakeholders who constitute the invisible hand, 'steering' corporations 'towards the public interest'.[20] The idea is that, while businesspeople themselves will indeed merely be guided by egoism and self-interest, without any intention of promoting common goods, their egoism is offset by the actions of stakeholders forcing business to promote the common good. This, in a nutshell, is the argument from common goods.

Problem of Effectiveness

The argument from common goods faces two serious problems: one concerns effectiveness, the other concerns legitimacy. The issue of effectiveness is not new and can be dealt with swiftly. The idea is that the generation of common goods often involves concerted actions from many sorts of actors besides the one single company whose SRI standing we evaluate: other corporations, consumers, governments, and non-profit organizations, often with radically opposing interests, and with differing moral and political ideologies. The most effective unit of policy if we want to address, say, climate change is certainly not going to be one specific oil company or airline. Only focusing on one corporation with its stakeholders most certainly reduces the effectiveness of SRI. I should emphasize that this first point of criticism tends to be taken on board in the SRI community—for instance, when SRI initiatives target entire industries, or work with portfolios of green technologies and their ilk.

Problem of Legitimacy

Still a second problem remains. Here it is. The link between the common good and the interests and concerns of shareholders and consumers is empirically tenuous and politically hard to justify. What counts as a common good in a particular society is often a contested issue, and it is generally to be preferred that democratic decision-making procedures determine what things should count as a common good. Leaving such decisions to stakeholder groups risks diminishing democratic legitimacy, in particular in a world in which around 70 per cent of the shares are owned by institutional rather than individual investors.

This point is reinforced by two observations. One is made by Ronald Mitchell, Bradley Agle, and Donna Wood.[21] These scholars observed that how salient a stakeholder is in the eyes of relevant decision makers (here: investors) is determined by the stakeholder's power, the perceived legitimacy of the claims they have against the company, and the perceived urgency of these claims. The concerns of more powerful stakeholders with greater perceived legitimacy and urgency are naturally more likely to be taken into account by managers, investors, and the general public.

The second observation comes from Thomas Jones and centres round the concept of moral intensity.[22] The moral intensity of an issue depends on the following range of properties: the magnitude of the consequences of the actions involved in the issue; the probability with which these consequences arise; the question of whether these consequences are concentrated on some specific and salient group of people, or dispersed across society; the question of whether there is consensus in society about the ethical prescriptions and proscriptions that should guide decision-making on the issue; and, finally, the question of whether the consequences of the actions are close to the evaluating agent in a social, cultural, psychological, physical, and/or temporal sense (temporal immediacy and proximity). Jones observed that the attention an ethical issue receives is proportional to its moral intensity.

It is certainly true that democratic decision-making does not guarantee that issues with high salience and moral intensity are privileged over less easily identified, or less popular, ethical causes. But there is at the minimum an attempt to afford the views of every citizen a hearing. Mechanisms forcing decision makers to consider stakeholders with justified claims of low salience and low moral intensity are, however, largely missing. Firms and SRI investors are free to determine what they consider to be relevant and justified stakeholder claims.

A Society of Teetotallers?

The alcohol industry provides a good example of legitimacy and effectiveness issues. I consider legitimacy first. It is beyond any reasonable doubt that alcohol abuse constitutes a sizeable global health issue, and many countries have adopted such tactics as excise taxes, licensing laws, advertising restrictions, minimum purchasing age, maximum traveller import allowances, education, and public information, or have restricted sales by such means as the Swedish *systembolag*, a state shop with a monopoly for selling alcohol.

Yet few countries have banned the production, sales, and consumption of alcohol altogether, and those that have banned it, have done so mostly for religious reasons rather than for reasons of some common good. Only in a few countries would democratic legitimacy be obtained for complete prohibition. This means that it is a dubious move for an SRI fund to adopt a negative screen on alcohol if the reason is that they want to contribute to the realization of some common good. Rather than contributing to a common good, investors divesting from the alcohol industry should be thought of as being committed to realizing a world without alcohol. Such a world is not seen as embodying a common good in most democracies, and hence the argument from common goods is unsuccessful in defending a negative screen on alcohol.

The second problem of the argument from common goods is that of effectiveness. It lies in the assumption that, when investors and consumers 'steer' the corporation, as Lydenberg and others maintain, the self-interested behaviour of the corporation (or its directors, managers and employees) will lead to public benefits. This is not generally true. To foster common goods, corporations have to act together with consumers, governments, and other stakeholders. Often they will do so only if they are so forced by law. Common goods need coordinated action. To see this, suppose, for the sake of argument, that decreasing the number of

alcohol-related deaths is a common good and that price regulation of alcoholic beverages is a sufficiently effective way to reduce mortality related
to alcohol (as it seems to be). Still, under such assumptions, it would be ut-
terly perverse to ask the stakeholders that Lydenberg focuses on (investors
and consumers) to steer a particular brewery or bottle factory into raising
its prices. This would put the company at an unfair, or at least unreasonable,
competitive disadvantage, which it is unlikely to accept.

If democratic support can be obtained for intervention with the pricing of alcoholic beverages in order to contribute to the common good of
decreasing alcohol-related mortality, considerations of efficiency and equity require that such intervention ought to maintain a level playing field
for all players in the alcohol industry. Consequently, it will have to be
the result of government intervention (by means of excise taxes, for instance) or from self-regulation of the entire industry. The argument from
common goods puts unreasonable and unrealistic demands on individual
companies.

Argument from Religious Values

The failure of the argument from common goods to undergird a negative
screen on alcohol does not entail that an individual investor may not have
good personal reasons to withdraw from the alcohol industry altogether.
This brings us to the argument from religious values. This is John Wesley's
line, and that of the Pax Fund, a Methodist fund, the first SRI fund in the
US. Even though individual investors can consistently use this argument
to defend completely ignoring the alcohol industry, institutional investors
have to exercise more care. As long as individual investors can voluntarily
select a fund (as for the Pax Fund), and the fund is explicit about its screens,
there is nothing morally objectionable about the fund's using religious values to back its selection criteria. But, if the relation between the individual
and the institutional investor is not voluntary, religious convictions of the
institutional investor are forced upon individuals with potentially different views. This is the case with pension funds, healthcare plans, insurance
companies, some commercial banks, and the European Central Bank. As
a result, the argument from religious values is a valid defence of a negative screen on alcohol only for funds that can be freely chosen by people
accepting the religious values the fund stands for.

Argument from Ethical Issues

If the arguments from common goods and religious values do not work, what should a social investor do instead? Am I not advocating the cynical position that nothing helps, or the nihilist position that nothing matters? Not at all. I am suggesting here an argument from ethical issues. I believe that a far preferable approach to social investing is to zoom in on specific ethical issues, to make them salient and public, to discuss them, to request changes, and sometimes indeed to use the power that institutional investors have to force changes by threatening to pull out by establishing a negative screen. Investors, that is, should be concerned about what happens in the firms they invest in, but it is their personal responsibility to do that.[23]

Marketing Alcohol

Take the alcohol industry again. Alcohol leads to 2.5 million deaths world-wide a year, is often involved in traffic accidents, crime, and child pro-tection cases, may lead to brain damage, decreased IQ, mental problems, addiction, aggression, liver cirrhosis, cancers, weakening of the immune system, and is also implicated in HIV and tuberculosis contagion, among others.[24] There are environmental concerns about the emission of carbon dioxide during fermentation processes, the management of waste (primar-ily the residue of fermentation), water and energy efficiency, packaging (bottles, cans), and shipping. For each bottle of beer, for instance, more than three bottles of water are used during production.[25] And, as Thomas Babor and colleagues argue, there are serious reasons to be concerned about conflicts of interest arising when the alcohol industry collaborates with research institutes, non-governmental organizations, or governmen-tal agencies, as this may inflate findings considerably.[26]

From a liberal point of view, however, we should be significantly more worried about some of the marketing practices that the industry uses, in-volving as they do ethically questionable sales techniques that reinforce gender stereotypes, create artificial wants, and target vulnerable consumers. Take stereotypes, for instance. There is evidence that the alcohol indus-try is quite heavily dependent on using sexual imagery in its advertise-ments to obtain consumer attention.[27] Nevertheless, there seems to be little evidence that alcohol marketing campaigns provide unacceptably stereotypical pictures of gender differences. Advertisements for washing detergents, pizzas, and instant dry soups and sauce mixes, to name a few, portray men and women in far more stereotypical fashion. And perhaps it might work the other way round: the conscious decision of marketers to treat men and women equally as potential consumers of alcohol and tobacco from the 1920s onwards may well have made several stereotypes disappear.[28]

But not all is well. A notorious case of questionable sales techniques involved so-called *beer girls* in Cambodia, where young women represent and promote certain beer brands in local pubs. More than 75 per cent of these women regularly and systematically supplement their income with paid sex, with a significantly increased risk of HIV. Breweries have, however, too long been reticent in countering these practices.[29] More outspoken shareholder advocacy should be more than justified.

Vulnerable Consumers

This brings us to what is arguably the most important ethical issue in alcohol marketing, and one that tends to be somewhat overlooked in the ethics literature: marketing of alcohol to minors. In particular, the topic of *alcopops* (flavoured alcoholic beverages also called *ready to drinks* or *malternatives*) such as Smirnoff Ice and Bacardi Breezer has not had as much attention as it should have had. Alcopops provide young consumers with a sweet alternative to beer. Such alternatives had been available already before. Think, for instance, of ciders, sweetened wines, flavoured beers. But these were hardly seen as premium products, did not typically feature such tastes as *grand melón, black razz, torched cherry, peach red*, or *wolf berry*. They were not sold in cans hardly distinguishable from soft drinks. And importantly—and unlike the alcopops—the ciders, sweetened wines, and flavoured beers had a clear alcoholic taste. Marketing alcopops, Diageo (of Smirnoff) and Anheuser–Busch (of Bacardi) were very successful in combining, on the one hand, a premium brand name with a hard liquor image with, on the other hand, something sweet that does not taste like alcohol, is sold in supermarkets, and is classified and taxed as beer.

Some observers might object to alcopops on such grounds as that the creation of artificial desires is ethically problematic, as John Kenneth Galbraith famously thought.[30] We have already encountered this when we discussed neuromarketing in Chapter 2. But, for an argument à la Galbraith to have minimal plausibility, one should be able to distinguish acceptable from unacceptable preference changes. This is difficult. Is a preference for, say, a touchscreen device an artificial want, created by Apple? I do not think a sufficiently widely embraced criterion can be developed here, and, even if it can, I believe that it is very hard to find a convincing argument showing there is something inherently wrong with designing a new kind of alcoholic beverage.

Alcopops: A Launch Pad for a 'Drinking Career'?

Alcopops are, however, ethically problematic for a different reason, which has to do with the phenomenon of target marketing. Market segmentation is an important contemporary marketing strategy, as it aims at finding significant and relevant differences between consumers and at targeting products at specific and sufficiently similar segments. When a segment contains vulnerable consumers, or when the products are seen as harmful, however, an ordinarily acceptable marketing strategy may become unethical.[31]

It is widely accepted among marketers that generally children and young adults must be treated as vulnerable consumers because they lack the capacity for full rational decision-making. The same applies *mutatis mutandis* to the elderly, people suffering from mental illness, and possibly other categories of consumers. Moreover, there is overwhelming evidence that non-targeted, general alcohol marketing contributes to underage drinking.[32] Watching alcohol commercials on television, exposure to advertisements in magazines, exposure to displays of alcoholic beverages in supermarkets and other stores, possession of alcohol merchandise (key rings, wallets), alcohol consumption in films—all these factors are correlated with early initiation of alcohol consumption.[33] But in the ethics literature the claim that the marketing of alcopops constitutes an unethical form of targeted marketing does not yet seem to have been defended.[34]

Even though research on alcopops is rather scant, a number of important findings underscore my claim that these drinks form an important ethical challenge to the industry. First of all, underage drinkers are a very significant source of revenue for the alcohol industry. An American study conducted by Susan Foster and colleagues estimated that underage drinkers (12–20 years of age) consume about 20 per cent of the total number of drinks consumed.[35] By itself, this is no evidence of targeted marketing. But alcopops are particularly attractive to consumers inexperienced with the taste of alcohol, because the flavouring hides the taste of alcohol.[36] Smirnoff Ice, for instance, tastes just like a variant of bitter lemon, the soft drink. The industry acknowledges as much:

> The beauty of this category [of beverages] is that it brings in new drinkers, people who really don't like the taste of beer.[37]

A study among Swiss children aged 13–16 years revealed that alcopops are often consumed in addition to other alcoholic drinks rather than replacing them. One research report from the UK Brewing Research Company argued that

> along with lager, [alcopops] are the launching pad for most young peoples drinking career.[38]

This is underscored by studies about taste development showing that earlier exposure to certain tastes raises the likelihood that similar tastes will be accepted later on. Again in the words of the UK Brewing Research Company, alcopops diminish the 'natural barrier of the strong and often unpleasant taste of alcohol against experimentation'.[39] Unsurprisingly, there is evidence that certain brewers and distillers actively perform marketing research among 15–17-year-olds.[40]

A Clean Conscience?

The argument from ethical issues I have proposed here is an alternative to the arguments from common goods and religious values. Applied to the case at hand, it would lead to the idea that social investors should not divest from the alcohol industry. Pension funds, university endowments, SRI funds, and the like should rather engage more actively with the alcohol industry. The argument from ethical issues gives such investors greater freedom in that the range of assets they can select is significantly larger than those for investors that have negative screens in place. But this freedom does not come cheaply. It comes with the responsibility to take action.

One additional reason to favour the argument from ethical issues is that it quite naturally adds support to the idea that firms should have a duty to provide information that enables investors to investigate ethical issues. Since such information will have to be communicated openly, it will as a matter of fact become common knowledge among the investing public, of which we have seen the benefits in Chapter 4. Whether current regulation is consistent with this idea is something I turn to shortly.

Another attraction of the argument from ethical issues is that engaging with corporations as well as campaigning for higher ethical standards is, with respect to such issues, often more effective than divesting. The divestment strategy, as sometimes embodied in the arguments from common goods and religious values, clears one's conscience; it gives investors a sense of having clean hands. But the feeling of a clean conscience may be spurious when, for instance, divesting creates room for less scrupulous investors; for, if financiers leave a company as soon as it engages in activities they deem unethical, only those investors remain who see no wrong in the corporate strategy. Unless the number of retreating investors is so large as to leave the company underfunded, the effect may well be that the directors of the company never have explicitly to confront the issue. No questions will be raised at the annual general meeting; no lawsuits will be filed; no discussions with management about alternatives will be held. If the industry is left to investors who do not care about ethics at all, we may be even further from home, ethically speaking.

Altogether, then, my claim is that the argument from ethical issues offers the most promising route to afford investors to assume their personal responsibility without compromising their freedom. In order to generate the value afforded by these arguments, however, we need known freedom. That was the lesson from Chapter 1. To see how that works in practice is something to which I now turn.

Informing Investors about the Risks of Climate Change

It is not too difficult to gain information about alcopops for most investors. Just have a look around you in the supermarket and do some straightforward searching on the Internet. For many potential ethical issues, however, retrieving reliable information is far more difficult. This is particularly true for what is arguably the most daunting ethical issue of our times: climate change. What a sustainable company is, and what we need to know about it to form accurate judgements here, remains quite elusive. Here it is interesting to see that lawmakers have gradually realized that investors may need reliable information about climate-related risks of firms they invest in, but that disclosure of such information will not be forthcoming if it is left to the discretion of corporate management. Here, as with more standard *financial* accounting information, a legal framework has to be in place to compel firms to disclose information about climate-related risks.

Some European developments in the 2010s are worth considering as an example of the legal techniques by means of which the epistemic assumptions that underlie the arguments from desire satisfaction and personal responsibility can be put to work. Consider the UK. The UK Stewardship Code determines principles to 'effective stewardship' for asset managers, asset owners, and further financial service providers, which includes such institutional investors as occupational pension schemes and insurers.[41] Principle 7 of the Code, for instance, requires that such investors will 'systematically integrate stewardship and investment, including material environmental, social and governance issues, and climate change, to fulfil their responsibilities'.[42] And, to demonstrate that they have fulfilled these obligations, these investors 'should explain how information gathered through stewardship has informed acquisition, monitoring and exit decisions, either directly or on their behalf, and with reference to how they have best served clients and/or beneficiaries'.[43]

It is not hard to see here a requirement to justify investment decisions by referring to the consequences of both the selected and the deselected investments, and as such a requirement for investors to be accountable for their investment decisions.[44] But, to assume responsibility, these investors need to know what they invest in and divest from. As Emily Webster notes, however, such information may not always be available and sufficiently reliable.[45] She attributes this to the fact that there seems to be no genuine mandatory requirement for directors of a company to disclose the relevant information.[46] While the larger companies are required under the Companies Act 2006 to disclose non-financial information in the annual report, which includes information about 'environmental matters', it is not further specified what that would mean, apart from saying that this should include information about 'the impact of the company's business on the environment'.[47] The Financial Reporting Council further clarifies this in a guidance that it has developed, stating that the report should answer such questions as: 'Will the entity's business be affected by climate change, either as a result of regulation or climate change affecting how the business can operate? What are the effects of an entity's activities on climate change?'[48] However, as Webster diagnoses, 'the current governance requirements are not adequate for promoting quality disclosures', and she approvingly cites the Green Finance Task Force to the effect that 'only if reporting is mandatory are we likely to see comprehensive and comparable risk disclosures'.[49]

Webster's concern is mostly that this soft-law, non-binding, approach fails to be effective in stimulating behavioural changes necessary to mitigate climate change. My perspective here is rather that a soft-law approach to information disclosure does not afford investors the opportunity to gain the knowledge necessary for satisfying their desires and assuming responsibility. If, as is the position embodied in the UK Stewardship Code, pension funds and insurance companies bear (some) responsibility for the climate risks of the companies they invest in, then clearly these investors should have relevant information about these risks. Reading the argument from responsibility as an argument for known freedom helps one to appreciate this point. One should not endow people or organizations with responsibilities they cannot bear; but to bear responsibility, one needs information.

The example of climate risk disclosures is interesting for another reason as well. This becomes especially clear if we follow Webster and compare the UK initiatives with those in France. According to the French Energy Transition Law 2015, listed companies must disclose such things as the 'financial risks related to climate change and the measures the company takes to reduce them' as well as the 'consequences on climate change of [the company's] activities and of the use of the goods and services it produces'.[50] As Webster observes, this means that, unlike in the UK, in France there is a 'clear, identifiable and consistent obligation' to climate risk disclosure.[51] What is interesting for our purposes, however, is that, also unlike in the UK, the information that companies provide about these climate-change-related risks has to obtain a seal of approval from independent third-party bodies, just as financial information has to be verified by auditors.[52]

Auditors, I believe, should be seen as providing justification to corporate management's statements, where *justification* is meant to be read in its epistemological sense: true beliefs become justified, and may ultimately become knowledge. The reasoning is as follows. Directors clearly have a plethora of disincentives when it comes to stating the truth, about both financial and non-financial risks. Good news will be overstated, bad news understated, repressed, or denied. The requirement to provide the investing public and other interested parties with annual reports is empty if it is not accompanied with a requirement for such reports to be truthful, and the development of the accounting profession over the past two centuries or so reveals that more is needed: someone independent has to check the veracity of the annual report if it is to have any value as a source of information to the investing public. There is a long tradition in auditing financial statements. Such practices as *integrated reporting*, where auditing firms develop standards to verify environmental and climate related risks—or further ethical issues—are, by contrast, still very much under construction. My hope is that this chapter has provided some reasons to support such initiatives.

Notes

1. Lloyd Kurtz, 'Socially Responsible Investment and Shareholder Activism', in Andrew Crane, Dirk Matten, Abagail McWilliams, Jeremy Moon, and Donald S. Siegel (eds), *The Oxford Handbook of Corporate Social Responsibility* (Oxford: Oxford University Press), 249–280, at 266 (poll conducted in 2005). See, generally, Chris Cowton, 'The Development of Ethical Investment Products', in Andreas Prindl and Bimal Prodhan (eds), *Ethical Conflicts in Finance* (Oxford: Oxford University Press, 1994), 213–232, and Chris Cowton, 'Playing by the Rules: Ethical Criteria at an Ethical Investment Fund', *Business Ethics: A European Review*, 8 (1999), 60–69.
2. See, e.g., John Parkinson, *Corporate Power and Responsibility* (Oxford: Oxford University Press, 1993).
3. See Robert Monks and Nell Minow, *Corporate Governance* (Malden: Blackwell, 2004), for further details on shareholder rights.
4. Russell Sparkes, 'Ethical Investment: Whose Ethics, Which Investment?' *Business Ethics: A European Review*, 10 (2001), 194–205.
5. See Craig Mackenzie, 'The Choice of Criteria in Ethical Investment', *Business Ethics: A European Review*, 7 (1998), 81–86, on dialogue, Anastasia O'Rourke, 'A New Politics of Engagement: Shareholder Activism for Corporate Social Responsibility', *Business Strategy and the Environment*, 12 (2003), 227–239, on engagement, and Russell Sparkes, 'Ethical Investment: Whose Ethics, Which Investment?' *Business Ethics: A European Review*, 10 (2001), 194–205, on advocacy campaigning.

6. Pieter Jan Trinks and Bert Scholtens, 'The Opportunity Cost of Negative Screening in Socially Responsible Investing', *Journal of Business Ethics*, 140 (2017), 193–208, show that there are substantial opportunity costs to negative screening, arising from the restriction of the universe of investment objects.

7. Social Investment Forum Foundation, *Report on US Sustainable and Impact Investing Trends 2020*, www.ussif.org/files/Trends%20Report%202020%20Executive%20Summary.pdf [perma.cc/3C47-923Z].

8. See, e.g., Andrew Crane, Dirk Matten, Sarah Glozer, and Laura Spence, *Business Ethics: Managing Corporate Citizenship and Sustainability in the Age of Globalization* (5th edn; Oxford: Oxford University Press, 2016), 262–274, for a thorough overview of these issues.

9. See, generally, Céline Louche and Steven Lydenberg, 'Responsible Investing', in John Boatright (ed.), *Finance Ethics: Critical Issues in Theory and Practice* (Hoboken: Wiley, 2010), 393–417.

10. S&P Global Switzerland, *The Sustainability Yearbook 2020*, www.spglobal.com/esg/csa/yearbook/files/482663_RobecoSAM-Year-Book_Final_med.pdf [perma.cc/6DCE-CVQH].

11. Lloyd Kurtz, 'Socially Responsible Investment and Shareholder Activism', in Andrew Crane, Dirk Matten, Abagail McWilliams, Jeremy Moon, and Donald S. Siegel (eds), *The Oxford Handbook of Corporate Social Responsibility* (Oxford: Oxford University Press), 249–280. See, generally, Steven May, George Cheney, and Juliet Roper (eds), *The Debate over Corporate Social Responsibility* (New York: Oxford University Press, 2009). Michael Hannis, *Freedom and Environment: Autonomy, Human Flourishing and the Political Philosophy of Sustainability* (London: Routledge, 2016), uses, among others, theories of liberalism and virtue ethics to develop a theory of ecological human rights, with important repercussions for business.

12. Harrison Hong and Marvin Kacpercsyk, 'The Price of Sin: The Effects of Social Norms on Markets', *Journal of Financial Economics*, 93 (2009), 15–36.

13. John Wesley, 'Sermon L: The Use of Money', in *The Works of John Wesley: Volume VI* (London: John Mason, 1856), 117–128.

14. Ibid. 119.

15. Ibid. 121.

16. Some commentators argue that the ECB (and perhaps other institutions) have a legal obligation to avoid certain asset classes. See, e.g., Jens van 't Klooster, *The ECB's Conundrum and 21st Century Monetary Policy: How European Monetary Policy can be Green, Social and Democratic*, Finanzwende/Heinrich-Böll-Foundation, 2021, transformative-responses.org/wp-content/uploads/2021/01/TR_Report_vant-Klooster_FINAL.pdf [perma.cc/L88X-AW9C]. One line of defence might be to observe that the ECB was designed to contribute to the

realization of the goals described in article 127(1) of the Treaty on the functioning of the European Union ('It shall work for the sustainable development of Europe' based among other things on 'a high level of protection and improvement of the quality of the environment'), in conjunction with article 3(3) of the Treaty on the European Union. It is to be foreseen that European courts will have to address these issues. Note that the typical definition of sin stock does not have an environmental or climate-change component as yet. As Van 't Klooster notes, treaties can also be changed. Ibid. 18 ff.

17. Harrison Hong and Marvin Kacpercsyk, 'The Price of Sin: The Effects of Social Norms on Markets', *Journal of Financial Economics*, 93 (2009), 15–36. Cf. Sadok El Ghoul, Omrane Guedhami, Chuck Kwok, and Dev Mishra, 'Does Corporate Social Responsibility Affect the Cost of Capital?', *Journal of Banking and Finance*, 35 (2011), 2388–2406, for evidence that alcohol may not be significantly related to cost of capital.

18. Lloyd Kurtz, 'Socially Responsible Investment and Shareholder Activism', in Andrew Crane, Dirk Matten, Abagail McWilliams, Jeremy Moon, and Donald S. Siegel (eds), *The Oxford Handbook of Corporate Social Responsibility* (Oxford: Oxford University Press), 249–280, and Steven Lydenberg, *Corporations and the Public Interest: Guiding the Invisible Hand* (San Francisco: Berrett–Koehler Publishers, 2005).

19. Lloyd Kurtz, 'Socially Responsible Investment and Shareholder Activism', in Andrew Crane, Dirk Matten, Abagail McWilliams, Jeremy Moon, and Donald S. Siegel (eds), *The Oxford Handbook of Corporate Social Responsibility* (Oxford: Oxford University Press), 249–280, at 256, attributes the Adam Smith problem to Joseph Schumpeter. Cf. James Otteson, 'The Recurring "Adam Smith Problem"', *History of Philosophy Quarterly*, 17 (2000), 51–74, for earlier sources.

20. Steven Lydenberg, *Corporations and the Public Interest: Guiding the Invisible Hand* (San Francisco: Berrett–Koehler Publishers, 2005), 107.

21. Ronald Mitchell, Bradley Agle, and Donna Wood, 'Toward a Theory of Stakeholder Salience: Defining the Principle of Who and What Really Counts', *Academy of Management Review*, 22 (1997), 853–886.

22. Thomas Jones, 'Ethical Decision Making by Individuals in Organizations: An Issue-Contingent Model', *Academy of Management Review*, 16 (1991), 366–395.

23. See Deepak Lal, *Reviving the Invisible Hand: The Case for Classical Liberalism in the Twenty-First Century* (Princeton: Princeton University Press, 2006), for a vigorous defence of liberalism with applications to free trade, financial markets, and sustainability, without, however, focusing on the informational aspects relevant to business ethics.

24. World Health Organization, *Global Status Report on Alcohol and Health 2018*, apps.who.int/iris/bitstream/handle/10665/274603/9789241 565639-eng.pdf [perma.cc/C72A-UUQD]. For benefits derived from alcohol consumption, see Stanton Peele, 'Exploring Psychological Benefits Associated with Moderate Alcohol Use: A Necessary Corrective to Assessments of Drinking Outcomes?', *Drug and Alcohol Dependence*, 60 (2000), 221–247, and, for economic effects, Christine Godfrey, 'The Financial Costs and Benefits of Alcohol', *Institute of Alcohol Studies: The Globe*, 2 (2004), www.ias.org.uk/What-we-do/Publication-archive/The-Globe/Issue-2-2004-amp-1-2004/The-financial-costs-and-benefits-of-alcohol-Christine-Godfrey.aspx [perma.cc/DD7X-XQPH].

25. Heineken N.V., *Heineken Annual Report 2019*, www.theheinekencompany.com/sites/theheinekencompany/files/Investors/financial-information/results-reports-presentations/heineken-nv-hnv-2019-annual-report.pdf [perma.cc/6LQR-XGA9].

26. Thomas Babor, Griffith Edwards, and Tim Stockwell, 'Science and the Drinks Industry: Cause for Concern', *Addiction*, 91 (1996), 5–9. See Catherine DeAngelis and Phil Fontanarosa, 'Impugning the Integrity of Medical Science: The Adverse Effects of Industry Influence', *JAMA* 299 (2008), 1833–1835, for an argument involving a perhaps broader range of research findings.

27. Michael Robert Solomon, Richard Ashmore, and Laura Longo, 'The Beauty Match-Up Hypothesis: Congruence between Types of Beauty and Product Images in Advertising', *Journal of Advertising*, 21 (2013), 23–34. I ignore the relevance of the literature on epistemic injustice on gender stereotype here, which might show an additional ethical issue with such marketing. See, generally, Miranda Fricker, *Epistemic Injustice: Power and the Ethics of Knowing* (Oxford: Oxford University Press, 2007), and see Boudewijn de Bruin, 'Epistemic Injustice in Finance', *Topoi*, 40 (2021), 755–763, for related observations about marketing of financial services.

28. Cheryl Krasnick Warsh, 'Smoke and Mirrors: Gender Representation in North American Tobacco and Alcohol Advertisements Before 1950', *Histoire sociale: Social History*, 32 (1999), 183–222.

29. Samantha Marshall and Steve Stecklow, 'Cambodia's "Beer Girls" Peddle the Product and Endure the Hassle', *Wall Street Journal*, 31 May 2000, www.wsj.com/articles/SB959726436649225479 [perma.cc/E3Z2-WGM2]. See also Andrea Kim, Ly Penh Sun, Chhea Chhorvann, Christina Lindan, Frits van Griensven, Peter Kilmarx, Pachara Sirivongrangson, Janice Louie, Hor Bun Leng, Kimberly Page-Shafer, 'High Prevalence of HIV and Sexually Transmitted Infections among Indirect Sex Workers in Cambodia', *Sexually Transmitted Diseases*, 32 (2005), 745–751.

30. John Kenneth Galbraith, *The Affluent Society* (Boston: Houghton Mifflin Company, 1958).
31. See, e.g., Craig Smith and Elizabeth Cooper-Martin, 'Ethics and Target Marketing: The Role of Product Harm and Consumer Vulnerability', *Journal of Marketing*, 61 (1997), 1–20.
32. Michael Mazis, Debra Jones Ringold, Elgin Perry, Daniel Denman, 'Perceived Age and Attractiveness of Models in Cigarette Advertisements', *Journal of Marketing*, 56 (1992), 22–37.
33. See Peter Anderson, Avalon de Bruijn, Kathryn Angus, Ross Gordon, and Gerard Hastings, 'Impact of Alcohol Advertising and Media Exposure on Adolescent Alcohol Use: A Systematic Review of Longitudinal Studies', *Alcohol and Alcoholism*, 44 (2009), 229–243, for a review of the relevant literature.
34. See Craig Smith and Elizabeth Cooper-Martin, 'Ethics and Target Marketing: The Role of Product Harm and Consumer Vulnerability', *Journal of Marketing*, 61 (1997), 1–20, for marketing to members of ethnic minorities.
35. Susan Foster, Roger Vaughan, William Foster, and Joseph Califano, Jr, 'Alcohol Consumption and Expenditures for Underage Drinking and Adult Excessive Drinking', *JAMA* 289 (2003), 989–995.
36. See, e.g., Kirsty Hughes, Anne Marie MacKintosh, Gerard Hastings, Colin Wheeler, Jonathan Watson, and James Inglis, 'Young People, Alcohol, and Designer Drinks: Quantitative and Qualitative Study', *British Medical Journal*, 314 (1997), 414–418.
37. Marlene Coulis, spokeswoman of Anheuser–Busch, the producer of two bestselling alcopops, Bacardi Silver and Bacardi Breezer, quoted by Hillary Chura, 'Beer Marketing: Brewers Binge on Malt Drinks', *Advertising Age*, 22 April 2002, adage.com/article/news/beer-marketing-brewers-binge-malt-drinks/52361 [perma.cc/WAM7-FY6M].
38. Quoted by Thomas Babor, 'Alcohol Research and the Alcoholic Beverage Industry: Issues Concerns and Conflicts of Interest', *Addiction*, 104 (2009), 39.
39. Quoted by Jan Copeland, Richard Stevenson, Peter Gates, and Paul Dillon, 'Young Australians and Alcohol: The Acceptability of Ready-to-Drink (RTD) Alcoholic Beverages among 12–30-year-olds', *Addiction*, 102 (2007), 1741.
40. Gerard Hastings, Oona Brooks, Martine Stead, Kathryn Angus, Thomas Anker, and Tom Farrell, 'Failure of Self Regulation of UK Alcohol Advertising', *British Medical Journal*, 340 (2010).
41. Financial Reporting Council, *The UK Stewardship Code 2020*, at 7 and 30, www.frc.org.uk/getattachment/5aae591d-d9d3-4cf4-814a-d14e156a1d87/Stewardship-Code_Final2.pdf [perma.cc/RN9W-TD5L].
42. Ibid. 15 (emphasis added).
43. Ibid.
44. Ibid. 7.

45. Emily Webster, 'Information Disclosure and the Transition to a Low-Carbon Economy: Climate-Related Risk in the UK and France', *Journal of Environmental Law*, 32 (2020), 279–308.

46. Ibid. 293–294.

47. Companies Act 2006, s. 414C(7).

48. Financial Reporting Council, *Guidance on the Strategic Report*, at 32, www.frc.org.uk/getattachment/fb05dd7b-c76c-424e-9daf-4293c9fa2d6a/Guidance-on-the-Strategic-Report-31-7-18.pdf [perma.cc/3RZ8-DVB4].

49. Emily Webster, 'Information Disclosure and the Transition to a Low-Carbon Economy: Climate-Related Risk in the UK and France', *Journal of Environmental Law*, 32 (2020), 279–308, at 300, and Environmental Audit Committee, *Greening Finance: Embedding Sustainability in Financial Decision Making (Seventh Report of Session 2017-19)* (HC 2017–2018, 1063), 31, publications.parliament.uk/pa/cm201719/cmselect/cmenvaud/1063/1063.pdf [perma.cc/483L-5PMG].

50. Loi 2015-992 du 17 août 2015 relative à la transition énergétique pour la croissance verte, article 173.

51. Emily Webster, 'Information Disclosure and the Transition to a Low-Carbon Economy: Climate-Related Risk in the UK and France', *Journal of Environmental Law*, 32 (2020), 279–308, at 302.

52. Ibid. 303.

6

Ethics Management and Informed Stakeholders

Despite its plain architecture and slightly unappealing location, the Great or St James's Church in The Hague is one of the best-known churches in the Netherlands. Constantijn and Christiaan Huygens, two prominent representatives of Dutch Renaissance diplomacy and scholarship, were buried here. It is the place where since the early seventeenth century members of the Dutch royal family have been baptized and where royal weddings have taken place. And it boasts an organ that has attracted attention from musicians all over Europe, including Camille Saint-Saëns and Albert Schweitzer.

On 11 January 2013, about five hundred people working in the Dutch financial services industry gathered here, knowing they were part of something truly unique. What was happening? In September 2008 Lehman Brothers had collapsed, and, while the Dutch financial world was not as internationally connected as American or British finance, the crisis seriously hurt. One Dutch bank had to be bailed out, another was nationalized, a third one was forced to merge, and the fourth received a fine of $1 billion after it was discovered that it had been part of a massive scam involving the manipulation of the Libor. In the early days of the crisis, however, Dutch finance was quick and optimistic in its reaction to the events unfolding on Wall Street. About a month after Lehman's collapse, the Dutch Banking Association installed a committee to advise the government on how to respond to the crisis. In early 2009, the committee published a report entitled *Restoring Trust*, which put forward suggestions concerning corporate governance, remuneration policies, risk management, and many other topics.[1] Important parts of the report were turned into law. The resulting Banking Code, published in September 2009, has operated as a code of conduct under the Dutch civil law since January 2010. The suggestions made in the report were not all entirely original, as significant parts were indebted to work carried out by other advisory groups. But it did contain a novelty

The Business of Liberty. Boudewijn de Bruin, Oxford University Press.
© Boudewijn de Bruin (2022). DOI: 10.1093/oso/9780198839675.003.0007

that made the Dutch response to the global financial crisis internationally unique. It recommended that every finance executive should pledge an oath—in bureaucratic parlance, a 'moral and ethical conduct declaration'.[2]

What happened in the church in The Hague in January 2013 was a public ceremony in which key representatives of Dutch finance pledged this oath. They read the text out loud, made relevant gestures, and ended with an appeal to the assistance of God Almighty, or a secular version thereof.

The Oldest Ethics Management Device

It is too easy to set the Dutch Banker's Oath aside as hopelessly naive. And it is probably too cynical to describe it as part of diversionary tactics designed by the finance industry. All the same, I believe there are very good prima facie reasons why we should seriously question the cogency of oaths as instruments to manage corporate cultures. To declare that one will act with integrity, obey the law, put client interests first, keep secret what one has been entrusted, and not abuse one's knowledge—people who follow these prescripts will follow them without an oath, and those who do not follow them will not change their attitude by swearing an oath. Oaths look powerless. And, indeed, while they may well be the oldest ethics instrument—the Hippocratic Oath dates back to 400 BC—they seemed to lose much of their appeal during the twentieth century, except for the Physicians' Oath and the Oath of Office.

Interestingly, however, the Dutch initiative is part of a reinvigoration of oaths, as is witnessed by the fact that we now have the University Manager's Oath, the Fiduciary Oath of the National Association of Personal Financial Advisors, the Financial Hippocratic Oath, the Modelers' Hippocratic Oath, the Banking and Finance Oath, the Asset Manager's Oath, the Microbanker's Oath, the Attorney's Oath, the Engineer's Hippocratic Oath, the Enterprise Architect's Professional Oath, the Oath of the Pharmacist, the Veterinarian's Oath, the Knowledge Engineer's Oath, the Pledge of the Computing Professional, the Public Health Oath, the Social Work Professional Oath, the Scientist's Oath, and the Accountant's Oath.[3] We also have the Economist's Oath, developed by George DeMartino, and, with highest global prominence, the MBA Oath, developed by Max Anderson and Peter Escher in 2010, two Harvard Business School graduates. The MBA Oath has attracted more than twelve thousand signatories (as of early 2021).[4]

I do not think oaths accomplish all they promise. But I believe that they can fulfil important functions once they are crafted as part of carefully designed, more comprehensive approaches to managing ethical culture, epistemic corporate culture in particular. Moreover, a second reason to look into oaths here is that, by investigating more closely what an oath really is, and what its preconditions are, we may gain insights helping organizations to change corporate culture for the better, even if you ultimately think oaths are, well, somewhat silly.

The starting point of my investigation is the platitude that, for a business to thrive, it needs freedom. Laws curtail an enterprise's freedom in the sense that they make certain courses of action highly unattractive. Laws make certain actions costly through punishments, fines, and other credible threats, provided the laws are sufficiently strictly enforced. Ethical climate and culture, personal integrity, moral values, and corporate virtues, by contrast, are meant to steer people towards ethical choices without limiting their freedom. Naturally, approaches based in ethics generate less immediately forceful instruments to influence behaviour than the interventionist approach of changing behaviour by means of fines. Yet it is also true that we cannot do without ethics. We cannot legislate everything away, even if you were to adopt entirely dictatorial management styles. There is a sense in which the freedom to act unethically is an essential given we have to accept, and perhaps even embrace. This underscores why ethical corporate culture is so important. Oaths may help here.

Characteristics of Oaths

So, what is an oath? I use and extend work by Daniel Sulmasy and distinguish seven conditions.[5] A typical professional oath is a promise, with the profession's beneficiaries (often society at large) serving as the promisees. Oaths typically satisfy a number of specific conditions, the effect of which is, I argue, to generate high-quality common knowledge of sorts.

Publicity

Oaths have a highly public character. The example with which I started offers the case in point. It involves a ceremony, in a central and well-known church in the Netherlands, with many people attending, covered by national television and other media. The publicity of an oath also comes to the fore in the way that individual oath-taking is documented. While there is no standard ceremony involved, the MBA Oath, for instance, has a high degree of publicity, because all signatories are listed online. Moreover, even though an oath-taking ceremony is not public in the medical profession, the way this profession is set up in countries such as the Netherlands ensures that (interested) patients know that every medical practitioner has pledged (a version of) the Hippocratic Oath.

Ceremony

The ceremonial aspect of oath-taking reinforces this point. An oath sworn during a ceremony is less easily forgotten than a promise made in between two business meetings, and the ceremonial gestures that often accompany oath-taking may also reinforce recall. An oath-taking ceremony has to be a unique and memorable event. Some business schools have, therefore, organized ceremonies for graduates to pledge the MBA Oath. These oath-taking ceremonies form common knowledge: every oath-taker witnesses every other oath-taker pledging the oath, and so on, and so forth.

Commitment

We should expect the content of an oath to be a general commitment. It would be ineffective to swear an oath every time you promised. There would be too many oaths to make a lasting impression. I promise to take good care of your dog, but I swear that I will never harm anyone, as the original Hippocratic Oath has it. A result of this generality is that breaking an oath negatively affects the promisor's moral standing as a whole person, rather than as, say, a good dog-sitter. It affects the oath-taker's integrity. Swearing the MBA Oath, for instance, commits one to ensuring that one's 'personal behavior will be an example of integrity, consistent with the values that [one] publicly espouse[s]'.[6] This means that, to the extent that people wish to maintain a positive view of their own moral standing, an oath provides them with a higher degree of moral motivation than a promise. It also seems plausible to say that the negative effects of breaking a promise concern the promisor's trustworthiness in the first place vis-à-vis the type of actions the promise is about (dog-sitting, say). Breaking a dog-sitting promise is less likely to affect the promisee's perception of the promisor's overall trustworthiness and, even less, their overall integrity. We are used to assigning different degrees of trust to promises about actions in different domains, made by one and the same promisor, based on what we have come to learn about their trustworthiness in these domains. But, while such distinctions make sense for trust and assignments of trustworthiness, they do not make good sense for evaluations of a person's moral standing.

The above is underscored by the fact that we tend to find that breaking a promise may become excusable (or even normatively expected) when relevant events intervene. Here is an example. I have promised a colleague that I will discuss a draft of a paper they want to submit to a journal. But, just when the colleague arrives, my daughter calls me about an urgent problem that needs immediate attention. In that case, I may be excused (and perhaps even required) to break the promise to my colleague, irrespective of whether they accept my reasons. The promise to discuss the working paper then and there was little more than an expression of an intention. I said, 'I promise', but if I had said 'I will', 'I plan', or 'I intend', I would have said almost the same thing. Oaths, by contrast, are not expressions of intentions or plans, but are about one's general moral standing.

Beneficiaries and Function

The fourth and fifth element of oaths are to do with the beneficiaries of the oath and the function the oath-taker fulfils. The fact that the commitment made through an oath is general does not mean that a good professional oath should not be very concrete and explicit about who its intended beneficiaries are. This often goes hand in hand with stating, as part of the oath, what the function is that the oath-taker, as a professional, fulfils to society. The Hippocratic Oath, for instance, stresses the admittedly unsurprising fact that the primary concern of the medical profession is the health of patients. Conversely, oaths that describe beneficiaries insufficiently clearly risk losing binding force. If it is unclear who the intended beneficiary (the promisee) is, then one may legitimately expect oath-takers to exploit the vagueness in the definition in such a way as to exculpate themselves in particular cases; they would easily deny that people raising complaints against them are in fact among the intended beneficiaries of the oath.

This may sound slightly theoretical, so let me illustrate. The MBA Oath mentions a whole array of beneficiaries, including shareholders, employees, consumers, civil society, government, and the natural environment. It excludes, however, suppliers and competitors. These stakeholders are indeed easily forgotten, as Laura Spence, Anne-Marie Coles, and Lisa Harris have shown.[7] Yet law and business ethics contain numerous provisions protecting them, and no manager taking an MBA Oath should assume that suppliers and competitors can be ignored, or that their concerns are less important than the stakeholders explicitly mentioned in the oath.[8]

Compliance–Sanction and Transcendence

I turn now to two more contentious elements of oaths: a stipulation of the consequences of oath-breaking or non-compliance (a *compliance–sanction* condition) and an invocation of a transcendent entity. Oaths no longer contain such phrases as 'May I suffer a painful and ignominious death if I fail to carry out my solemn oath to defend the honour of the King', and for good reasons.[9] We no longer find it plausible to see an oath the way Francis Hutcheson defined it—namely, as a 'religious action in which we invoke God as a witness and avenger so as to assert something that is uncertain'.[10] To some extent, however, one must wonder if a twenty-first-century update of these two elements (compliance–sanction, and transcendence) might be preferable.

The goal of the first type of phrase is to stipulate what happens if the oath is broken. Generally, professional oaths are part of larger systems of laws and internal rules that do in fact describe sanctions on transgressions. However, it may add to the strength of an oath if the repercussions of breaking an oath are made common knowledge among promisor and promisee—that is, between professionals and society at large. Oath-takers may then know that society expects them, for instance, to confront a disciplinary council in the case of oath-breaking, and that it will be a matter of public scrutiny whether these disciplinary councils fulfil their tasks with sufficient energy and vigour.

Another reason why it may be good to create common knowledge and inform society about the sanctions and repercussions that oath-breakers face is that this allows society to judge the effectiveness of the incentives thus created. If oath-breaking leads to expulsion from the profession no matter what, this would probably do more to boost compliance than if oath-breakers have to suspend their activities only for a month or so.

Considering the difference between oaths and promises offers another perspective on sanctions and repercussions. Since oaths involve the person's integrity—that is, their moral standing as a person as a whole—repercussions of oath-breaking can be more general—namely, less dependent on the precise way in which the oath was broken. Without implying a judgement about merits, it is worth pointing out that, in the wake of the global financial crisis, several countries have started examining the possibility of introducing jail sentences for high-level finance professionals, even though so far only one person has been put behind bars.[11] Whether including the threat of jail (or perhaps more realistically 'dismissal with disgrace') in an oath would be a good idea is, however, something that should be further examined.

The Dutch Banker's Oath ends with one of two sentences: 'So help me God!' or 'This I pledge and promise!' The choice is up to the oath-taker. Traditionally, most oaths have referred to something transcendental, such as a religious deity, or other objects or concepts held in high regard, such as a religious text or the constitution. In a religious context, this created an additional witness to the oath-taking, or, in terms of the model that I am proposing here, it made God a participant in the common knowledge. If God or any transcendent entity held in high regard knows that you have committed yourself to do something, this gives you an additional—religious—reason to stick to it. And, while in a more secular context such arguments may become less persuasive, some scholars suggest even non-religious people may undergo the additional motivating force of pledging by a transcendent entity.[12]

Just as numerous oaths have been drafted to accommodate the compliance–sanction condition without mentioning specific sanctions themselves, it is not necessary for an oath to refer to religious entities for the transcendence condition to be met. In the Netherlands, for instance, the Oath of Office allows civil servants either to 'swear', or to 'affirm', their allegiance to the monarch and their respect for the constitution; and it allows the oath-takers to conclude by saying either 'So help me God Almighty!', or 'This I declare and affirm!' These alternatives are not just meant to accommodate secular objections to the use of religion as a source of transcendence. A significant number of Dutch citizens have objected to 'swearing by God' on religious grounds: for their religion prohibits them from referring to God when making a promise. The 'secular' alternatives in usage are also intended to address these religious concerns. More generally, the moral weight and binding force of oaths are increased when use is made of particular opening formulas that involve verbs such as *swear, pledge, affirm, solemnly declare*, and so forth. These phrases may refer to the oath-taker's dignity, honour, or conscience, or gain force by the ceremonial placing of the oath-taker's hands on important texts, such as a country's constitution, or other revered objects. This is not to say that reference to transcendent entities will never increase the moral force of an oath. But it is not necessary that the characteristic of transcendence be interpreted in religious terms.

Function of Oaths

What function can professional oaths reasonably be expected to fulfil?

Fostering Professionalism

One function is that they may foster professionalism. It has been observed that a solemn oath-taking ceremony is a kind of *rite de passage* concluding a professional's formal training.[13] This observation not only emphasizes the fact that members of a profession share a body of specific technical knowledge, expertise, and skills, but also calls attention to a set of norms and values that are specific to the profession.[14] The oath brings into the open the fact that members of the profession can count upon each other to possess these skills, and that they are justified in assuming that they subscribe to these norms and values. In other words, oaths are common knowledge creators par excellence. This is nicely illustrated by the fact that Michael Chwe's monograph on common knowledge, which I discussed in detail in Chapter 4, features an oath-taking ceremony on the cover of the second edition.[15] It is not so much that the oath here creates common knowledge among practitioners; formal professional training has already generated such common knowledge. The point is rather that the oath makes things salient to practitioners. Work in medical ethics shows that, when the intended beneficiaries are aware of the oath, the oath creates reasons for beneficiaries to trust professionals to conform to professional standards of expertise and integrity.[16]

Facilitating Moral Deliberation

Apart from fostering professionalism, oaths may also facilitate moral deliberation. Common knowledge has a role to play again. As research in medical ethics shows, the Hippocratic Oath functions as an instrument for moral analysis for individual medical practitioners and moral deliberation among colleagues.[17] This function is underscored by the fact that doctors and medical ethicists use the Hippocratic Oath (or variants thereof) as a source of information and inspiration in debates about topics such as euthanasia and physician-assisted suicide, health-insurance reforms, the role of physicians in professional sports, quality control in hospitals, and many others.[18]

The force of common knowledge becomes clear when one considers the way in which oaths stimulate moral deliberation among professionals. If professionals have mutually acknowledged a set of norms and mutually acknowledge their freedoms and unfreedoms, as characteristic of their profession, a result is that debates among professionals will tend to focus on those aspects of the problem at hand that, from the point of view of the profession, are the most relevant. It creates, so to speak, a set of 'default' moral reasons or considerations, and concomitant 'taboo' reasons and considerations. The consequence is not just that moral deliberation among professionals typically centres round the key values of the profession. More than that, it creates a sense that strong reasons must be provided in favour of the relevance of any argument that is *not* backed by the oath. The Hippocratic Oath, for instance, does not specify anything about cost efficiency. The health of the patient is the first and foremost concern. A result of this characteristic is that the participants who introduce financial considerations into a debate bear the burden of proof during any discussion about the costs of healthcare informed by the Hippocratic Oath.

Enhancing Compliance

You might object that, for most beneficiaries, the most pressing issue in the end is above all whether the oath (or any other business ethics instrument) induces compliance. So far, I have stressed the relevance of two things—namely, that oaths can contribute to generating knowledge and common knowledge. The thought was that promises establish common knowledge among the promisor and the promisee, and that such common knowledge increases the binding force of the commitment made through the promise because, among other things, it creates expectations in the promisee that the promisor is aware of.[19] To the extent that oaths are promises, they generate common knowledge of this type. Clearly, however, the act of promising may be more or less successful in making normative expectations common knowledge. I may mumble words. You may not pay full attention. I may not be entirely sincere, or I may fail to see that you cannot hear my promise. These nuances would make for a more secret or private affair, which does not capture the central social sense of promising; in such cases, the requirement that a promise can be publicly acknowledged by the promisee cannot be met.

The idea now is that the above characteristics of the oath (publicity, ceremony, commitment, beneficiaries, function, compliance–sanction, transcendence) offer mechanisms to bring the commitment expressed in the oath into the open in a way that increases the chance of successfully establishing common knowledge. This goal is certainly no guarantee. Oaths may also misfire. But the solemn ceremonial character of oath-taking and the fact that it is public and open to witnesses (potentially strengthened by the invocation of transcendent entities) increase the likelihood that common knowledge is established and maintained. By pledging the oath, the oath-taker openly and publicly creates expectations among the beneficiaries, and this establishes an additional reason to keep the commitments specified in the oath. That is to say, the commitment itself specifies reasons, and the oath-taking creates extra reasons. It is quite reasonable to assume that people are generally interested in maintaining a view of themselves as individuals of sufficiently high moral standing. We are keen not only to view ourselves as moral individuals, but also to be so viewed by others. As a result, once a commitment becomes common knowledge and is mutually acknowledged among people, we have an extra reason to keep the commitment. Breaking the commitment not only decreases our own view of our moral standing, but also causes those who were aware of the commitment (those who were party to the acknowledgement) to downgrade their assessment of our moral standing.

If this line of argumentation sounds a tad theoretical, think about how it may help us to keep some resolutions by making them common knowledge among family and friends. We want to save face. We want to show the strength of our commitment to our friends. We have, in a sense, partly externalized our internal motivation. We not only have an interest in keeping our commitment to practise the piano more often for our own benefit, but we are now also interested in keeping this commitment because we want to avoid appearing weak-willed in the eyes of friends and family. We may want to avoid their criticism or their sarcasm. It is true that there is some empirical evidence that oaths indeed accomplish what they are meant to, and some of the research points in a direction that confirms the postulated mechanism, as we shall see. I hasten to say, however, that the evidence is still fairly scant, and that some of it does counter the idea that oaths are effective as ways of managing ethics. There is also some evidence that sharing one's intentions (as in the resolution example given) may not help to keep them.[20] Clearly, much more empirical work is needed on this subject, but it is interesting in its own right to consider some potentially relevant findings.

Some research concerns virginity pledges, where oath-takers pledge not to engage in premarital sexual intercourse. These turn out to work best in a community of people that mutually reinforces compliance.[21] Such a community may work because it monitors compliance, but it also reinvigorates the public acknowledgement of the commitment. It keeps common knowledge alive. Further evidence is from the classroom, albeit quite anecdotally, recounted by Dan Ariely to show that transcendental references may be effective even in fairly secular environments. Ariely described a Middle Tennessee State University professor who made students swear that they would not cheat on their exams, and that, if they did, they 'would be sorry for the rest of their lives and go to Hell'; and Ariely noted that, despite the highly controversial approach taken by the professor, the oath as such may have been successful by making the oath-takers visualize the stakes as 'very high', even for those who, as Ariely put it, 'did not necessarily believe in Hell'.[22] Less anecdotal evidence exists to the effect that oaths make people more likely to tell the truth, even though some of that research involves only children.[23] Moreover, apart from the above-mentioned virginity pledges, pledges to eat healthy food, not to smoke, or to reveal one's actual preferences in a second-bid auction seem to have at least some positive effect on behaviour, as has a pledge for the auditing profession.[24]

Yet evidence is assuredly mixed, and research on professional oaths is still in its infancy; moreover, oaths may have undesirable side effects.[25] A pledge to tell the truth does indeed make people more likely to tell the truth, but it does not decrease the probability of someone making a false statement. In the context of corporate ethics, a potentially undesirable effect of emphasizing doing good may be that it primarily inspires ethical behaviour at the philanthropic level, at the expense of shareholders, employees, or consumers. Similarly, oaths may be taken as an indication of untrustworthiness rather than as a promotion of trust. Some research also shows that publicity may negatively affect compliance. Yet, in the end, the question of whether oaths are successful instruments to generate compliance through common knowledge remains unanswered.

Powerful Idealism, or Misplaced Response?

Professional oaths have been hailed as giving an 'ethical foundation' to business;[26] or as embodying 'powerful idealism'.[27] But equally they have been denounced as inviting 'a violation of fiduciary responsibilities', and described as a 'misplaced response' to ethical misconduct.[28] You may even think that oaths harm integrity. Well-meaning professionals may see an oath as a condescending expression of distrust in their ability to judge and act ethically and may become cynical as a result. Since oaths summarize what is already contained in laws or codes of conduct, they may be seen as redundant, or as stating the obvious. Oaths may be found to create an unjustified illusion of trustworthiness. And, perhaps most seriously, they might lead to moral error. For recall that the MBA ignores the concerns of competitors and suppliers. Or observe, similarly, that many oaths contain prescriptions to keep secret what one is entrusted with, which is unhelpful, if not straightforwardly immoral, when, for example, revealing secret client data may save lives.

A more practical objection is that generating sufficiently widespread awareness of the oath among its intended beneficiaries may be difficult. A small-scale investigation around the Banker's Oath in its early years showed that Dutch citizens were very unlikely to stumble upon information about the oath.[29] Before the larger event in The Hague with which I began this chapter, if you had not seen or read the news, you would not have known about the oath; at least, logging on to your online banking portal would not have given you any relevant information. And, despite attention on national television and in national newspapers, even the event in The Hague failed to reach most Dutch citizens.

A final objection against oaths may be that proposing a professional oath for businesspeople commits oneself to an unjustified assumption that business (banking, financial advice, management, and so on) is a genuine *profession*. Some scholars have indeed made suggestions in that direction, but their arguments will not convince everyone.[30] One problem with such a view is that (unlike paradigmatic professions such as medicine) business and management do not rest on a body of specialized technical knowledge and transferable skills that are acquired through years of training, maintained, and improved over a career, and developed further on the basis of research carried out primarily by members of the profession themselves. Surely workers in the banking industry need specific and highly technical knowledge. But that knowledge is still fairly general: your knowledge of financial economics may qualify you for a job in a bank, but also for academic work. If we were to zoom in on management as a profession, we would see that training is often of little importance. Despite what professors may believe, one can become a great manager or businessperson without attending business school. A medical career without medical school, by contrast, is out of the question.

Ethics Management beyond the Oath

Back to the Banker's Oath. Surely the Dutch realized that pledging integrity cannot be more than the starting point to incorporate ethics into the financial industry as a whole. The oath, though meant to be highly visible, was only a small part of a new and perhaps even more innovative regulation.[31] Bank executives were explicitly obligated to develop concrete policies to ensure that the principles embodied in the Banking Code and the Banker's Oath were translated into concrete and consistent practice within their organizations.

Let me situate the discussion. In the first part of this book, I argued that knowledge of freedom increases the chances that people satisfy desires and assume moral responsibility for their actions, and I alluded to something that could be summarized thus: knowledge of morality increases the chances that the desires people satisfy conform to morality, where knowledge may be more of the know-that type (as with consequential-ist and deontological norms), or more of the know-how type (as perhaps is more characteristic of virtue ethics). Moreover, I have argued in the present chapter that common knowledge of moral commitments increases the chances that people stick to the moral commitments they make. Now, while I have so far focused on the last claim, I believe that oaths can also be made relevant to the first two, and that is why I conclude by making a number of observations about how we may manage ethics in organiza-tions more generally in ways that incorporate the insights behind all three claims. In other words, I explore how the epistemic insights garnered so far can help us to incorporate integrity into organizations.

Traditional Models

A traditional, but still useful, model of ethical decision-making is proposed by James Rest and distinguishes four stages.[32] First, there must be recog-nition of the issue at stake and one must conceptualize it as calling for ethical reflection. Reflection then leads to a judgement about what actions morality requires in this particular case, which is followed, if at all, by the formation of an intention actually to perform the actions one judges to be right. Finally, if one carries out the intention, the result is actual ethical behaviour.

Things may go wrong at any of the four stages. I may fail to recognize because of a lack of sensitivity, awareness, concentration, or empathy. I may recognize but fail to judge because of lack of time, resources, ethical knowledge and expertise, or distraction. I may judge but not form a com-mitment or intention because of countervailing, selfish reasons. And I may intend but not display the intended behaviour because of weakness of will or forgetfulness.

Ethics management addresses all four levels. Mission statements, corpo-rate codes of conduct, ethics officers, compliance teams, ethics committees, ethics hotlines, CSR departments, ethics training, culture change pro-grammes, integrity consultants—these instruments are all in the end meant to make people recognize, judge, intend, and behave with integrity. The epistemic perspective offers, I believe, a more general way to assess such initiatives and to make suggestions for improving them. The idea is simple. In order to recognize an issue as ethically laden, and to form a judgement about what morality requires, you need knowledge about its potential consequences. You need knowledge about the alternatives, because, as long as there are no alternatives, morality has little to say. You need knowledge about the consequences of these alternatives to weigh them against each other. In sum, you need knowledge about freedom and knowledge about morality. But such knowledge about morality is often lacking. As we saw in the previous chapter, the way a case is presented to us may considerably distort our thinking about the moral intensity of the issue at stake, or by the perceived salience of particular stakeholders.[33] Acquiring deeper knowledge is a way to counter such biases and avoid being misled. As we deepen our knowledge of the opportunity set we are facing (the available actions and their probabilistic consequences), and about the preference orderings morality licenses or prescribes, we are less likely to be influenced by irrelevant considerations that otherwise may have given an issue unjustifiably high (or low) moral intensity or salience.

Here is one concrete suggestion as to how we can accomplish this. Recall that research on stakeholder salience showed that what determines the chances of a stakeholder being recognized, and being included in ethical judgement, is proportional to the extent to which management sees the stakeholder as possessing power, and sees their claims as legitimate and sufficiently urgent.[34] Clearly there is often a substantial discrepancy between management's perceptions of power, legitimacy, and urgency, and what an impartial moral view would have to say on the matter. It may be laudable that HSBC's Malaysian Forest Dialogue engages with stakeholders such as the World Wildlife Fund. But how sure can we be that the interests of poor individual farmers, say, or small enterprises are also recognized and included in their ethical judgements, intentions, and behaviour?

The epistemic perspective I champion here helps by urging decision makers to perform extensive impartial research in order ultimately to act with integrity. This solution may sound innocuous. It is meant to be very wide-ranging. I am inclined to think that, when you have experienced ethical debates in organizations, you must conclude that a great deal of moral decision-making in business suffers from a lack of knowledge about relevant facts. This conclusion is actually true, not only in for-profit organizations, but also in the non-profit sector, as is witnessed by the way in which Greenpeace ostensibly failed to do justice to dissenting opinions in the Brent Spar case.[35] Stakeholder engagement may go some way to expand one's knowledge, but more is clearly needed.[36]

Creating Knowledge and Common Knowledge among Stakeholders

Let me conclude. I have elsewhere recommended the use of Deliberative Polling as an alternative knowledge-generating technique.[37] This tool was designed by James Fishkin (and his colleague Robert Luskin) primarily to boost buy-in in political decision-making, but it may provide value in business contexts as well.[38] Suppose I need to decide about an issue and want to obtain information. I can send around a questionnaire to gather input and then perhaps decide the issue in a majoritarian fashion. But people may fill out questionnaires with different levels of expertise and knowledge about the issue, which may significantly decrease the reliability of the procedure.

By contrast, the idea behind a deliberative poll is that it brings people together to discuss and deliberate. They engage experts. They learn from each other. They subsequently revise their views. Then they vote. And this vote, the thought is, then reflects the 'considered judgements' of the participants. If the group of people involved in the poll is representative of the relevant population, this vote captures what the population were to think about the issue, if they had access to relevant information and experts and rigorously engaged with the issue.

Although decision makers should exercise care to avoid bias in selecting participants, the precise setting of the poll forces them to gather information more carefully than the usually quite rigidly structured stakeholder dialogues most businesses organize today. Deliberative polls confront decision makers with details about the experiences, fears, and concerns of individual stakeholders, thus creating knowledge about freedom (about opportunity sets) and about morality (norms and values). This tactic gives a voice to stakeholders that might otherwise be forgotten. And, while a deliberative poll will look very different from the oath-taking ceremony with which I started—it will not typically take place in a church, and it will be less solemn, less formalized, less ceremonial—it may well have a greater impact.

Notes

1. Adviescommissie Toekomst Banken, *Naar herstel van vertrouwen* (2009), www.nvb.nl/media/1863/001152_rapport-adviescommissie-toekomst-banken-cie-maas.pdf [https://perma.cc/J5R4-5U9A].

2. See, e.g., Rob Schotsman, 'Wordt de bankierseed wel op de juiste wijze getoetst?', *Tijdschrift voor Compliance*, 2 (2019), 133–137 (evaluating the way in which compliance with the oath is ensured), and Jonathan Soeharno, 'Tuchtrecht en de wens tot integere bankiers: Een kritische beschouwing', *Tijdschrift voor Financieel recht*, 6 (2014), 243–251 (a critical evaluation of introducing concerns about integrity in financial law).

3. For suggestions similar to the Dutch oath, e.g. by the British government, the Australian Banking and Finance Ethics panel, and individuals including James Montier, Barry Morgan, the Archbishop of Wales, and HSBC chairman Douglas Flint, see George Lekakis, 'Industry Ponders "Oath" with Exit Clause', *Banking Day*, 30 July 2012, www.bankingday.com/article/industry-ponders—oath—with-an-exit-clause [perma.cc/J2SR-CW2C], Louisa Peacock, 'HSBC: Banks Should "Reward Staff Who Escalate Concerns"', *Telegraph*, 22 April 2013, www.telegraph.co.uk/finance/newsbysector/banksandfinance/10011061/HSBC-Banks-should-reward-staff-who-escalate-concerns.html [perma.cc/6BHG-7CDA], and Tim Webb, '"Hippocratic Oath" for Bank Workers Meets with Scepticism', *Guardian*, 18 April 2010, www.theguardian.com/business/2010/apr/18/banking-business-code-of-conduct [perma.cc/E4UX-EUES].

4. George DeMartino, *The Economist's Oath* (New York: Oxford University Press, 2010), and Max Anderson and Peter Escher, *The MBA Oath: Setting a Higher Standard for Business Leaders* (New York: Portfolio, 2010). The MBA Oath signers are listed at mbaoath.org/view/oath-signers [perma.cc/25S5-JSTU]. Oaths for the business world were suggested in discussions at the 2002 World Economic Forum in Geneva, and by Jai Ghorpade, 'Ethics in MBA Programs: The Rhetoric, the Reality, and a Plan of Action', *Journal of Business Ethics*, 10 (1991), 891–905, at 903.

5. Daniel Sulmasy, 'What Is an Oath and why Should a Physician Swear One?', *Theoretical Medicine and Bioethics*, 20 (1999), 329–346. See also Kostas Amiridis 'The Shadow of Sophocles: Tragedy and the Ethics of Leadership', *Business Ethics Quarterly*, 28 (2018), 15–29, Vincent Blok, 'Bridging the Gap between Individual and Corporate Responsible Behaviour: Toward a Performative Concept of Corporate Codes', *Philosophy of Management*, 16 (2017), 117–136, and Sareh Pouryousefi, The Economist's Oath: On the Need for and Content of Professional Economic Ethics', *Journal of Business Ethics*, 24 (2014), 283–287.

6. MBA Oath, Legacy Version, mbaoath.org/wp-content/uploads/2009/05/mba-oath2.pdf [perma.cc/JQJ5-TY86].

7. Laura Spence, Anne-Marie Coles, and Lisa Harris, 'The Forgotten Stakeholder? Ethics and Social Responsibility in Relation to Competitors', *Business and Society Review*, 106 (2002), 331–352.

8. See, generally, Edward Freeman, *Strategic Management: A Stakeholder Approach* (Boston: Pitman, 1984). Sam Mansell, *Capitalism, Corporations and the Social Contract: A Critique of Stakeholder Theory* (Cambridge: Cambridge University Press, 2013), provides an argument against stakeholder theory inspired by Milton Friedman's defence of shareholder wealth maximization, of which the *locus classicus* is Milton Friedman, 'A Friedman Doctrine: The Social Responsibility of Business Is to Increase its Profits', *New York Times*, 13 September 1970, www.nytimes.com/1970/09/13/archives/a-friedman-doctrine-the-social-responsibility-of-business-is-to.html [perma.cc/Y2K9-VEZU]. Joseph Heath, *Morality, Competition, and the Firm: The Market Failures Approach to Business Ethics* (New York: Oxford University Press, 2014), collects essays on a new strand in business ethics, the markets failure approach, which is gaining traction in business ethics as an important alternative to stakeholder theory and corporate social responsibility.

9. The example comes from Daniel Sulmasy, 'What Is an Oath and why Should a Physician Swear One?', *Theoretical Medicine and Bioethics*, 20 (1999), 329–346, at 333. This is no longer plausible, not only because few *oath-takers* will believe it, but also because an oath-taker who does believe it might find it odd to utter such words as long as they think that their *audience* does not believe it (or does not believe that the oath-taker believes it). Common knowledge is required here too. Cf. Dan Ariely, *The Honest Truth about Dishonesty: How we Lie to Everyone—Especially Ourselves* (New York: HarperCollins, 2012), 44–45, for some evidence that an oath-taker may change behaviour even though they do not believe (all of) the oath.

10. Francisco Hutcheson, *Philosophiæ Moralis Institutio Compendiaria* (Dublin: Guliel. McKenzie, 1787), bk. II, ch. XI, 'De Jejurando et Votis', 155 (own translation).

11. See, generally, e.g., the contributions to Joe McGrath (ed.), *White-Collar Crime in Ireland: Law and Policy* (Dublin: Clarus Press, 2019).

12. See, e.g., Dan Ariely, *The Honest Truth about Dishonesty: How we Lie to Everyone—Especially Ourselves* (New York: HarperCollins, 2012), 44–45.

13. See, e.g., Mark Rutgers, 'Will the Phoenix Fly Again? Reflections on the Efficacy of Oaths as a Means to Secure Honesty', *Review of Social Economy*, 71 (2013), 249–276.

14. See Rakesh Khurana and Nitin Nohria, 'It's Time to Make Management a True Profession', *Harvard Business Review*, October (2008), 70–77, for an argument that management should be thought of as a profession.

15. Michael Chwe, *Rational Ritual: Culture, Coordination, and Common Knowledge* (2nd edn; Princeton: Princeton University Press, 2013).

16. See, e.g., Clifford Perlis and Noah Shannon, 'Role of Professional Organisations in Setting and Enforcing Ethical Norms', *Clinics in Dermatology*, 30 (2012), 156–159.

17. See, generally, Steven Miles, *The Hippocratic Oath and the Ethics of Medicine* (Oxford: Oxford University Press, 2004).

18. See, e.g., Linda Emanuel, 'Facing Requests for Physician-Assisted Suicide', *JAMA* 280 (1998), 643, on euthanasia and physician-assisted suicide, Andrew Hohenstein, 'Team Physicians: Adhering to the Hippocratic Oath or Just Plain Hypocrites?', *Marquette Sport Law Review*, 19 (2009), 579–612, on sports, Donald Lighter and Douglas Fair, *Quality Management in Health Care: Principles and Methods* (London: Jones and Bartlett, 2000), on quality control, and Mark Waymack, 'Health Care as a Business: The Ethic of Hippocrates versus the Ethic of Managed Care', *Business & Professional Ethics Journal*, 9 (1990), 69–78, on insurance.

19. See Lon Fuller, *The Morality of Law* (New Haven: Yale University Press, 1964), 159, on how the principles of legality, including generality and promulgation, increase public scrutiny and thereby the chance that lawmakers can be taken to account. Fuller's interactional view of law sees law as a 'co-operative effort—an effective and responsible interaction between lawgiver and subject' (ibid. 219). This is not unlike the relation between sender and recipient in common knowledge generating contexts, such as oath-taking.

20. Peter Gollwitzer, Paschal Sheeran, Verena Michalski, and Andrea Seifert, 'When Intentions Go Public: Does Social Reality Widen the Intention–Behavior Gap?', *Psychological Science*, 20 (2009), 612–618.

21. See, e.g., Peter Bearman and Hannah Brückner, 'Promising the Future: Virginity Pledges and First Intercourse', *American Journal of Sociology*, 106 (2001), 859–923, Melina Bersamin, Samantha Walker, Elizabeth Waiters, Deborah Fisher, and Joel Grube, 'Promising to Wait: Virginity Pledges and Adolescent Sexual Behaviour', *Journal of Adolescent Health*, 36 (2005), 428–436, and Janet Rosenbaum, 'Patient Teenagers? A Comparison of the Sexual Behavior of Virginity Pledgers and Matched Non-Pledgers', *Pediatrics*, 123 (2009), 110–120.

22. Dan Ariely, *The Honest Truth about Dishonesty: How we Lie to Everyone—Especially Ourselves* (New York: HarperCollins, 2012), 44–45.

23. See, e.g., Tobias Beck, Christoph Bühren, Björn Frank, and Elina Khachatryan, 'Can Honesty Oaths, Peer Interaction, or Monitoring Mitigate Lying?', *Journal of Business Ethics*, 163 (2020), 467–484, for evidence that an honesty oath increases moral awareness, and Thomas Lyon and Joyce Dorado, 'Truth Induction in Young Maltreated Children: The Effects of Oath-Taking and Reassurance on True and False Disclosure', *Child Abuse & Neglect*, 32 (2008), 738–748.

24. See John Hallaq, 'The Pledge as an Instrument of Behavioral Change', *Journal of Social Psychology*, 98 (1976), 147–148, on smoking, Nicolas Jacquemet, Robert-Vincent Joule, Stéphane Luchini, and Jason Shogren, 'Preference Elicitation under Oath', *Journal of Environmental Economics and Management*, 65 (2013), 110–132, on preferences, and Sekar Raju, Priyali Rajagopal, and Timothy Gilbride, 'Marketing Healthful Eating to Children: The Effectiveness of Incentives, Pledges, and Competitions', *Journal of Marketing*, 74 (2010), 93–106, on food. Christophe Van Linden and Kris Hardies, 'Entrance Requirements to the Audit Profession within the EU and Audit Quality', *International Journal of Auditing*, 22 (2018), 360–373, find mixed evidence for the effect of professional oaths on audit quality.

25. See, e.g., John Boatright, 'Swearing to be Virtuous: The Prospects of a Banker's Oath', *Review of Social Economy*, 71 (2013), 140–165, as well as the other contributions to a special issue on oaths in the same journal, with editorial Boudewijn de Bruin and Wilfred Dolfsma, 'Oaths and Codes in Economics and Business: Introducing the Special Issue', *Review of Social Economy*, 71 (2013), 135–139. See also Matthew Braham and Friedel Bolle, 'A Difficulty with Oaths: On Trust, Trustworthiness, and Signalling', *European Journal of Law and Economics*, 22 (2005), 219–232, for the view that oaths may be thought to signal lack of trust, and Xiao-Ping Chen, 'The Group-Based Binding Pledge as a Solution to Public Goods Problems', *Organizational Behavior and Human Decision Processes*, 66 (1996), 192–202.

26. Barry Morgan, 'MBA Oath Provides an Ethical Foundation', *Financial Times*, 6 February 2011, www.ft.com/content/5c7b7592-307c-11e0-9de3-00144feabdc0 [perma.cc/EPK5-UHZS].

27. Edward O'Boyle, 'Anderson and Escher's the MBA Oath: Review Essay' (2011), *Journal of Business Ethics*, 101, 285–295.

28. Theo Vermaelen, quoted by Roger Thompson, 'The MBA Oath Debate', www.alumni.hbs.edu/stories/Pages/story-bulletin.aspx?num=1862 [perma.cc/765Y-5HXW].

29. Boudewijn de Bruin, 'Professional Oaths in the Financial Services Industry', in Robert Chandler (ed.), *Business and Corporate Integrity: Sustaining Organizational Ethics, Compliance and Trust* (Santa Barbara: Praeger, 2014), 121–140.

30. See, e.g., Rakesh Khurana and Nitin Nohria, 'It's Time to Make Management a True Profession', *Harvard Business Review*, October (2008), 70–77.

31. See, e.g., the assessment of Stephen Scott, 'Trust and Technology: A New Paradigm for Culture and Conduct Risk Management', *Seattle University Law Review*, 43 (2020), 765–806, and of Ciaran Walker, 'Role of the Board in Improving Culture in Financial Services Firms', *Seattle University Law Review*, 43 (2020), 723–764.

32. James Rest, *Moral Development: Advances in Research and Theory* (New York: Praeger, 1986).

33. See Thomas Jones, 'Ethical Decision Making by Individuals in Organizations: An Issue-Contingent Model', *Academy of Management Review*, 16 (1991), 366–395, on moral intensity, and Ronald Mitchell, Bradley Agle, and Donna Wood, 'Toward a Theory of Stakeholder Salience: Defining the Principle of who and what Really Counts', *Academy of Management Review*, 22 (1997), 853–886, on stakeholder salience. See, more generally, Daniel Kahneman, *Thinking, Fast and Slow* (New York: Farrar, Straus and Giroux, 2011), on cognitive biases clouding our judgements.

34. Ronald Mitchell, Bradley Agle, and Donna Wood, 'Toward a Theory of Stakeholder Salience: Defining the Principle of Who and What Really Counts', *Academy of Management Review*, 22 (1997), 853–886.

35. See, e.g., Stelios Zyglidopoulos, 'The Social and Environmental Responsibilities of Multinationals: Evidence from the Brent Spar Case', *Journal of Business Ethics*, 36 (2002), 141–151.

36. See, e.g., John Elkington and Shelly Fennell, 'Partners for Sustainability', *Greener Management International*, 24 (1998), 48–60, and Cathy Hartman and Edwin Stafford, 'Green Alliances: Building New Business with Environmental Groups', *Long Range Planning*, 30 (1997), 184–196.

37. Boudewijn de Bruin, 'Ethics Management in Banking and Finance', in Nick Morris and David Vines (eds), *Capital Failure: Rebuilding Trust in Financial Services* (Oxford: Oxford University Press, 2014), 255–276.

38. See, generally, James Fishkin, *Democracy when the People Are Thinking: Revitalizing our Politics through Public Deliberation* (Oxford: Oxford University Press, 2018). James Fishkin, 'The Deliberative Corporation', *Management Innovation Exchange*, 18 July 2011, www.managementexchange.com/hack/deliberative-corporation [perma.cc/T8KA-QTTZ], contains suggestions for applications to business.

7
Freedom of Speech and Consumer Autonomy

My freedom ends where I begin to harm you. This, in a nutshell, is John Stuart Mill's harm principle. If this is applied cautiously, policymakers may find justification in it for the idea that, if some *X* causes something harmful *Y*, there is a prima facie reason to ban *X*, or at least to regulate *X*. But there is one exception, and it is epistemic. It is to do with freedom of speech and expression. However large, say, is the harm that a journalist's uncovering a money-laundering scheme does to the implicated bank, it is no reason to silence the journalist. Spelling out the reasons why we can set aside the harm principle once we consider speech requires a great deal of further thinking, however, and many different arguments for freedom of speech and expression have been designed over time—for instance, in terms of the contributions of free speech to democracy, truth finding, tolerance, or diversity.[1]

Most of these arguments will offer only limited special protection to media violence, the topic of the present chapter. It is true that depictions of violence may play an important role in democracy and truth finding. As Luc Bovens once observed, early photography was key in raising awareness of the colonial atrocities perpetrated in the Congo Free State under the rule of King Leopold II.[2] But it is much harder to think in these terms of the value of depictions of fictitious violence in films and video games. That is why, in debates about the regulation of pornography, hate speech, fascist propaganda, 'fake news', and so forth, liberal policymakers typically employ only one special protection argument: the argument from autonomy.

Argument from Autonomy

Autonomy typically signals something like the Kantian ideal of being able to form beliefs and desires, independently of others, and being able to decide

The Business of Liberty. Boudewijn de Bruin, Oxford University Press.
© Boudewijn de Bruin (2022). DOI: 10.1093/oso/9780198839675.003.0008

to act on these beliefs and desires, again independently of others.[3] Autonomously believing, desiring, and acting is believing, desiring, and acting without inward or outward interfering influences. While this definition of autonomy is admittedly rough, it excludes at least cases where other agents influence the formation of your beliefs and desires by such means as brainwashing, subliminal advertising—or, as is not prima facie implausible to think, by exposing you to media violence.

The argument from autonomy (or, more precisely, the hearer version thereof) holds that freedom of speech and expression must not be curtailed, as this would unjustifiably limit belief (and desire) formation opportunities of the hearers of speech. The thought is that hearers should be able to decide for themselves what they want to hear, and what they want to do with what they hear, and that banning, for instance, incendiary hate speech or the spreading of falsehoods would betray a disrespectful attitude towards hearers' capacities to evaluate the content of the speech as well as to decide for themselves what actions, if any, would be supported by the speech.[4]

The argument from autonomy depends on a crucial distinction with paradigmatic cases of harmful behaviour that are *not* protected by the harm principle. In the speech case, the harmful consequences are *mediated* by the hearer. After a speaker has uttered some words, the hearer interprets and evaluates their words, and decides on a course of action (or omission). It is that course of action (or omission) that, we assume here, harms someone. There is no direct or *unmediated* connection between speech and harm. We need the hearer in between. Applied to media violence, the argument from autonomy states that a restriction of exposure to media violence removes an opportunity to form beliefs and desires, and to act on them independently, and on our own; and it does not add new opportunities to do so. It decreases our autonomy, and hence exposure to media violence should not be restricted.

Combining Psychology, Neuroscience, and Cognitive Science

Psychologists such as Craig Anderson and colleagues, and Susan Hurley, a philosopher, have used psychological and neuroscientific research to cast doubt on the application of the argument from autonomy to media violence.[5] The thought is that this body of research shows that the connection between speech and harm is much less mediated than the argument from autonomy presupposes. If these authors are right, the connection between speech and harm in the case of media violence is more like that between a blow and a bruise, a typical example of unmediated harm. If cogent, this line of attack on media freedom has repercussions that go far beyond the entertainment industry, as is witnessed by related attempts to do away with the relevance of the argument from autonomy as affording special protection to advertisements that may spread gender and minority stereotypes, hate speech, and defamatory speech.[6] If the link between exposure to media violence and harmful aggressive behaviour is not as the argument from autonomy claims it is, then this is probably true of the relation between advertisements (or any producer-provided information) and purchasing behaviour as well. Since for most consumers what the producer says may well be the main source of information determining what they buy, it is important to see whether we should set aside the argument from autonomy so easily. I argue we should not.

Psychology

Let us begin with the social psychology evidence that proponents of regulating media violence call upon. To define things, exposure to media violence is exposure to violence in the news, as part of a film in a cinema or on television, or as part of a video game. Aggressive behaviour, in turn, embraces all kinds of intentional production, or threats of production, of physical harm.

The empirical evidence we are talking about is that exposure to media violence causes an increase in aggressive behaviour in a significant proportion of the viewing population. Important meta-analyses of research on violence on television by Haejung Paik and George Comstock, and of research on video games by Craig Anderson and Brad Bushman, plus a review by Anderson and co-authors, are typical sources supporting the existence of a correlation between exposure to media violence and aggressive behaviour, of around $r = 0.30$.[7] Here is one example. A longitudinal study by Jeffrey Johnson and colleagues showed that the amount of television watching at age 14 was associated with assaults or fights and other aggressive acts at age 16 and 22.[8] Here are some further examples attributed to

Leonard Berkowitz.[9] In an oft-cited experiment, the level of aggressiveness of institutionalized delinquent boys was measured prior to the experiment. One half, chosen at random, were subsequently shown violent films, while the others were exposed to non-violent films. Participants in the treatment group, who were shown violent films, were significantly more aggressive in the following days than those in the control group, and this was especially true for those who had scored low on aggressiveness before the experiment. Another study observed that individuals were more likely to respond aggressively to provocation if they had watched a film in which a villain was beaten up. And a further longitudinal study established that 8-year-old boys viewing media violence showed significantly more aggression at age 18 as well as at age 30 than boys in the control group. The results were independent of socioeconomic status, intelligence, and parental aggression, and held across five nations.

Neuroscience and Cognitive Science

This research is all taken from social psychology. The idea now is to pair this body of research with a different body of research, from neuroscience and cognitive science. Let me explain the research. The prime example in this respect is the chameleon effect, introduced by Tanya Chartrand and John Bargh.[10] This effect is that your merely perceiving someone doing something is already sufficient to increase the probability that you will engage in the same behaviour yourself. This involves copying the goals of the action as well as the exact bodily movements that constitute the means of achieving the goal. Experimental data reveal, for instance, that adults engaged in a conversation with an experimenter rubbing his or her feet from time to time start rubbing their own feet after a while too. The striking point is that the participants in the experiment were aware only of the experimenter rubbing feet, not of their own behaviour.

Two theories are put forward in this regard. The mechanism explaining the possibility of imitation is the mirror neuron system, research on which was pioneered by Giacomo Rizzolati and colleagues.[11] Mirror neurons discharge when we perceive others interacting with objects, irrespective of what type of object it is, and whether the interaction takes place at a great distance from us, or close to us. Given the mirror neuron system, the second mechanism is that of ideomotor theory, which explains how perceiving or imagining certain bodily movements in others evokes the movement that it represents, often unconsciously.[12]

Argument for Regulation of Media Violence

Altogether, we have two empirical hypotheses. One is from social psychology: exposure to media violence causes aggressive behaviour. The other is from cognitive science and neuroscience: humans have an innate tendency to copy behaviour in ways that bypass conscious deliberation. Susan Hurley, and, slightly earlier, Craig Anderson and co-authors, combine these two hypothesis in one.[13] In Hurley's words:

> I now suggest that it is reasonable to believe two propositions, on the basis of the empirical evidence I have surveyed. First, exposure to media violence causes an increase in violent behaviour of significant effect size across the population of viewers, in both the short and long terms. Secondly, that it often does so directly, in ways that are unrecognized and bypass the individual viewer's autonomous deliberative processes.[14]

I call this the *combined empirical hypothesis*. Even though Hurley does not put much stress on it, it is important to see that the combined empirical hypothesis is an additional hypothesis over and above the earlier two. Nothing in social psychology, cognitive science, or neuroscience suggests that the chameleon effect, mirror neurons, and ideomotor systems are at work precisely whenever individuals who have watched violent films or played violent video games engage in aggressive acts. The combined empirical hypothesis is that the aggressive behaviour studied by social psychologists is exactly—or at least in a significant number of cases—the kind of unconscious imitation investigated by neuroscientists and cognitive scientists. This is an additional claim.

Back to the argument from autonomy. Applied to media violence, it says that restricting exposure to media violence removes, in the hearer, an opportunity to form beliefs and desires, and to act on them independently, and on their own, without creating new such opportunities; therefore, no such restrictions are justifiable. The champions of regulation attempt to show that, if we accept the combined empirical hypothesis *and* the argument from autonomy for freedom of speech and expression, no special protection for media violence follows. They purport to show that, when we assume the combined empirical hypothesis to be true, we can show that a restriction of exposure to media violence does not, in fact, decrease our autonomy. The thought is that (under that assumption) a person exposed to media violence will, with some non-zero probability, act on beliefs and desires that they have not formed independently, and on their own, and that, consequently, removing an opportunity to be exposed to media violence does not decrease one's autonomy as a hearer.

Problems with Causes, Effects, and Policies

This argument for regulation of media violence has a lot of initial appeal. To the extent that we have reason to value freedom, we should look at non-autonomous belief formation with suspicion, for, if, bluntly put, media violence works the way brainwashing and the other mechanisms surveyed in Chapter 2 work, we have very good prima facie liberal reasons to ban it.

Correlation, Reversed Causation, and Third Causes

But the argument for regulation is not quite as rigorous as it may seem. Let me start with some very elementary statistical observations. When policy-makers find that some X has to be regulated because X causes something harmful Y, the evidence they have is almost always statistical in nature. A statement that exposing people to media violence leads to aggressive behaviour is ideally based on statistical inferences drawn from observations of instances of exposure to media violence, on the one hand, and instances of harmful aggressive behaviour, on the other. What this means can be easily illustrated by means of a scatter diagram. Observations are represented as dots on a two-dimensional plane, where the values on the X-axis and the Y-axis indicate, for instance, the hours of exposure to media violence, and the intensity of subsequent aggression, respectively. Each dot represents one observation.

Regression analysis is a statistical tool that brings order in the scatter diagram. It summarizes the data by means of one straight line. If all observations are already on a straight line, there is nothing interesting for regression analysis to do. But such straight-line cases hardly ever occur.

Rather, the observations will look more or less like a cloud, in which the untrained eye cannot see any structure. The regression line—meant rationally to interpolate and extrapolate the data—may look rather 'artificial'. It is the concept of correlation that encapsulates the degree to which the scatter diagram is more like the straight-line case, or more like the cloud case. The stronger the correlation, the closer we are to the straight-line case, and that is why, the stronger the correlation, the more confident researchers are of having found something of a genuine link. An influential classification offered by Jacob Cohen takes a correlation of $r = 0.1$ to be small, $r = 0.3$ to be mid-size, and $r = 0.5$ to be large.[15] Or, for policymakers: the stronger the correlation, the more confident they can be that, when they develop appropriate regulation of variable X, this has an effect on variable Y. Large correlations are rare, and are not always needed, though. Consider two well-known policy issues: passive smoking in the workplace (regulated because of its association with lung cancer), and exposure to asbestos (regulated because of laryngeal cancer). They both have a correlation of around $r = 0.10$ only, but still support policy. Yet policy based on a correlation lower than $r = 0.10$ does not seem to be justifiable.

A decent correlation coefficient is a necessary condition for regulation, but not sufficient. We also need some evidence of a causal link between the relevant variables. What you see on the scatter diagram may, for all you know, reflect the fact that, indeed, X causes Y. But it may equally mean that Y causes X (*reverse causation*), or that there is some Z (a so-called *third cause*) that causes both X and Y. Given the way statistics work, it may even be the case that we are in one of those cases where the found correlation is entirely spurious. Clearly, only if X causes Y will barring or regulating X limit the harmful Y.

Back to media violence and aggressive behaviour. First, we should not be too quick to dismiss the possibility of reverse causation. It has some initial plausibility that more aggressive individuals are more likely to engage in violent video games, rather than the other way round. And neither should we rule out a third cause, as certain personal or situational factors might explain both a person's preference for consuming violent media and their tendency to engage in aggressive behaviour. As it stands, there is little in the way the social psychology and neuroscience/cognitive science results are combined that addresses these concerns, and there is little we need to say to appreciate why this endangers the legitimacy of regulation.[16]

Unintended Effects

A number of further issues undermine the initial plausibility of the argument for regulation as well. One is to do with the unintended or unpredicted consequences of policy. Establishing that some X causes something harmful Y is insufficient for policymaking as long as it provides no insights into what would happen if X were to be banned (or otherwise be regulated)—in particular, as long as it offers no guarantee that, when X is regulated, then the harmful Y is not replaced by something even more harmful. An example of how regulating can have undesired effects is the following. Criminalizing the possession and use of alcohol in the US is claimed to have led to an increase in the number of minors with criminal records, making it significantly more difficult for them to find a job, or to take out a mortgage. Similar observations have been made about prevention programmes in Europe. These effects are generally considered to be the unintended and undesired consequences of a policy that in itself makes sense to begin with.[17]

Back to our case. We seem to have less evidence of what would happen if we restricted exposure to media violence, so we can only speculate here. But the existing evidence does not allow us to exclude that limiting exposure to media violence would lead to a situation where the net crime rate *increases*. Just as barking dogs do not bite, people playing violent video games do not, while playing, engage in criminal aggressive behaviour. This is a platitude. But it may well be that the decrease in criminal aggressive behaviour resulting from an increase in hours spent playing violent video games (or watching violent films or videos) outweighs the increase in aggressive behaviour that, based on the combined empirical hypothesis, one should expect to result from playing these games or watching these videos.[18]

Policy Principles

A related point of criticism is that it is unclear what policies the combined empirical hypothesis could possibly support. Only a proportion of the viewer population is affected by the adverse effects of exposure to media violence. Numerous viewers are unaffected. Some people do not view media violence. Many people will never be confronted with the unconscious, imitated aggression of affected media-violence viewers. Therefore, while increasing the autonomy of some, limiting exposure of media violence decreases the autonomy of others. It seems therefore that, if we adopt Pareto efficiency as a criterion for distribution of autonomy (if that makes sense), barring media violence cannot be justified. Pareto efficiency forbids increasing the extent of some person's autonomy at the cost of that of others. If, on the other hand, we take it that the extent of autonomy of the *average* individual should be maximized, a ban on media violence might be defended. At the minimum, this shows that the policy repercussions are heavily dependent on the deployed distributive principle.

Policies that Are Too Broad

A further point of criticism is to do with the question of how broadly our variable X (the thing to be regulated) must be defined. The combined empirical hypothesis involves research about media violence and aggressive behaviour, but also research on more general unconsciously copied behaviour, such as the chameleon effect. If the latter sort of empirical findings takes the upper hand in the argument for regulation, the risk is that one will have to regulate more than makes sense.

Consider this: exposure to instances of 'nice' behaviour in the media will also be imitated in ways that bypass autonomy. Consequently, outlawing 'grandson-helps-grandmother films' will increase the extent to which certain individuals (boys, grandsons) exercise their autonomy in certain realms because, without the prohibition of such films, they may sometimes non-autonomously copy caring behaviour. This risk is real—at least for champions of regulation who adopt both the argument from autonomy and the combined empirical hypothesis, and who want to argue that the empirical evidence is to the effect that banning exposure to media violence increases the autonomy of viewers. The example of copying nice behaviour shows that, if that is the position you adopt, you should consider regulating a whole lot more, which few people will find a palatable idea.

Problems with Measurement and Operationalization of Variables

These observations weaken the initial appeal of the argument for regulating media violence construed earlier in this chapter. I now turn to a more specific argument attempting to show that the research that underpins the combined empirical hypothesis is not of the right kind to support liberal policymaking. It centres round the issue of how researchers measure, or 'operationalize', the X and Y variables. The underlying thought is that advocates of regulation sometimes fail to realize that the research they cite often demonstrates an association, not so much between variables X and Y that are relevant to policymaking, but rather between *something-like-X* and *something-like-Y*. But, if the something-like-Y is not a genuine form of harm, the harm principle will have to remain inoperative.

How do researchers measure the two variables of *exposure to media violence* and *aggressive behaviour*? At least three different kinds of operational definition have been used for the *media-violence* variable. First: a temporal measure of hours per day spent playing (violent or non-violent) video games or watching (violent or non-violent) television. Second: subjects' expressed preference for violent video games. And third: in experimental contexts, a random assignment of watching either a violent or a non-violent film.[19] Many more operational measures have been used for the *aggression* variable. First: teacher ratings of a student's aggressiveness. Second: experimenter's rating of observed behaviour (hitting, kicking, pushing). Third: aggression reports by parents, teachers, or peers, or aggression self-reports of subjects. Fourth: the number of recorded times a child hits another child. Fifth: play with aggressive toys. Sixth: physical measures (shock or noise intensity). Seventh: the number of convictions for crime.[20] Further distinctions are made between simulated aggressive behaviour such as hitting a doll, self-reports of aggressive intent, and playing with aggressive toys; minor aggressive behaviour such as non-illegal verbal or physical violence against objects or human beings; and illegal activities such as burglary, grand larceny, and criminal violence against human beings (homicide, rape, assault).[21]

Legal or Illegal Aggression?

What is the point of knowing all this? It should not come as a surprise that the correlation between two variables differs dramatically depending on which operational definitions are used. As long as the *aggression* variable ranges over non-illegal activities, many policymakers will feel no need to take measures. There is no need to curb watching media violence if it does not lead to criminal violence (or other criminal activities). Given that most of the research involves non-illegal activities such as hitting a doll, or reporting aggressive fantasies, we have some reason for suspicion here. This is underscored by Paik and Comstock's meta-analysis of the literature on violence on television and aggression.[22] They find a correlation of $r = 0.31$ for all observations in which the *aggression* variable measures simulated or minor aggression. They find $r = 0.17$ for illegal activities, and $r = 0.10$ for criminal violence against human beings. As long we are interested in preventing illegal activities, only the last two figures are important.

To appreciate this point, suppose that, in defence of regulating media violence, a policymaker were to cite research demonstrating a correlation between the following two variables: *hours per day watching television* and *playing with aggressive toys* (and assume that this link is causal). What regulation would follow? Since *hours per day watching television* includes any kind of television programme, policymakers using such research findings cannot distinguish between violent and non-violent television programmes. The X variable is not subtle enough. Equally problematic, *playing with aggressive toys* is not immoral or illegal by any liberal standards. The Y variable does not measure genuine criminal harm. As a result, such research is quite meaningless for regulatory purposes.

Bypassing Autonomy?

To exploit the full force of the combined empirical hypothesis for the purposes of an argument for regulating media violence, a further issue is crucial: the *aggression* variable must be restricted to only non-autonomously copied criminal violence. To see why, let us briefly consider existing forms of policy based on information about statistical correlations. In the earlier mentioned cases of passive smoking and exposure to asbestos (which were examples of correlations of around $r = 0.10$), the potentially harmed person is the person who is exposed to smoke or asbestos, and the policy is meant to decrease the chances that that person will experience harm.

This is different in the case of media violence, for reasons that have to do with the fact that the harm resulting from speech and expression is *mediated*, as I called it earlier. In the media-violence case, the potentially harmed person is a third person Q, who may suffer from the criminal behaviour of a person P exposed to media violence.[23] The logic here is not the same as that of smoking and asbestos, because, as long as P can be held personally responsible for their actions, many policymakers will see little reason to regulate media violence, no matter how large the correlation coefficient may be.

To summarize, for the data to be relevant to policymakers, there has to be a correlation between exposure to media violence and criminal violence (the social psychology part of the combined hypothesis) that is non-autonomously copied, which means bypassing autonomy and responsibility (the neuroscience/cognitive science part). And here is the crux: the precise value of the relevant correlation cannot be gathered from the research underlying the combined empirical hypothesis.

It is not unlikely that the correlation will be smaller than $r = 0.10$, though. First, while social psychologists found a correlation between exposure to media violence and subsequent illegal activities of $r = 0.17$, this figure ($r = 0.17$) is irrelevant here, because these activities do not involve copying media violence. Stealing a candy bar after seeing a film in which someone was killed with a rifle is a case of subsequent illegal activity, but not one of violence. And we are interested only in non-autonomously copied criminal violence. A more relevant coefficient is therefore the correlation between exposure to media violence and criminal behaviour, $r = 0.10$. This coefficient, however, is in all likelihood still too high for our purposes, because it correlates exposure to media violence with any form of criminal violence, whereas only some instances of criminal violence are imitation in the strict, literal sense in which it is used in the literature on the chameleon effect and mirror neurons. If I watch a film in which a villain is killed with a rifle, I do not copy behaviour in the relevant sense if I punch someone in the face.

Nor is that all, because not only should the violence be copied; it should be non-autonomously copied. Typical school, college, and university shooting incidents, for instance, involve an aggressor who very consciously and autonomously decided to buy a gun to copy what they saw on television or in video games. Because no bypassing of autonomy takes place, this type of incident is, perhaps surprisingly, not covered by the argument for regulation that is the topic of this chapter. This means that the only relevant correlation coefficient is one relating exposure to media violence to *non-autonomously copied criminal violence*, where each of the emphasized words is necessary. And, while it is theoretically possible that this correlation is (much) higher than $r = 0.10$, in all likelihood it is smaller. But a correlation smaller than that is too small for liberal policy.

A Way Out for the Regulation Advocate?

Let me take stock. I argued that the combined empirical hypothesis does not give us reason to think that the argument from hearer autonomy fails to protect exposure to media violence. Furthermore, I showed that the correlation between exposure to media violence and non-autonomously copied criminal violence is too low to support general regulation. But suppose that a champion of regulation grants all this. Would it still be possible for them to argue that, at least in certain particular cases, exposure to media violence ought to be banned? They might be inspired by Justice Holmes's famous remark: 'The most stringent protection of free speech would not protect a man in falsely shouting fire in a theatre and causing a panic.'[24] This remark indicates that any sensible argument for freedom of speech leaves some cases unprotected. While Justice Holmes's remark was not made in such a context, these unprotected cases are often such that they involve significant damage resulting from the physical manifestations of the utterance rather than from its (propositional or expressive) content. An example is when one bars a person from voicing their political opinions through a megaphone causing nearby listeners' eardrums to break.[25] The range of unprotected cases may be rather extensive, at least in principle. If someone can express themselves only in ways that physically damage others—they have too loud a voice and no ability to communicate their views in any other way—then all their utterances are unprotected. In a world in which there are many such unprotected cases, there will de facto be many restrictions of free speech that can be defended without any need to retract even the slightest bits of the argument from autonomy (or any other argument for freedom of speech and expression, for that matter).

A champion of the regulation of media violence might therefore try to reason in the following way. They could grant that the argument from hearer autonomy is left untouched by the findings underlying the combined empirical hypothesis, and they could grant that the relevant correlation coefficient is too small to support general regulation. Nonetheless, they could try to describe particular unprotected cases. If these cases are many, and the combined empirical hypothesis plays a role in demarcating them, then they would still be able to succeed in making use of that very hypothesis in an argument for regulation of media violence.

This last-ditch attempt is, however, doomed to fail. To see this, three routes have to be examined along which one might go about construing unprotected cases. First: unprotecting certain quantities of exposure; second: unprotecting certain kinds of media violence; and, third: unprotecting certain viewers.

With respect to the quantity of exposure to media violence, the combined empirical hypothesis gives precise and relevant conditions. It entails that not only long-term, severe exposure, but also one-shot exposure to a single violent episode, can cause aggression, often in the short term. As a result, there is no such thing as a moderate, non-dangerous dose of media-violence consumption. This means that regulations involving a quota such as a one-hour game a day, or a film a week, do not make any sense. If regulation is to be developed along the lines of unprotected cases, then it will not allow for quotas.

Similar reasoning applies to the kind of media violence. While the psychological research on which the combined empirical hypothesis rests reveals that different kinds of media violence give rise to different levels of aggression, even such cartoons as *Tom and Jerry* lead to significant increases in aggressive behaviour. A consequence of this is that the class of unprotected cases, if it can meaningfully be defined, will include a fairly wide spectrum of kinds of display of violence, and will certainly not coincide smoothly with the boundaries set by current age limits on films and video games. The restrictions will be more or less total. If a champion of regulation wants to unprotect, they will have to bite the bullet and unprotect exposure to any form of media violence.

Third: can we single out certain viewers and define a class of unprotected cases? Here too the answer is negative. The combined empirical hypothesis reveals a statistical, not a deterministic, correlation between exposure to media violence and subsequent non-autonomously copied aggressive behaviour. Not all viewers become aggressive after watching media violence, and instances of exposure to these non-aggressors should not, of course, be unprotected. Moreover, on the basis of the combined hypothesis, it is impossible to single out beforehand which viewers will show aggression, and which ones not. There is no evidence that, say, only individuals with already increased levels of aggression are susceptible, or that certain individual characteristics indicate higher susceptibility, or that, in particular environments, certain individuals have a higher disposition to imitate violence. As a result, there is no class of individuals to unprotect. This gives us a further reason to believe that regulation of media violence on the basis of the combined empirical hypothesis will not fly. Since the combined empirical hypothesis is by far the most sophisticated body of empirical evidence available to that end, we must conclude that the chances of defending regulation of media violence are dim.

The Epistemic First Amendment

The focus of this chapter is on depictions of violent behaviour, on television, in films, or in video games. To conclude, I ask the question whether my argument applies to other forms of speech and expression as well, such as hate speech, fake news, or puffery. I start here with what looks like the typical thought behind freedom of speech: that, in a market where people exchange their ideas and opinions, truth will come out winning. In a well-known case that came before the US Supreme Court in 1919, Justice Holmes phrased it thus:

> The best test of truth is the power of the thought to get itself accepted in the competition of the market, and … truth is the only ground upon which [people's] wishes safely can be carried out.[26]

Holmes is perhaps not the founding father of this idea, which is generally thought to go back at least as far as John Milton's *Areopagitica*.[27] It is this statement, however, that has become the *locus classicus* of the marketplace of ideas model of freedom of speech. But, as Richard Posner observed, Holmes's arguments 'owe their distinction to their rhetorical skill rather than to the qualities of their reasoning'.[28] This seems underscored by a wealth of findings from psychology, behavioural economics, and other fields.[29] One might be led to think that the observations discussed in this chapter only reinforce this conclusion; for, indeed, it is hard to see how a marketplace of ideas could be conducive to collective truth-finding when market participants process information in ways that bypass their autonomous decision-making. If the market is to do its work, then participants should consciously evaluate, and if necessary criticize, each other's views. Sheepishly copying views is far removed from doing that.

I happen to think that contemporary social science offers less than conclusive evidence to back such radical conclusions, because, it seems to me, there is sufficient room for personal responsibility regarding belief formation to make genuine cases of bypassing autonomous control rare. This is not to say, however, that these empirical findings should be set aside without further ado. To see why that is so, it is instructive to consider a new strand of defence of the First Amendment, the piece of American law guaranteeing freedom of speech. Building on earlier applications of epistemology to conceptualize the First Amendment, Joseph Blocher has proffered what he calls a *knowledge-based approach* to free speech.[30] His account centres round the idea that the constitutional value of free speech should not so much be located in truth, but rather in justification, thought of as among the elements that give a belief the status of knowledge. The goal of free speech is, according to Blocher, not to maximize the number of truths (or true beliefs), but rather the 'development of knowledge'.[31] Among the key observations supporting this claim is the observation that knowledge is a 'guide to action'.[32] Here Blocher's position seems to be close to those of Timothy Williamson and John Hawthorne, discussed in Chapter 3. The idea is that, when you know, say, the way to Larisa, your beliefs (constituting knowledge) are less easily lost than if you happened to possess only mere true beliefs.[33] Knowledge is practically relevant.

Back to the main line. I argued in this chapter that the empirical findings from social psychology and neuroscience/cognitive science do not support further regulation of media violence. Yet, if the constitutional value of free speech is to be located in the acquisition of practically relevant knowledge, then one could ask if perhaps some restrictions of freedom of speech may be defended if we take epistemic freedom, as conceptualized in Chapter 2, as our point of departure. Here is the (admittedly tentative) idea. Typically, an account of the constitutional value of freedom of speech (such as the marketplace of ideas, democracy, autonomy) protects speech (that is unprotected by the harm principle) to the extent that it contributes to the value underlying the account. Typical arguments in this domain—not only as relayed by the US Supreme Court, but also in other jurisdictions as well as in academia—involve the question of whether a particular restriction of free speech should be permitted in the light of such accounts.[34]

One way to read Hurley's argument about autonomy is, however, that sometimes promoting the value underlying the account should require restricting freedom of speech. Hurley submits that fostering autonomy might require restricting exposure to media violence. If knowledge is the central ideal that free speech fosters, then one might reason à la Hurley that some person S's freedom to utter speech φ may have to be curtailed if uttering φ obstructs another person R's freedom to gain knowledge. Such an argument could be derived for the alethic version of the marketplace of ideas account of free speech, in the sense that an omniscient state might be in the position to silence every falsehood. This is, however, empirically implausible, to say the least.[35]

Let me conclude. I do not want to be taken to exclude the possibility that some restriction of freedom of speech could be defended on the basis of the fact that some speech might sometimes bypass autonomous control in some people. But we should be very cautious when we think we have found evidence that shows such bypassing actually happens, and, even if we find the evidence sufficiently reliable, there are additional reasons not to move to regulation immediately. It is part of our psychology that some bypassing will happen in all of us, and it seems to me a far better strategy for the state—except where there is genuine vulnerability and incapacity— to spend money on helping citizens become more epistemically resilient, and to endow them with the skills and knowledge necessary to mitigate the influence of problematic speech and expression.[36] This is not my main concern in this book, though.

Notes

1. See, generally, Thomas Emerson, *The System of Freedom of Expression* (New York: Random House, 1970).
2. Luc Bovens, 'Moral Luck, Photojournalism, and Pornography', *Journal of Value Inquiry*, 32 (1998), 205–217, at 205.
3. See, e.g., Thomas Scanlon, 'A Theory of Freedom of Expression', *Philosophy and Public Affairs*, 1 (1972), 204–226, at 215 ('To regard himself as autonomous in the sense I have in mind a person must see himself as sovereign in deciding what to believe and in weighing competing reasons for action. He must apply to these tasks his own canons of rationality, and must recognize the need to defend his beliefs and decisions in accordance with these canons'.) His definition of autonomy underlies Susan Hurley, 'Imitation, Media Violence, and Freedom of Speech', *Philosophical Studies*, 117 (2004), 165–218, Susan Hurley, 'Applying the Science of Imitation to the Imitation of Violence', in Hurley and Nick Chater (eds), *Perspectives on Imitation: From Neuroscience to Social Science: Volume 2: Imitation, Human Development, and Culture* (Cambridge, MA: MIT Press, 2005), 380–385, and Susan Hurley, 'Bypassing Conscious Control: Media Violence, Unconscious Imitation, and Freedom of Speech', in Susan Pockett, William Banks, and Shaun Gallagher (eds), *Does Consciousness Cause*

Behavior? An Investigation of the Nature of Volition (Cambridge, MA: MIT Press), 301–337, which inspired this chapter. See also Thomas Scanlon, 'Freedom of Expression and Categories of Expression', *University of Pittsburgh Law Review*, 40 (1979), 519–550, for a revised view.

4. See, for a critical evaluation of this argument, e.g., Susan Brison, 'The Autonomy Defense of Free Speech', *Ethics*, 108 (1998), 312–339.

5. See, e.g., Craig Anderson and Brad Bushman, 'Effects of Violent Video Games on Aggressive Behaviour, Aggressive Cognition, Aggressive Affect, Physiological Arousal, and Prosocial Behaviour: A Meta-Analytic Review of the Scientific Literature', *Psychological Science*, 12 (2001), 353–359, Craig Anderson, Leonard Berkowitz, Edward Donnerstein, Rowell Huesmann, James Johnson, Daniel Linz, Neil Malamuth, and Ellen Wartella, 'The Influence of Media Violence on Youth', *Psychological Science in the Public Interest*, 4 (2003), 81–110, Susan Hurley, 'Imitation, Media Violence, and Freedom of Speech', *Philosophical Studies*, 117 (2004), 165–218, and Susan Hurley, 'Applying the Science of Imitation to the Imitation of Violence', in Hurley and Nick Chater (eds), *Perspectives on Imitation: From Neuroscience to Social Science: Volume 2: Imitation, Human Development, and Culture* (Cambridge, MA: MIT Press, 2005), 380–385. Cf. Gordon Dahl and Stefano DellaVigna, 'Does Movie Violence Increase Violent Crime?', *Quarterly Journal of Economics*, 124 (2009), 677–734, for an empirical argument that exposure to media violence *decreases* violent crime in the short and medium run.

6. See, e.g., Susan Brison, 'The Autonomy Defense of Free Speech', *Ethics*, 108 (1998), 312–339, Moshe Cohen-Eliya and Yoav Hammer, 'Advertisements, Stereotypes, and Freedom of Eexpression', *Journal of Social Philosophy*, 35 (2004), 165–187, and Filimon Peonidis, 'Freedom of Expression, Autonomy, and Defamation', *Law and Philosophy*, 17 (1998), 1–17. Cf. Kenton Machina, 'Freedom of Expression in Commerce', *Law and Philosophy*, 3 (1984), 375–406.

7. Haejung Paik and George Comstock, 'The Effects of Television Violence on Antisocial Behaviour: A Meta-Analysis', *Communication Research*, 21 (1994), 516–546, Craig Anderson and Brad Bushman, 'Effects of Violent Video Games on Aggressive Behaviour, Aggressive Cognition, Aggressive Affect, Physiological Arousal, and Prosocial Behaviour: A Meta-Analytic Review of the Scientific Literature', *Psychological Science*, 12 (2001), 353–359, and Craig Anderson, Leonard Berkowitz, Edward Donnerstein, Rowell Huesmann, James Johnson, Daniel Linz, Neil Malamuth, and Ellen Wartella, 'The Influence of Media Violence on Youth', *Psychological Science in the Public Interest*, 4 (2003), 81–110.

8. Jeffrey Johnson, Patricia Cohen, Elizabeth Smailes, Stephanie Kasen, and Judith Brook, 'Television Viewing and Aggressive Behavior during Adolescence and Adulthood', *Science*, 295 (2002), 2468–2471.

9. These examples are mentioned by Susan Hurley, 'Imitation, Media Violence, and Freedom of Speech', *Philosophical Studies*, 117 (2004), 180–181, who attributes them to Leonard Berkowitz, *Aggression: Its Causes, Consequences, and Control* (New York: McGraw-Hill, 1993), 204–205, 210 ff. See also ibid. 205–207, 228–229.

10. Tanya Chartrand and John Bargh, 'The Chameleon-Effect: The Perception–Behavior Link and Social Interaction', *Journal of Personality and Social Psychology*, 76 (1999), 893–910.

11. See, e.g., Giacomo Rizzolatti and Laila Craighero, 'The Mirror-Neuron System', *Annual Review of Neuroscience*, 27 (2004), 169–192. Cf. Vittorio Gallese and Alvin Goldman, 'Mirror Neurons and the Simulation Theory of Mind-Reading', *Trends in Cognitive Science*, 2 (1998), 493–501.

12. For a discussion of ideomotor theory relevant to the present context, see Wolfgang Prinz, 'An Ideomotor Approach to Imitation', in Susan Hurley and Nick Chater (eds), *Perspectives on Imitation: From Neuroscience to Social Sciences: Volume 1* (Cambridge, MA: MIT Press, 2004), 141–156.

13. Susan Hurley, 'Imitation, Media Violence, and Freedom of Speech', *Philosophical Studies*, 117 (2004), 165–218, Susan Hurley, 'Applying the Science of Imitation to the Imitation of Violence', in Hurley and Nick Chater (eds), *Perspectives on Imitation: From Neuroscience to Social Science: Volume 2: Imitation, Human Development, and Culture* (Cambridge, MA: MIT Press, 2005), 380–385, Susan Hurley, 'Bypassing Conscious Control: Media Violence, Unconscious Imitation, and Freedom of Speech', in Susan Pockett, William Banks, and Shaun Gallagher (eds), *Does Consciousness Cause Behavior? An Investigation of the Nature of Volition* (Cambridge, MA: MIT Press), 301–337, and Craig Anderson, Leonard Berkowitz, Edward Donnerstein, Rowell Huesmann, James Johnson, Daniel Linz, Neil Malamuth, and Ellen Wartella, 'The Influence of Media Violence on Youth', *Psychological Science in the Public Interest*, 4 (2003), 81–110.

14. Susan Hurley, 'Imitation, Media Violence, and Freedom of Speech', *Philosophical Studies*, 117 (2004), 165–218, at 186.

15. Jacob Cohen, *Statistical Power Analysis for the Behavioral Sciences* (San Diego: Academic Press, 1969).

16. Joanne Savage, 'Does Viewing Violent Media Really Cause Criminal Violence? A Methodological Review', *Aggression and Violent Behavior*, 10 (2004), 99–128, casts doubt on the causality claim that underlies the argument for regulation of media violence.

17. See, e.g., Mark Wolfson and Mary Hourigan, 'Unintended Consequences and Professional Ethics: Criminalization of Alcohol and Tobacco Use by Youth and Young Adults', *Addiction*, 92 (1997), 1159–1164.

18. See, e.g., Gordon Dahl and Stefano DellaVigna, 'Does Movie Violence Increase Violent Crime?', *Quarterly Journal of Economics*, 124 (2009), 677–734.

19. Craig Anderson and Brad Bushman, 'Effects of Violent Video Games on Aggressive Behaviour, Aggressive Cognition, Aggressive Affect, Physiological Arousal, and Prosocial Behaviour: A Meta-Analytic Review of the Scientific Literature', *Psychological Science*, 12 (2001), 353–359, Craig Anderson, Leonard Berkowitz, Edward Donnerstein, Rowell Huesmann, James Johnson, Daniel Linz, Neil Malamuth, and Ellen Wartella, 'The Influence of Media Violence on Youth', *Psychological Science in the Public Interest*, 4 (2003), 81–110, Haejung Paik and George Comstock, 'The Effects of Television Violence on Antisocial Behaviour: A Meta-Analysis', *Communication Research*, 21 (1994), 516–546, also for subcategories used to mark the content of a video game or television show as *violent, violent–erotica, cartoon or fantasy, sports, action or adventure or crime, news or current affairs,* and *westerns.*

20. Craig Anderson and Brad Bushman, 'Effects of Violent Video Games on Aggressive Behaviour, Aggressive Cognition, Aggressive Affect, Physiological Arousal, and Prosocial Behaviour: A Meta-Analytic Review of the Scientific Literature', *Psychological Science*, 12 (2001), 353–359.

21. Haejung Paik and George Comstock, 'The Effects of Television Violence on Antisocial Behaviour: A Meta-Analysis', *Communication Research*, 21 (1994), 516–546.

22. Ibid.

23. See Barrett Prettyman Jr and Lisa Hook, 'The Control of Media-Related Imitative Violence', *Federal Communications Law Journal*, 38 (1987), 317–382, for forms of damage to one's own person resulting from copying the behaviour of, e.g., a stunt man in a television show.

24. *Schenck* v. *United States* [1919] 249 US 52.

25. See also Thomas Scanlon, 'A Theory of Freedom of Expression', *Philosophy and Public Affairs*, 1 (1972), 204–226, at 210.

26. *Abrams* v. *United States* [1919] 250 US 616, 630 (Holmes, J., dissenting).

27. Vincent Blasi, 'A Reader's Guide to John Milton's *Areopagitica*, the Foundational Essay of the First Amendment Tradition', *Supreme Court Review*, 2017 (2018), 273–312.

28. Richard Posner, 'Introduction', in Posner (ed.), *The Essential Holmes: Selections from the Letters, Speeches, Judicial Opinions, and Other Writings of Oliver Wendell Holmes, Jr* (Chicago: University of Chicago Press, 1992), p. xvii.

29. Joseph Blocher, 'Free Speech and Justified True Belief', *Harvard Law Review*, 133 (2019), 439–496, at 441.

30. Ibid. 445. See also Paul Horwitz, 'The First Amendment's Epistemological Problem', *University of Washington Law Review*, 87 (2012), 445–493, Douglas Husak and Craig Callender, 'Willful Ignorance, Knowledge, and the "Equal

Culpability" Thesis: A Study of the Deeper Significance of the Principle of Legality', *Wisconsin Law Review*, 1994 (1994), 29–70, and Christian Turner, 'The Burden of Knowledge', *Georgia Law Review*, 43 (2009), 297–365.

31. Joseph Blocher, 'Free Speech and Justified True Belief', *Harvard Law Review*, 133 (2019), 439–496, at 459.

32. Ibid. 470.

33. Ibid. 471. Blocher suggests that this was Socrates' view. See Chapter 3 for textual evidence that in the *Meno* Socrates may have thought that a true-belief guide is just as good as a knowing guide when it comes to helping you reach Larisa.

34. See also Onora O'Neill, 'Ethics for Communication?', *European Journal of Philosophy*, 17 (2009), 167–180, at 167–170.

35. See Joseph Blocher, 'Free Speech and Justified True Belief', *Harvard Law Review*, 133 (2019), 439–496, at 473–474.

36. See Reid Standish, 'Why Is Finland Able to Fend off Putin's Information War?', *Foreign Policy*, 1 March 2017, foreignpolicy.com/2017/03/01/why-is-finland-able-to-fend-off-putins-information-war/ [perma.cc/ZV5T-73YS], for a suggestion that Finish education may instil such skills and knowledge, more than elsewhere.

8
Liberal Privacy and Legal Protection

Liberals often wrestle with privacy, especially liberals operating with a negative conception of freedom. Some even hold that privacy has little liberal value and ought not to receive much special legal protection. Such people see the pursuit of privacy as self-interested economic behaviour, aimed at concealing 'discreditable' facts about oneself, which is opposed to liberal interests such as freedom of speech, freedom of market transactions, or security.[1] Generally, therefore, they do not object to the presence of surveillance cameras in public spaces, to bookshops forwarding information about customers to companies or government agencies, or to airlines requiring numerous items of data from travellers boarding planes. Naturally, these sceptics about the value of privacy acknowledge that the disclosure of private information can have unpleasant—even harmful—effects, but they assert that such effects are outweighed by the value of freedom (or economic growth, or security, and so on). Most problems arising from invasions of privacy should, they think, therefore be left to individual consumers and companies rather than the state to organize and redress.[2]

I argue in this chapter that this view, while initially plausible, should be revisited. Before proceeding, however, let me stipulate: an invasion of the privacy of a person P involves a person S disclosing some fact about P to a third person R. Here P and S may be identical. Privacy is consequently a triadic relation between a sender, a subject, and a recipient.[3] Moreover, it is important to realize that the liberal sceptic is not putting forward the argument that privacy lacks value to the extent that people have nothing to hide. This nothing-to-hide argument, perhaps more often voiced by laypeople than legal scholars, is to the effect that, as long as I do not perform any illegal and immoral acts, I have nothing to be afraid of. Consequently, I do not have to hide anything, and so my privacy lacks value. In contrast

The Business of Liberty. Boudewijn de Bruin, Oxford University Press.
© Boudewijn de Bruin (2022). DOI: 10.1093/oso/9780198839675.003.0009

to proponents of the nothing-to-hide argument, liberal privacy sceptics acknowledge that, even though I do not perform illegal or immoral actions, others may use information about me in ways that harm (or benefit) me.[4]

Arguments for Privacy

It is not only this naive nothing-to-hide argument but also more theoretically inspired arguments for privacy that fail to convince the liberal sceptic.

Perspective Change

Take the argument from perspective change, put forward by Stanley Benn and Robert Gerstein, and already discussed to some extent in Chapter 4.[5] It is to the effect that, if I were to discover someone observing me while I am engaged in certain activities, I would change from being a genuine participant in the action to being an observer of it, which—the defenders of this argument opine—is bad. However, many privacy sceptics are not troubled overmuch by subjective feelings of perspective change. They will hold that, after all, it is possible to carry out the tasks irrespective of whether or not someone is watching you.

Relationships

Take the argument from relationships, developed mainly by Charles Fried and James Rachels.[6] According to these authors, privacy is a necessary condition for many human relationships, because relationships involve the mutual giving of gifts in the form of information exchange; and such gift-giving prospers only when individuals have secure possession of what they want to give—namely, private information. Yet, does another person's listening into a conversation between friends really make it impossible to share intimate thoughts and feelings? The privacy sceptic will doubt that. The friends may *feel* inhibited, but that does not mean that they *are* inhibited.

Dignity

Or take the argument from human dignity, introduced into the literature by Samuel Warren and Louis Brandeis as well as by Edward Bloustein.[7] It is to the effect that invasions of a person's privacy go against their dignity. The source of this argument is a famous case that came before the Michigan Supreme Court in 1881.[8] A woman laid a complaint against a man who had been present when she was giving birth and who was presumed to be connected to the medical profession whereas in fact he was not. Thereby, it was claimed, he had affronted the woman's dignity. Now, in this case, privacy sceptics will not be so callous as to ignore the fact that the woman suffered feelings of 'shame and mortification', as was argued, but what they will condemn is the man's pretending to have a false identity, rather than an invasion of privacy.

Autonomy

Finally, take the argument from autonomy, which has been propounded by Beate Rössler, among others.[9] Starting from the assumption that the possession of correct beliefs about what others know about me fosters my autonomy, this argument claims that it is in my interest to be in control of what others know about me. It matters, for instance, in terms of my decision to practise the salsa in my office whether or not I know someone is watching me. But, again, liberal privacy sceptics would not be moved. Someone peeping through my office window in no way obstructs me from dancing. I must not be too squeamish.

Acting under Some Description

Can we not sway the liberal sceptic? Perhaps we could, if we showed that, upon closer inspection, they should admit that invasions of a person's privacy do decrease the extent of their freedom. A first attempt is the following. Strictly speaking, activities such as having sexual intercourse, exchanging secret information, or giving birth can, as the sceptic correctly notes, also be performed if someone were to keep you under observation. But, one might think, the logic of these activities requires that they be performed unwatched. If someone listens in, it is just not possible, for example, to exchange secrets, or to correct a friend's mispronunciation of a particular foreign term in a discreet manner. Similarly, it is impossible to give birth in the typical way if someone unrelated is watching you.[10] Or so one might think. This attempt can be successful, however, only if we assume a rather broad manner of describing actions, which is not universally accepted. How can I make a distinction between two opportunity sets, one containing the option of correcting mispronunciation, the other correcting it discreetly, if both actions involve uttering exactly the same words? We also risk circularity here, since absence of a privacy invasion now becomes part of the description of the action.

Privacy and Freedom

I propose a different way to meet the liberal sceptical challenge. I defend the claim here that disclosures of private information lead to changes in our freedom and/or to changes in the knowledge we have concerning the extent of our freedom. This means that our interest in privacy reduces to an interest in freedom and known freedom, as developed in Chapter 3. My approach has the advantage that it allows us to cast arguments about the protection of a person's privacy in a uniform normative vocabulary. Whether or not to protect a person's privacy in a certain situation is almost always a question of balancing; it involves trade-offs. But the traditional arguments surveyed here put a rather heterogeneous collection on the scales: perspective changes or human dignity, on the one side, for instance, and freedom of speech or freedom of market transactions, on the other. As soon as we cast the value of privacy in terms of freedom and known freedom, only one currency is needed—liberty.

Recall the conception of freedom set out in Chapter 1 according to which I am unfree to perform some action A if someone interferes with my performance of A or if someone has the disposition to interfere with my performance of A, were I to attempt to A, as proposed by Matthew Kramer.[11] Observe that it does not matter here whether the interference is intentional or not. To use the earlier examples, my freedom to travel home is obstructed by the police blocking the road (they interfere), by a highway robber forcing me to stop at gunpoint (who has the disposition to interfere as soon as I attempt to drive on), or by a bridge superintendent forgetting to close the open bridge (unintentionally). But also observe that my freedom is not restricted by my ignorance of topography, my lack of driving skills, or my absentmindedness, as these factors do not involve external obstacles. These things affect my knowledge about my freedom.

Some Examples

To start my argument for the liberal value of privacy, I begin with a number of examples of how disclosures of private information decrease freedom. I keep the dialectic restricted to examples that have frequently featured in the literature on privacy.

First: a top-ranking midshipman at the Naval Academy, Joseph Steffan, told his chaplain about his own homosexuality.[12] The chaplain passed this information on to his superiors, who forced Steffan to resign (on the basis of old Pentagon regulations barring gay people from the military, still operative in the late 1980s).

A second example comes from Amitai Etzioni.[13] It involves a banker who was illegally given access to a Maryland government database of medical records. Obtaining knowledge about the medical situations of a number of his bank's clients, he forced customers diagnosed with cancer to pay off their loans.

Third: subsequent to the rape and murder of a 7-year-old-girl, Megan Kanka, numerous states in the US implemented laws requiring sex offenders to register with a public database allowing every interested individual access to information about the sex offenders' home addresses, offences, photographs, and many other personal data. This has led, in some cases, to harassment of sex offenders (and bystanders mistaken for them), to actual vigilantism, and even to the death of registered sex offenders.[14]

Fourth: employers increasingly consult social networking websites such as Facebook in order to check the profiles of candidates they consider hiring, and some even admit to having decided against candidates because of the *risqué* pictures such profiles contain or the wild student life boasted about. One student interviewed by a *New York Times* journalist reported that, as soon as he had removed some material from the Internet, he began to receive invitations to job interviews.[15] Telling, even if anecdotal.

Disclosure, Belief Revision in Recipient, and Actions

I have introduced these examples as I take them to suggest that the connection between privacy and freedom has a three-step structure. The first step is the very disclosure of information. A sender S discloses information about a subject P to a recipient R. (Note that P and S may be identical.) Disclosure is used in a general sense here, as it may involve not only speaking and writing but also drawing R's attention to a certain scene involving P that is happening right now, sending R a photograph capturing P in a certain situation, showing video footage of P, passing on P's criminal or medical records, or S allowing R to hack S's website containing P's home address or other data.

The second step covers belief revision. On the basis of the information obtained from S, person R revises their earlier beliefs about P. This may amount to adding more information, more detail, and leaving earlier beliefs intact; often, though, it will involve a real change of belief. There are three options. First, R may update their beliefs about P, and adopt a doxastic attitude of belief towards some proposition φ (about P) about which they had so far suspended judgement. Second, R may change their disbelief that φ to a belief that φ (or their belief that φ to a disbelief that φ). And third, sometimes, of course, R may reject information about P that S provides and neither update nor change any of their beliefs.

The third and final step involves action. The changed or updated beliefs concerning φ (the proposition about P) may motivate P to perform a certain action they would not have performed had S not provided the information concerning P. The simple thought now is: if performing this action constitutes interference with P, then P's freedom has been reduced as a result of an invasion of privacy. Clearly, just as much as the information that S provides (and the resulting belief about φ) may lead R to perform some action, it may also lead them to omit an action, and both may constitute interference. I can actively block the road, or refrain from letting the bridge down. I will not stress this all the time, but what I say about actions is true, with the necessary changes, of omissions as well.

Dispositions to Action

Here is another key observation: the new doxastic attitude towards φ can offer a reason for R to perform some action (or to omit it), but also merely to adopt a disposition to perform some action (or to omit it). Consider the following two cases.

First: having learned that a convicted sex offender moved into her neighbourhood, a woman in Timberlane (Washington) decided that she would gun him down if he came too close to her house.[16] The sex offender never came close to her house, but, if the woman's decision was genuine enough (as there seems no reason to assume it was not), the man would not have survived if he had tried. Many sex offenders are equally unfree to enter areas around kindergartens and other schools. Most of them do not try, but, if they did, watchful and informed parents would stand in their way.

Second: several airline companies use information about travel itineraries to decide on whom they choose to put on their 'no-fly lists'.[17] Many of the individuals appearing on such lists never buy tickets from these airline companies, but, if they did, they would be barred from flying to certain destinations.

The woman in Timberlane did not use the new information concerning the sex offender to perform an actual interfering action, but she did use it to change her disposition to act. The no-fly policy similarly embodies a changed disposition towards certain potential customers. Following Kramer's concept of freedom in use here, these changed dispositions constitute a decrease of freedom, just as much as actual interference. This means that we have slightly to revise the formulation of the third step in the connection between privacy and freedom: it may involve not only the performance or omission of an action, but also the adoption of a disposition to perform or omit some action.

It is important to reiterate my response to a potential objection to the effect that referring to dispositions might lead to the inclusion of counterfactual or hypothetical obstacles, making the conception of freedom too broad. The reply is that the counterfactuality resides not in the interferer's actions or dispositions. The woman's decision to kill the sex offender and the no-fly policy have nothing counterfactual, but are very real. Rather, the counterfactuality resides in the interferee's performance of the action.[18] The sex offender never actually entered her neighbourhood, the person on the no-fly list never actually bought a one-way ticket from, say, Tehran to London, and so the very real disposition was never triggered.

To reinforce this point, an example along the lines from Chapter 2 may help. Suppose that I am working in my office. In one scenario, the door has been locked and I do not have a key. I am unfree to leave. In another scenario, someone is waiting outside my office. They have the key in their hands, and, if they heard me approaching the door, they would lock it. I do not have the key myself, so in this scenario too I cannot leave my office; for, if I attempted to leave the room, I would find the door locked. I am unfree in both situations. Many unfreedoms are exactly of this form. That I am unfree to protest against the government, or to travel abroad, may involve actual barriers. More often, though, my unfreedom will reside in the fact that, if I attempted to protest or travel, I would be interfered with. Excluding dispositions to interfere would give rise to an implausible evaluation of the freedom of, for instance, citizens of totalitarian regimes. Therefore, it is preferable to have a conception of freedom that takes dispositions to interfere as reductions of the extent of a person's freedom.

General Form of Privacy Invasions

Back to privacy. Disclosure of private information leads to belief revision, which in turn leads to the performance of actions, or dispositions to perform actions. This framework is entirely general. To be sure, it can be expected that the privacy cases that are brought before courts typically involve some decreases of freedom, but there is no reason why disclosure of information should decrease freedom at all times.

If agent S discloses information φ about P to R, the information may not be new to R (they already believe that φ, say), in which case R has no reason to change the plan of action they settled on before S provided the information about φ to R. And, even if the information is new to R, the beliefs revised in accordance with that information need not offer a reason for R to change their planned actions vis-à-vis P. To go back to the earlier examples, a banker obtaining information about a client's cancer diagnosis, or an employer learning about a prospective candidate's behaviour at student parties, may simply find no grounds therein to change their (dispositions to) actions.

In fact, disclosing private information may just as often be essential to *increase* one's freedom. A large number of services are impossible to obtain if customers do not identify themselves (entrance to a night club, hospital, banking, and so on), and many market transactions also require one to disclose a great deal of private information (buying a house, starting a business). James Whitman even goes so far as to argue that the strictness of the European privacy legislation in comparison to that in the US is one

of the factors that determine differences in individuals' wealth.[19] He argues that, as it is easier in the US, especially in terms of time and costs, for
banks to obtain information about someone's credit record, it is also easier for customers to obtain credit. In such cases, the business updates their
beliefs about the customer, but the actions (or dispositions) motivated by
their updated beliefs do not restrict the customer's freedom; they increase
it. It is true that the examples of privacy invasions given by alarmist authors
typically involve decreases of freedom, but this should not obscure the fact
that disclosures of private information may lead to decreases as well as to
increases of freedom, or to no change at all. It is impossible to conduct
business without giving up some parts of one's privacy.

Difference with Competing Accounts

How does this approach to privacy and freedom differ from the traditional
arguments from perspective change, relationships, and so forth? If someone
is peeping through my office window all the time I am working on a project,
the argument from perspective change suggests I may resent this, because
it forces me to adopt the observer's point of view, thereby making it harder
(or even impossible) for me genuinely to participate in my activities. And, if
someone overhears me talking to a friend, the argument from relationships
implies this makes it harder (or even impossible) to engage in the mutual
gift-giving essential to friendship. It might seem that this shows that the
arguments from perspective change and relationships also indicate ways in
which disclosures of private information make individuals less free. I am
less free to work on the project and to maintain relationships.

But these privacy invasions do not influence my negative freedom to
work on the project or to perform gift-giving actions, because the peeper
and the eavesdropper do not establish external impediments to, say, my
typing at the keyboard or my uttering certain words to my friend. Moreover, unlike the traditional arguments, my analysis is concerned not with
the (perspective on) actions the agent is presently performing, but rather
with the influence an invasion of privacy has on a decision-maker's degree
of freedom at some future point in time. The point is not that the eavesdropper makes it less easy to talk to my friend, but that the eavesdropper
may use what they learn from my conversation with my friend in ways that
frustrate my *future* freedom. Imagine, for instance, that the eavesdropper is

a government informant in the—let us assume—totalitarian country I live in, and my friend and I have talked disparagingly about the current president. Altogether, by focusing on external impediments to future actions, my approach is very different from the traditional ones.

Privacy and Known Freedom

People often resent invasions of their privacy. The traditional arguments explain the feeling of resentment in terms of a perceived frustration to be a genuine participant in a certain action, by feeling affronted, or by feeling obstructed in realizing a certain friendship. The problem with such views, however, is that it is hard to distinguish between a situation in which a person is peeping through your window observing you typing a paper, and a situation in which you share your office with a colleague who observes you typing a paper. Both would be cases of perspective change, yet most people feel resentment only in the former case.

While the traditional arguments find it difficult to account for such forms of resentment, the approach I put forward can be used to proffer an explanation. To that end, it is insufficient to consider the ways in which freedom is compromised, because peeper and colleague may change my freedom to the same degree. Rather, we have to consider the influence of privacy invasions on a person's known freedom.[20] Knowing my colleague sufficiently well, I know that they will not plagiarize my work, use the credit card that is lying on my desk to buy books on the Internet, or gossip to my students about my habit of talking to my computer. My knowledge of the peeper, by contrast, is very limited. I do not know why they are watching me at all. For all I know, they may be trying to find some pattern in my working hours to plan a burglary of my house; they may be attempting to get hold of research secrets; they may be checking whether the office contains anything worth stealing; or they may be doing anthropology fieldwork. This only serves to increase my ignorance about the likelihood of interference with future actions of mine. I am just less sure about what I can do.

More Examples

First: customers of Old National Bancorp, a US bank, filled in online forms requesting personal information from applicants for certain banking services.[21] A hacker got into the bank's computer server, thereby gaining access to confidential information on more than ten thousand individuals. Numerous of these individuals decided to buy credit monitoring services to insure themselves against the risks of future identity theft, thereby reflecting their increased uncertainty about future interference.

Second: three undercover police officers investigated a drug conspiracy in a violent gang in Columbus (Ohio).[22] When some gang members were tried, their lawyers requested access to the personnel files of the officers—and got it. Such files contain information about names, home addresses, phone numbers, driver licence numbers, and information about the officers' family members. None of the officers seems to have suffered from any harm to date; no lawyer seems to have passed on the information to their clients. Clearly, though, the officers' uncertainty about the risk of harmful interference has increased. For all they know, the information might come into the hands of some of the gang's members, and, for all they know, this might lead them to suffer retaliation.

Belief Revision in the Subject

These two examples motivate the following further additions to the small model of privacy invasions already given. The connection between an invasion of privacy and reduced known freedom is a kind of 'internalization' of the earlier connection between privacy and freedom. A sender S discloses private information about a person P to a recipient R. The subject of the information P learns about the disclosure and, internalizing the three-step process linking privacy to freedom, forms the belief that R may use the information to motivate either the performance (or omission) of certain actions, or the adoption of certain dispositions to perform (or omit) certain actions.[23]

First, if P knows R well, P has some information about R's current beliefs, about the ways R changes and updates their beliefs, and about R's desires, norms, values. As a consequence, P can predict the influence that the disclosure of private information will have on R's actions and dispositions, and P's known freedom may be just as accurate as it was before the privacy disclosure. Of course, P's freedom may be less, but, if that is so, then P knows it. Secondly, if P does not know R, however, P will not be able to infer much about what R will do with the information. P may not be able to predict R's action or disposition, and, consequently, P's known freedom will be reduced.

Clearly, whenever P is unaware of the fact that S discloses private information about P to R, the internalization will not take place. This means that, if novel information about P makes R interfere with P, then P will not anticipate such interference. P's known freedom is then reduced, not because P has changed their beliefs (as in the case in which internalization takes place), but because P's freedom has changed in a way that is not matched by a change in P's beliefs. This is far from a hypothetical example. Many recent incidents to do with identity theft and computer fraud are of this type: unbeknownst to you, someone may make use of your social security number in a credit application. If, on the other hand, P knows that S has disclosed private information about them to R, but P does not know what R will do with the information (how they will revise their beliefs, and what actions or dispositions they will settle on, if any), then P will have to suspend a number of beliefs about future opportunities and their probabilistic consequences. A lot hinges on whether P can predict R's belief revision and on R's actions or dispositions.

Suppose I believe that I can fly to London from Tehran. In one scenario I subsequently learn that my travel itineraries have been publicized, and I also learn that, because of that, my name has been put on no-fly lists of all airline carriers connecting Tehran and London. Consequently, I know I am no longer free to fly to London directly. This constitutes a reduction of freedom, but not a reduction of knowledge about my freedom and unfreedom, as I do have accurate beliefs about my unfreedom to fly to London. In another scenario, the only thing I learn is that my past travel itineraries have been sold to some airline carriers. Not knowing much about the criteria that underlie no-fly lists, but knowing that my travel itineraries may be thought of as suspicious, I do not know for sure that I will be barred from flying. But neither am I sure that I will not be barred, so I have to suspend my initial belief that I can fly to London. This constitutes a genuine reduction of known freedom. This is as in the two motivating examples. A hacker gained access to the financial records of a bank's customers, and lawyers of a criminal gang obtained information contained in the personnel files of undercover police officers who had investigated the gang's alleged drug conspiracy activities. This led to a decrease in the victims' known freedom. Upon learning about the privacy invasion, the victims suspended their beliefs about their freedom and unfreedom.

Reasonable and Demonstrable Belief Revision

Not all decreases in known freedom should be taken seriously when we weigh liberal interests, though. Some S informs R, a notorious car thief, about the fact that P is the owner of a fancy Ford Mustang Convertible. P learns about the disclosure and claims no longer to know their car to be safe. But P still parks the car in front of their house, often even leaving it with the key in the ignition. They still act on the belief that the car is safe. In that case, there is no demonstrable change of belief. Or, suppose that S informs R, a reliable and law-abiding friend of P, about the fact that P is the owner of such a car. P learns about the disclosure and decides to hire a person to guard the car twenty-four hours a day. In this case, P's known freedom did in fact decrease—they did revise their beliefs about the likelihood of car theft—but they deployed an irrational, paranoid belief revision policy. They ended up with less knowledge and more confusion. These two cases show that the belief change underlying the decrease in knowledge about freedom has to meet two conditions: it has to be demonstrable and reasonable. To grasp something of what this concretely means, let us look at a number of court cases. While set in America, they are highly instructive and relevant to other jurisdictions.

Examples Again

First, a court case that is often invoked as an illustration in the privacy literature: *Stollenwerk* v. *Tri-West Healthcare Alliance*.[24] This case is about a burglary leading to the theft of laptops and computer hardware on which personal information was stored about customers of Tri-West, a health benefits organization—that is: names, home addresses, and social security numbers. The personal data of one of the claimants (Brandt) were used on several occasions in attempts illegally to obtain a credit account; those of the other claimants (Stollenwerk and his wife) were not. Stollenwerk judged the risk of identity theft high enough to buy credit monitoring services and additional insurance and wanted to be compensated for this by Tri-West. The court, however, rejected this claim.

Stollenwerk's known freedom decreased in demonstrable and reasonable ways. Stollenwerk's action of buying credit monitoring services and extra insurance clearly demonstrates that he changed his beliefs about the likelihood of future interference. He would not have bought such services had he thought that he had incurred no additional risks because of the burglary. Moreover, his beliefs were reasonable to adopt. Computer servers may be stolen for their hardware, but they are also stolen for the data stored on them. The fact that the data of the other claimant (Brandt) were in fact misused (which the court accepted, but Stollenberg allegedly did not know) suggests that Stollenwerk's suspicions were at least minimally reasonable. He did not, for instance, change his beliefs in paranoid ways, claiming an increased likelihood of, say, kidnapping or burglary of his house; and the court documents suggest that he was careful enough to request advice from insurance specialists. The burglary was even covered by national newspapers, in which many experts pointed out the risks run by the victims. Two weeks before Brandt and Stollenwerk filed their claim, the *New York Times* published an article quoting Tri-West's president saying that '[i]t is unlikely that people were breaking in for resale value', as the burglars 'left things that were more valuable and easier to hock'.[25]

Second: *Giordano* v. *Wachovia Securities, LLC* is an example of a decision in which it was concluded that the claimants lacked standing to pursue their claims. In this case, a customer sued her financial services company because a package containing information about customers' names, addresses, and social security numbers was lost in transit by UPS, the package delivery company. The court found that the claimant lacked constitutional standing to bring this action, on the grounds that, as the claimant's claims about the possibility of future identity theft were 'at best … speculative', she had been unsuccessful in proving that she had suffered a compensable injury.[26]

Third: *Ruiz* v. *Gap, Inc.* is an example of another line of decisions, in which courts do rule that claimants have standing to bring suit.[27] In this case, the claimant entered personal information on a website when he applied online for a job at Gap, the clothing retail company. A laptop was stolen containing his and other applicants' information. Unlike in the *Giordano* case, the court in *Ruiz* relied on an expert opinion about the probability of suffering identity theft. It accepted that in the first year after the breach the probability of identity theft is about five times as high as the average probability of identity theft (it rises from 4 per cent to 19 per cent), and therefore concluded that the claimant had standing to sue. However, since the claimant could not demonstrate any *actual* damage, the court did not find the increased risk of identity theft a compensable injury.

How Courts and Lawmakers Should Think about Privacy

These examples illustrate that rather than requesting companies to compensate—and to pay for such things as additional insurance—the trend in data-breach cases is only to require that companies notify customers of data breaches. Clearly notification adds to a person's known freedom. Using the statistics from *Ruiz*, if my personal information is breached, there is a 19 per cent chance that I will become the victim of identity theft within a year. As a victim of identity theft has to spend, on average, about eighty hours and \$850 to alleviate the consequences of that theft, it constitutes a significant form of interference.[28] Accordingly, learning about the increased likelihood of identity theft advances one's known freedom.

Even if liberals favour mandatory disclosure of data breach, they have good reasons to question the conception of the predicament of data-breach victims that underlies these court decisions, as well as the views of lawmakers and regulators. To start with, they should, I think, dispute the courts' belief that the larger risk of future identity theft is 'speculative'. There are reliable statistical data about identity theft available in many countries, and to set these data aside as speculation does not do justice to the methodology that underlies them. While it may be that the courts' judgments about speculative probabilities concern the size of the probabilities rather than the source of information about the probabilities, this latter line of reasoning would be equally dubious. A chance of 19 per cent that you will have to spend eighty hours and some \$850 to right the consequences of identity theft is a very substantial risk. Moreover, from a statistical point of view, what is perhaps just as important to characterize the situation is not the mere figure of a 19 per cent chance of identity theft, but rather the fivefold increase from 4 per cent (average citizen) to 19 per cent (after data breach), as opposed to say an increase from 18 per cent to 19 per cent. There is no ground to set aside the probabilities as 'speculative'.[29]

But there is another reason to find fault with the view that privacy invasions should not matter as long as the gained information has not been used against the victim. It takes issue with the assumption that underlies such views to the effect that a risk of future identity theft does not constitute an actual harm. Following the approach to privacy that I advocate here, there are two ways in which disclosure of private information may harm the subject of that information. The first is a decrease of freedom: it may lead others to interfere, or to form dispositions to interfere. Admittedly, as no claimant in our examples was able to demonstrate such harm in court, this first form of harm does not apply here. Yet, as I have argued, the second way in which disclosure of private information may harm the subject is that it decreases their known freedom: the person's beliefs about their freedom and unfreedom deteriorate.

What is important now is that the inadequacy of these beliefs about freedom is far from hypothetical. They are faulty, not in a hypothetical future, but at the very moment of the data breach. A direct consequence of this is that the person's present decision-making capacities are frustrated. The decision maker is less adequately positioned than they were before the data breach when it comes to engaging in responsible planning and decision-making, because they have to incorporate, in their current planning, the fact that their beliefs about certain freedoms and unfreedoms are less adequate than before the breach.

To conclude, the idea of looking at privacy invasions from the point of view of freedom and known freedom has led to the insight that there are very good reasons for courts and lawmakers alike to rethink their reliance on a principle of 'no harm, no foul' in data-breach cases (and elsewhere). There are two clear criteria that should guide the way in which victims of privacy invasions change and update their beliefs: demonstrability and reasonableness. Invasions of privacy decrease a person's freedom and known freedom, and thereby frustrate their desire satisfaction and personal responsibility. These are good reasons for lawmakers and regulators to take into account.

A Way out for the Privacy Sceptic?

Liberal privacy sceptics may concede that I have linked privacy invasions to changes in a person's freedom, but they can still refuse to draw any normative conclusions from my analysis on the grounds that whether or not the recipient R of the private information uses the information to interfere with subject P is up to R's moral and legal responsibility. If, upon receiving new information about P, agent R decides to use P's credit card number, or to fire P because of sexual prejudices, then R does something that is already prohibited by law, so there is no ground for protecting privacy here. And if, upon receiving the information about P, recipient R decides to put an end to their friendship with P, then that is something P simply has to cope with, however unpleasant that may be.

This move to moral and legal responsibility is standard in many cases where liberal values are balanced. Take media violence and aggression, as discussed in Chapter 7. Proponents of legal measures suggest that the statistical correlation is strong and that the interests of the potential victims of aggression outweigh the interests of the viewers of certain films and television shows. Opponents of regulation, by contrast, point out that, as long as the individual viewer can be held morally and legally responsible for the aggressive acts, there is no need for the regulation of media violence. It suffices to have laws prohibiting homicide, assault, and so on. As we have seen, such an argument against regulation of media violence succeeds only if it is possible to assign responsibility to the perpetrators of aggressive acts subsequent to exposure to media violence (and, potentially, assuming also that regulation offers sufficiently strong deterrence). As I have argued, the champions of regulation do not succeed in making this proviso plausible, because copycat crime and other forms of aggression following exposure to media violence often involve a huge amount of advance planning, which is incompatible with decreased or bypassed autonomy.

But matters may be different in the case of privacy. Recipients of private information may be credulous, they may overgeneralize on the basis of limited information, and they often suffer from prejudices, all without their being aware of this. Moreover, the collective effect of the actions performed by individual recipients of private information is often considerable, even though the individual agents' contributions are small. Add to this the observation that recipients frequently remain anonymous, and we have some reason to believe that in many cases it is hard or impossible to assign moral or legal responsibility to the recipients of private information for the effects of their actions.[30] This, I am inclined to think, makes it not less, but even more important for liberals to consider protecting the freedom and known freedom of victims of privacy invasions.

Notes

1. Richard Posner, *The Economics of Law* (Cambridge, MA: Harvard University Press, 1981), 233 ff. See also Andreas Kapsner and Barbara Sandfuchs, 'Nudging as a Threat to Privacy', *Review of Philosophy and Psychology*, 6 (2015), 455–468, for a discussion of libertarian paternalism and privacy.

2. See, e.g., Isaac Taylor, 'Data Collection, Counterterrorism and the Right to Privacy', *Politics, Philosophy & Economics*, 16 (2017), 326–246, for balancing security and privacy interests. Sceptical positions about privacy have been articulated by such authors (not all of them liberals) as Anita Allen, *Why Privacy Isn't Everything: Feminist Reflections on Personal Accountability* (Lanham: Rowman and Littlefield, 2003), Richard Epstein, 'Deconstructing Privacy: And Putting it Back Together Again', *Social Philosophy and Policy*, 17 (2000), 1–24, Amitai Etzioni, *The Limits of Privacy* (New York: Basic Books, 1999), Catharine MacKinnon, *Towards a Feminist Theory of the State* (Cambridge, MA: Harvard University Press, 1989), Richard Posner, *The Economics of Law* (Cambridge, MA: Harvard University Press, 1981), Jesper Ryberg, 'Privacy Rights, Crime Prevention, CCTV, and the Life of Mrs Aremac', *Res Publica*, 13 (2007), 127–143, and Michael Sandel, *Democracy's Discontent: America in Search of a Public Philosophy* (Cambridge, MA: Harvard University Press, 1996).

3. This sets the notion apart from the way the term is used in such oft-cited court cases as *Griswold* v. *Connecticut* [1965] 381 US 479 and *Roe* v. *Wade* [1973] 410 US 113, where privacy is rather defined in terms of abilities to decide and act. See also Judith DeCew, 'The Priority of Privacy', *Social Philosophy and Policy*, 17 (2000), 213–234, Raymond Frey, 'Privacy, Control, and Talk of Rights', *Social Philosophy and Policy*, 17 (2000), 45–67, Robert Hallsborg Jr, 'Principles of Liberty and The Right to Privacy', *Law and Philosophy*, 5 (1986), 175–218, and Adam Moore, 'Privacy: Its Meaning and Value', *American Philosophical Quarterly*, 40 (2003), 215–227.

4. See Daniel Solove, '"I've Got Nothing to Hide" and Other Misunderstandings of Privacy', *San Diego Law Review*, 44 (2007), 745–772, for a critical evaluation of the nothing-to-hide argument for privacy.

5. Stanley Benn, *A Theory of Freedom* (Cambridge: Cambridge University Press, 1988), 271–278, and Robert Gerstein, Intimacy and Privacy', *Ethics*, 89 (1978), 76–81.

6. Charles Fried, 'Privacy', *Yale Law Journal*, 77 (1968), 475–493, and James Rachels, 'Why Is Privacy Important?', *Philosophy & Public Affairs*, 4 (1975), 323–333.

7. Samuel Warren and Louis Brandeis, 'The Right to Privacy', *Harvard Law Review*, 4 (1890), 193–220, and Edward Bloustein, 'Privacy as an Aspect of Human Dignity: An Answer to Dean Prosser', *New York University Law Review*, 39 (1964), 962–1007.

8. *DeMay* v. *Roberts* [1881] 46 Mich. 160.

9. Beate Rössler, 'Privacy as a Human Right', *Proceedings of the Aristotelian Society*, 117 (2017), 187–206, and Beate Rössler, *Die Wert des Privaten* (Frankfurt am Main: Suhrkamp, 2001).

10. For this line of argument, see James Rachels, 'Why Is Privacy Important?', *Philosophy & Public Affairs*, 4 (1975), 323–333. My treatment of the matter here has benefited from a discussion with Luc Bovens.

11. See Matthew Kramer, *The Quality of Freedom* (Oxford: Oxford University Press, 2003), 3.

12. *Steffan* v. *Perry* [1994] 41 F.3d. 677.

13. Amitai Etzioni, *The Limits of Privacy* (New York: Basic Books, 1999), 140.

14. Jon Nordheimer, '"Vigilante" Attack in New Jersey Is Linked to Sex-Offenders Law', *New York Times*, 11 January 1995, www.nytimes.com/1995/01/11/nyregion/vigilante-attack-in-new-jersey-is-linked-to-sex-offenders-law.html [perma.cc/SZ4M-YMTG]. See Mark Tunick, 'Privacy and Punishment', *Social Theory and Practice*, 39 (2013), 643–668, for the legitimate interest of convicted criminals in informational privacy to avoid non-legal punishment.

15. Alan Finder, 'For Some, Online Persona Undermines Resumé', *New York Times*, 11 June 2006, www.nytimes.com/2006/06/11/us/11recruit.html [perma.cc/B6XD-9YQ9].

16. Linda Keene, 'Warning Signs: A New State Law Alerts Parents to Predators in the Neighborhood and the Struggle to Cope Begins', *Seattle Times*, 15 September 1991.

17. See, e.g., Sally Donnelly, 'You Say Yusuf, I Say Youssouf...', *Time.com*, 25 September 2004, content.time.com/time/nation/article/0,8599,702062,00.html [perma.cc/TVP6-QRNN]

18. See, for more details, Matthew Kramer, 'On the Counterfactual Dimension of Negative Freedom', *Politics, Philosophy & Economics*, 2 (2003), 63–92.

19. James Whitman, 'The Two Western Cultures of Privacy: Dignity versus Liberty', *Yale Law Review*, 113 (2004), 1151–1221.

20. See Alan Rubel, 'Justifying Public Health Surveillance: Basic Interests, Unreasonable Exercise, and Privacy', *Kennedy Institute of Ethics Journal*, 22 (2012), 1–33, at 14 ff., for an application of my argument to health information, such as concerning a person's HIV status or body weight. Also see Michele Loi, Christian Hauser, and Markus Christen, 'Highway to (Digital) Surveillance: When Are Clients Coerced to Share their Data with Insurers?', *Journal of Business Ethics*, published online 8 November 2020, for a discussion of the privacy and knowledge issues arising out of life and health insurers requesting information about policyholders' lifestyles.

21. *Pisciotta* v. *Old Nat. Bancorp* [2007] 499 F.3d. 629.

22. *Kallstrom* v. *City of Columbus* [1998] 136 F.3d. 1055.

23. See Jamie Grace, 'Privacy, Stigma and Public Protection: A Socio–Legal Analysis of Criminality Information Practices in the UK', *International Journal of Law, Crime and Justice*, 41 (2013), 303–321, for an application of the idea of belief revision to information about criminality.

24. *Stollenwerk* v. *Tri-West Healthcare Alliance* [2007] 254 Fed. Appx. 664.

25. Adam Clymer, 'Threats and Responses: Privacy; Officials Say Troops Risk Identity Theft after Burglary', *New York Times*, 12 January 2003, www.nytimes.com/2003/01/12/us/threats-responses-privacy-officials-say-troops-risk-identity-theft-after.html [perma.cc/B3FC-JN59].

26. *Giordano* v. *Wachovia Securities, LLC* [2006] WL 2177036.

27. *Ruiz* v. *Gap, Inc.* [2009] 622 F. Supp. 2d 908.

28. Eric Eisenstein, 'Identity Theft: An Exploratory Study with Implications for Marketers', *Journal of Business Research*, 61 (2008), 1160–1172. See Keith Anderson, Erik Durbin, and Michael Salinger, 'Identity Theft', *Journal of Economic Perspectives*, 22 (2008), 171–192, for more details on the economic consequences of identity theft.

29. The burden of demonstrability and reasonableness would seem to be easily been met in various cases, including *Caudle* v. *Towers* [2008] 580 F. Supp. 2d. 273, *Dyer* v. *Northwest Airlines* [2004] 334 F. Supp. 2d. 1196, and *Forbes* v. *Wells Fargo Bank* [2006] 420 F. Supp. 2d. 1018. Acknowledging a connection between known freedom and liberty interests seems to have a precedent in a number of cases where the publication of certain data affects the knowledge a person has about future (employment) opportunities, such as *Asbill* v. *Housing Authority of Choctaw Nation* [1984] 726 F.2d 1499, *In re Smith* [1981] 656 F.2d 1101, and *McGregor* v. *Greer* [1990] 748 F. Supp. 881. My discussion has benefited from email correspondence with Daniel Solove.

30. See Boudewijn de Bruin, 'The Liberal Value of Privacy', *Law and Philosophy*, 29 (2010), 521–527, for details on this argument from responsibility.

Conclusion

How Freedom Can Be Sufficient

It is Twitter's mission 'to give everyone the power to create and share ideas and information instantly, without barriers'.[1] Where ideas and information meet resistance, and Twitter is called upon to remove abusive messages, the company responds that 'the tweets must flow'.[2] They have, they claim, a 'mandate' to safeguard their users' right to free speech.[3] I have argued in this book that we should not think of freedom without thinking about knowledge and acknowledgement. While there is freedom without knowledge, freedom gets its value only if it is accompanied by knowledge. It may seem, then, that Twitter's mission is consonant with this ideal, for to gain knowledge one needs information, and to gain information, others need to share their knowledge with you.

When I started writing this book, the world was a different place. It was early in 2011 when Twitter wrote that 'the tweets must flow'. Ten years later, on 8 January 2021, Twitter suspended the account of the then US president because it deemed two of his tweets to violate its Glorification of Violence Policy.[4] One may debate whether two tweets—which taken in isolation seem fairly innocuous to the outsider—justify the suspension, or whether, arguing in the other direction, Twitter's policies should already have been used to suspend the account at a much earlier stage. One can also ask oneself the question of whether it should be up to the arbitrary will of a corporation to decide to whom to give a voice, or whether in concrete cases the limits to the right to free speech of a head of state should ultimately be set by the judiciary. But my sense is that most observers think that somehow limiting free speech is more and more justified in view of the spread of factually untrue statements and morally abhorrent opinions.

As I said in the Introduction, it is my sense that the philosophical literature on freedom lost its appeal to application-minded scholars after the outbreak of the financial crisis in 2008. The debate about global finance was

The Business of Liberty. Boudewijn de Bruin, Oxford University Press.
© Boudewijn de Bruin (2022). DOI: 10.1093/oso/9780198839675.003.0010

largely left to neo-Marxists and other critics lambasting 'neo-liberalism'. This was regrettable, and it would be similarly regrettable if the undeniably daunting problems to do with climate-change denial, vaccination scepticism, and other irrational and unjustifiable beliefs and normative opinions would lead us to blame freedom again. My sense is that you should look elsewhere if you are really interested in developing political remedies to these challenges.

Building on analytical insights from liberal and republican thought, I have developed the view that realizing freedom's value presupposes intricate informational conditions that agents have to satisfy in order to benefit from their freedoms. Apart from developing theory, I have looked at a range of concrete cases of practical relevance, including the production and marketing of violent video games and freedom of expression, privacy, socially responsible investing, and the management of epistemic corporate culture. I have defended two normative ideals: known freedom and acknowledged freedom.

I have not been too interested in defending a political ideology in this book. Rather, my inspiration has been to draw from a range of more neutral sources from several empirical disciplines, philosophy, and legal scholarship. I have made use of insights on consumer behaviour from psychology and economics. I have examined court decisions and the scholarly legal literature on privacy, free speech, and consumer protection. And I have looked into neuroscience/cognitive science research on how people gain and process information—for instance, regarding the techniques of neuro-marketing. The result of avoiding a bias towards any political ideology is that many of the things I have said will be relevant just as much to, say, libertarians as to followers of Rawls or Marx.

Yet, to conclude, let me speculate on one particular political consequence of the view that what is ultimately valuable is not freedom per se, but freedom you know of that is acknowledged. My thought is that, once you take known freedom and acknowledged freedom as key normative ideals, the right to education gets a *very* different form from what it now has. Article 26 of the 1948 Universal Declaration of Human Rights introduced a right to education, free for elementary and fundamental stages. The 1950 Convention for the Protection of Human Rights and Fundamental Freedoms, which was meant to 'take the first steps for the collective enforcement of certain of the Rights stated in the Universal Declaration' among a number of countries in or near Europe, did, however, not include this right.[5]

In both documents freedom is the value par excellence, embodied in the rights to life, liberty, and security, and driving most other normative concerns. But, if we take the lessons from this book seriously, we should see that the right to liberty is quite meaningless if it is not accompanied with significant epistemic guarantees. It is hard to see how this could not entail a much more substantive conception of the right to education. I am inclined to think that when we propose to limit speech as a solution to the spread of false beliefs this is nothing more than admitting a deeply worrying unconcern among citizens, politicians, and policymakers for a malfunctioning educational system (or at least an inexcusable unawareness thereof).

It is also plausible that my view would entail much wider informational rights for citizens towards governments and businesses. Here, too, the apparent appeal of limiting free speech betrays, if I am right, a lack of sufficient institutional warrants of information provision that states should put in place.

Finally, I believe that taking an epistemic reading of the right to liberty seriously should have far-reaching consequences for the quality of the evidence that lawmakers and courts should be required to provide. Far too often are laws made without any apparent concern for the fact that only if they are based on evidence can they be rationally adopted as measures aimed at creating particular effects. Examining these political repercussions of my views was not on my agenda when I started this project. Right now it is the most pressing direction for future investigations.

Notes

1. help.twitter.com/en/rules-and-policies/twitter-services-and-corporate-affiliates [perma.cc/4ALY-7Z3L].
2. blog.twitter.com/en_us/a/2011/the-tweets-must-flow.html [perma.cc/EAB2-2V4U].
3. Ibid.
4. blog.twitter.com/en_us/topics/company/2020/suspension.html [perma.cc/2F6U-9JRM].
5. Article 2 of the Protocol to the Convention for the Protection of Human Rights and Fundamental Freedoms, which dates from 1952, captures the right to education.

Index